# PLATEAUX,
# GATEAUX,
# CHATEAUX

For Esme and Michael Ash, with love

# PLATEAUX, GATEAUX, CHATEAUX

## Mary Davies Parnell

seren

seren is the book imprint of
Poetry Wales Press Ltd
2 Wyndham Street, Bridgend
CF31 1EF, Wales

A CIP record for this title is available from
the British Library CIP Office

ISBN 1-85411-207-4

*The publisher works with the financial assistance of the
Arts Council of Wales*

Cover Illustration: Lorraine Bewsey

Printed in Plantin by
WBC Book Manufacturers, Bridgend

# Contents

# List of Illustrations

# 1. O Level Showdown

My best friend's brother was trying to distract my attention to make me pour the bottlefull of brown sauce over my breakfast sausages, when my O level results arrived. We were on holiday – Caryl, her parents, brother Graham and me – staying at an hotel in Weymouth in late August. "Telegram for Mary Davies", announced the bell-boy on the threshold of the dining room, "Mary Davies – telegram". Focus of all eyes and scarlet-faced, with my heart doing a wild drum solo while leaping uncontrollably around my chest, I rather ungraciously snatched the ochre envelope from the boy, tore it open and fumbled at the sheet inside to read, "All passed, except Mathematics. Well done. Mam & Dad." Relief and a certain pleasure must have been evident in my demeanour as other guests who, interested in the breakfast-time diversion, had paused in the transferring of forked bits of bacon, fried bread, tomato and egg to their mouths to enquire, "Everything all right then?" and "Good news by the looks of it."

Caryl plucked the telegram out of my hand. "Lessee! Oh, you lucky so and so! I've got to wait 'til half past nine before I can phone Margaret for my results." Then, after further inspection, "You failed Maths you daft thing. Wouldn' be surprised if I have too," she added gloomily.

Whether she did or not I don't remember. I didn't care about Maths and hadn't expected to pass. I'd left the Algebra exam well before full time. It was mid-June then and in Tydraw, my uncles' farm, they were washing the sheep in the brook nearby, and I couldn't possibly miss that. The water was being dammed up by the bridge, one of the iron rails across the middle removed, and the hundred and fifty or so sheep, contained on the road by the dogs, were to be shoved through the gap into the brook about two feet below. I could see the scene. The men, my uncles, cousins and neighbouring farmers who came to help, would be concentrating on the job but with time for a laugh and a joke, the dogs would be excited, barking and dancing about, and the sheep bleating protestingly as they wandered aimlessly about or made mad dashes for nowhere. Occasionally one would try to make a frantic, awkward bid for freedom up the impossible slope of the dingle to be confronted by a crouching sheepdog, then seeing its escape barred, trot off resignedly with a pathetic baa to find a bit of grass to crop. No, I couldn't miss that, O level Maths or not!

My mother had been a little surprised to see me. "I thought you had an exam," she said as I pulled off my green and yellow tie and draped it over one of the ancient, chipped, heirloom-type jugs hanging on the dresser.

"I did. 's finished."

"Oh, you're home earlier than usual then," she said looking a bit perturbed.

"Yeah, I finished early."

"Oh Lord, that doesn't sound too 'opeful. What was it today?"

"Maths. Algebra."

Perturbation turned to peevishness. "Oh Mary, that's an important subject that is. You can't afford to neglect Maths you know. You should have tried extra hard with that. What are you going to do if you fail Mathematics?"

Seeing her clearly anxious I tried to re-assure her by being casual.

"Try it again nex' year I s'pose. Anyway they're washing the sheep over Tydraw today."

"Well, what's that got to do with anything?"

"I'm goin' over there now, that's what. Jus' goin' to change and go. Is there anythin' to eat?"

"Oh Jawl, I don' know!" My mother went off muttering then shouted from the pantry, "Corned beef sandwich and a slice of apple tart?"

Shortly before, as I was walking up Bryn Eirw hill from the bus stop at the Vaughan's Arms, I'd glanced up at the mountain. Gwyn Tylawinder who delivered the milk around Trehafod, was a tiny figure in the distance, returning over the mountain to his farm near Tydraw, with the empty churns strapped over his pony. He was approaching the bend in the mountain path towards Jacob's Well spring about half way to the top. I thought I'd try and catch him up for a bit of company on the way to Tydraw after I'd called in at home. I did too, and he was glad to see me to have a chat as we walked. No, I wasn't bothered about my lack of proven competence in Maths. I'd quite enjoyed the subject over the years with the constantly retiring, somnolent, easily red-herringed, newspaper-addict Miss Bird from Bristol, then the Irish Miss Sandys in Form 5. No surprise we couldn't understand Maths. We couldn't understand the latter speaking English, but would simply listen, charmed, to the soft, musical vowel sounds and practise them in whispers when she was writing on the board with her back to us.

It was Chemistry I was pleased to have passed. Since Form 2 we'd had Miss Long. She was the antithesis of her name, being positively Lilliputian, an energetic, forthright north Walian with hair cropped in no-nonsense fashion and incredibly piercing bright-blue eyes. She marched around the Chem lab in her long white coat, her splayed-out feet, unusually large for such a little person, clattering in solid, no-nonsense shoes that matched her direct character.

"Naow girlss, gather rraound and pay attention pleass," she would say in her strong north Welsh accent. "Can you all ssee? Naow, in this Wolfe'ss bottle arre twoo grrammes of sinc dust. I'm going to add dilute ssulphuric acid throough thiss funnel. What's the correct name for thiss funnel Maureen Griffiths?"

"Umm. Thistle funnel Miss Long."

"Goodt. And whaey iss it called that Pamela Nichollss?"

"Because the top looks like a thistle Miss."

"Rraight. Naow, hydrogen iss given off in the reaction and collects under water in thiss graduated jar. Can you all ssee?"

She would introduce bangs and rattles into the experiment whenever possible, and sparks and flames with magnesium ribbon and phosphorus. She delighted in making horrid odours with hydrogen sulphide and ammonia and gleefully relished the consequent class unpopularity with the rest of the school. Although the gas would be dispersed in the fume cupboard, bad smells would invade the inside of the building, worst in the proximity of the lab, and Miss Long would wickedly grin at the pained expressions of unsuspecting, passing pupils.

"Oh come on naow girlss. If you don't laike it, go outsaide. It's not rraining verry hard!" she'd say, offering little comfort.

She would tell us chemical horror stories of how someone had once broken into a school lab's secure cupboard, dipped his finger into a jar of prussic acid, licked it and dropped dead on the spot. A careless pupil had dropped a jar of sulphuric acid and lost all the skin off her legs as well as a few ounces of flesh into the bargain. But it wasn't one of Miss Long's girlss! A story we were particularly fond of, which Miss Long was ever eager to relate was about the scientist who wanted to convert a chunk of coal into another carbon molecular arrangement, that of a diamond. A piece of coal, encased in an iron globe, was heated to great temperatures, then plunged into icy water to cool the carbon quickly. The scientist was successful in obtaining a tiny diamond, but unfortunately, in the ferocious blast caused by the red hot, glowing globe being immersed in the $H_2O$, the intrepid experimenter lost a hand. Apparently the reverse experiment, transferring a diamond into coal was fairly easy and Miss Long quite eager to perform it if anyone was obliging enough to bring in a sample of those jewels for her. She taught us Chemistry with charisma and to our dismay decided to remove herself back to north Wales at the end of my first fifth year. Myself and a few other girls in the class of '47 were selected for a second one by the then Minister of Education, Florence Horsbrugh, who didn't wish to award O levels to people who hadn't achieved the age of 16, clearly the age of wisdom, reason and sense, by the end of August.

We returned for our second voyage through Form 5 in September '52 to find a new Chemistry teacher, a Miss Goodman, as large as Miss Long was little. We soon found that she too belied her name. 'Good' appeared most inapplicable to her temperament *vis à vis* pupils, though she did seem to be as tough as a man. Counsel to new teachers is usually, "Be firm with the kids at first so they know exactly who's boss. Don't let them get away with anything or they'll take advantage. You can ease up on the strictness a bit later." Or as I was told to say a few decades after, "I'll play ball with you if you'll play ball with me. But don't forget it's my ball!" Someone had either told Miss Goodman only the first part of the advice or she had decided to ignore the second. Cold, disdainful and disapproving eyes, set in a rosy-cheeked face with a high forehead topped by wiry hair swept back in a bun, regarded us from around six feet up in the Chem lab's gaseous air. Much flesh adorned the chin and neck area and the upper lip sported a not unobtrusive hint of moustache. The hitherto blameless fifth form returners were soon dubbed "the residue" by their new teacher – a term possibly in context with the subject, but inappropriate in the circumstances. We, the residue that is, hated her on the spot and vowed we would revise only Miss Long's notes for the O level exam. Feeling trapped, betrayed and confused, we were unwilling participants in her humourless lessons. A mere trifle would incur her wrath and through clenched teeth and words spat out as though she'd been chewing wasps she informed me, "You will never pass Chemistry O level, girl, not if you revise from now until Doomsday. You're a lost cause if ever I saw one!"

Through reciprocally clenched teeth I thought, "Oh won't I, you old harridan?", determined at that moment to pass Chemistry if I had to sacrifice all else, "We'll see about that!"

"And don't narrow your eyes at me in that saucy manner you insolent child!", she added vituperously as she clearly read my thoughts in my expression.

The left-overs, me, Maureen Griffiths, Anne Morris, Mary Price and Margaret James huddled together at a bench on our own in the Chem lab and moaned while waiting for her to arrive at the start of the lesson.

"Oh, that woman! She drives me up the wall. She doesn't know how to be civil."

"No I know. She hates us because we've done the course with Miss Long."

"Well it's not our fault she left. And we haven't failed or anything. Not yet anyway! Why did she come here if she doesn't like schoolchildren?"

"P'raps she's jealous 'cos Miss Long taught us better."

"Imagine having to re-sit Chem and having her for another year! I'd rather commit suicide I would."

"Well," Maureen Griffiths said, "it won't apply to me thank God, 'cos I'm leaving." The rest of us looked at her enviously.

"D'you know what she did after the lesson last Monday?" complained Anne Morris. "Oh! I hate Mondays because of Chem, aye. Well, see, everybody was ready to go on the bell. She let the ones who catch the Treorchy bus out first, then the Ferndale lot, then the Porth. An' she knows I don't catch a bus 'cos she's seen me walking home. Anyway she kept me behind to wash some dusty ol' test-tubes an' stuff she found in a cupboard."

"Cor, she didn't! There's cheek!"

"Yeah, she did," continued Anne, pink with indignation, "an' I'm definitely not 'ere to be her skivvy. 'Now then Anne Morris,' she said, 'I just want you to do a little job for me before you go'."

"Why didn' you say no?" someone suggested, "I would 'ave. Cheeky bitch!"

"Well, I couldn' very well. She'd be even nastier to me then."

"I'd've made an excuse that I had to be home on time that day," I said.

"What did your mother say when you got 'ome?"

"Nothin'. She didn' see nothin' wrong in it. She told me to stop complainin'," Anne tutted. "I dunno! Parents! Not much better than teachers sometimes!"

"Were you very late?"

"Yeah, about ten minutes."

"Oh, that's not much!"

"Huh! Ten minutes in her company longer than I need!"

"What an ol' cow though, an' I hate her callin' us the residue. All the rest think it's funny. An' we know more Chem than them an' all."

"If you ask me she looks more like a bull than a cow. She's sort of wide at the top and gets narrower lower down."

"Huh, apart from her legs, that is. She's got massive calves."

"An' a snorty sort of face." Criticism of our least favourite teacher provoked much mirth. It continued.

"An' the way she looks at you, you'd think she was gonna charge like a bull and toss you off your stool over the Bunsen burners into the sink."

We laughed like carefree mitchers, wishing we were, at the imminent approach of Chemistry. Perched on the tall lab stools we could just see through the high window and Miss Goodman, grim-faced, turning the corner from the staffroom.

"*Olé, olé*, here comes the Bull," said Maureen, giggling. "Books out ready, Matadors, or she'll have your blood!"

And thus was invented the unflattering nickname, the Bull, a nickname which stayed with Miss Goodman throughout her decades at Porth County. It and she became so renowned throughout the Rhondda that visitors to the school in ensuing years were known to ask to see Mrs Bull, the headmistress. The 'residue' gave themselves the name of the Peeved Picadors, and had the satisfaction of some sort of long-term revenge although none of us were there to really appreciate it.

I devoted 600% more time to revising Chemistry (Miss Long's notes) than I did any other subject. I know it was 600% because some time before the start of O levels, the teacher being absent for one of our lessons, I went along to Mrs Hopkins, the Games mistress, to ask if I could play tennis if one of the courts was free. Her chiding response, to my surprise, was "But Mary, what about your revision? O levels start in six weeks!" I didn't play tennis. I got out my Chemistry books and swotted as I did every day from then until the exam. The other subjects weren't so lucky, only having once weekly attention. So in late August 1953 I smiled heavenward and gave thanks to the Good Lord for letting me pass O level Chemistry and sparing me the torment (in the event of a re-sit had I failed) of coming into contact with Miss Goodman again.

We probably returned to school, to go into 6B (which is what Porth County called the Lower 6th) on September 6th – we usually did – to spoil my birthday. By now, to our amazement, Miss Goodman had become Mrs Watkins. Poor Mr Watkins! He was widely sympathised with, but then, so they say, love is blind.

# 2. Dubious Delights of the Sixth Form

In the euphoria of success on a comparatively low rung of the educational ladder, meeting relieved classmates and friends who had similarly worried the summer away until results day, and wearing the new 6th form uniform of white blouse, tie and navy skirt instead of the hitherto dreaded gymslip, I don't recall much of that first day of term. I do however remember an interview with Miss Hudd in the library to determine my course of A level study.

"And now then, Mary. Mmm, you must be quite pleased with your results. Creditable marks." (This was the era before anybody had thought of giving grades at O level). She scanned my sheet. "Some marks are excellent. Pity about Maths though. Still, you can re-sit in November. You only failed by three marks. Now then, your A level subjects. What are you going to do? Science, I imagine. Chemistry of course, that's your top mark."

I looked at her horrified and speechless. My jaw almost dislocated as my mouth fell into a catatonic gape. I managed to squeak, "Oh no, no. Arts. I'm Arts."

"Are you sure?" She looked at me with that searching gaze of hers, over the top of her glasses. "I would have thought Chemistry certainly. It's your best subject. Chemistry with Botany and Zoology. Your Biology mark is good too. You'll need Maths of course to do Science, but I shouldn't have thought there'd be a problem there."

"No," I said, mustering as much conviction as I could in a voice tremulous with shock, and shaking my head to urge home the point, "No, I want to do English, French and something else."

"Why, Mary?" she persisted, "Why not Science? Not enough girls are doing Science you know."

"I don't like Science much Miss Hudd," was my lame answer.

"But you have such good marks in the Science subjects...." she tailed off looking baffled. For my part I could hardly tell her I'd rather drink a potion of prussic and sulphuric acids followed by a dessert of crushed glass, than tangle again with one particular member of her staff, so I just looked woebegone.

"What do your parents say?"

Mam and Dad hadn't any definite thoughts on the matter. Since I'd only failed one O level, they were fairly pleased with me, thought I was reasonably smart and left such decisions up to me.

When I was small, Mam used to say that I'd end up scrubbing the stone floors of the local pub, the Vaughan's Arms, if I didn't work in school. Then when I managed to pass the exam to the County school, her career ideas for me moved up a step or two and she thought it would be nice for me to be a doctor or a lawyer. On those occasions when I failed to intercept my termly report to make a few judicious alterations in my favour, it was back to the stone floors again. I didn't fancy any of those jobs. I wasn't too keen on blood, particularly somebody else's, and when I'd accompanied my mother to the solicitor's to see about the lease of our house, we were ushered into a dark, untidy office with dirty windows, unwashed cups and the most uninspiring-looking tomes propping each other up on shelves. The solicitor was thin, bent, harrassed and unhealthy looking and I certainly had no wish to resemble him! No, I saw myself as an international traveller of some sort – doing what, I had no idea. Either that or living on a farm in some picturesque part of the country, helping out in an advisory, managerial role rather than a working one.

So, to Miss Hudd's question, I could truthfully answer, "They don't mind. They want me to take the subjects I like and will be good at."

She wasn't giving up. "Well, give it some thought, talk it over with your parents tonight and tell me tomorrow." That evening then, I informed them that English, French and Geography were the subjects I'd be studying at A level and looked forward to returning to school the next day, wondering who 6B's form mistress would be.

It was the custom in Porth County to line up outside your form room after the bell for registration and recess in double rows, but the Sixth form stood in a single row outside the Library and the Hall opposite the First form. When the lines were ready and all was quiet, the staff emerged from their sanctum and walked to stand facing their form.

On the first morning of the autumn term there was much craning of necks and balancing on tip-toe to see which teacher was approaching your form. *Sotto voce* preferences were uttered and sighs of disappointment whispered when a favourite member of staff passed or came to a halt elsewhere.

"Oh, look! Miss Llewellyn's coming. Hope we have her! Oh blow, she's stopped opposite 3A."

"Never mind, here's Mrs Hopkins. Hope she's going to be our form mistress!" Disappointed eyes watched her walk past.

"Surely we're not gonna get Dai Lat. We'd have to do the register ourselves!" No, she was going to take a second form.

The Bull hove into sight. Anxious glances were exchanged in the 6B line. No-one said anything. She marched resolutely down the middle of the corridor and with sinking hearts we saw her smilingly stop, facing us. The girls immediately in front of her attempted to grin back, forcing lips back over teeth, but most only managed a grimace, while those at the extremities simply looked at each other in disbelief. "Just our bloody luck!" murmured Dorothy Jones.

"Am I having a bad dream or something?" asked Anne Morris, "I don't believe that out of thirty or so staff, we end up with her!"

Others just looked at each other in desperation.

In fact, 6B's relationship with their form tutor was not infelicitous, which is not saying it was particularly felicitous. The Bull seemed reasonably human outside the learning situation and we were, after all, mature people now, having passed our O levels. She never spoke directly to me other than to call my name when marking the register and never mentioned my Chemistry pass. This was fine as far as I was concerned. I kept my sights lowered and did my best to keep out of any possible line of fire.

School Assembly took place every morning in Porth County after registration. Classes filed into the Hall to stand, facing the dais, Form 1 at the front, Form 5 at the back. The Sixth form were led in by the Prefects in 6A who stood at the end of a row starting at the front. There were usually more rows than Prefects so 6B girls took up positions at the end of half a dozen or so rows while the rest thankfully went to stand at the back where they couldn't be seen not singing the hymn and reciting the prayers. You could even have a few sinful yawns or make some murmured comments out of sight of the staff who stood or leaned against the brown-tiled wall near their class. When all was ready, ordered and waiting, Miss Hudd would sweep in, academic gown billowing, to conduct proceedings from the stage. These consisted of a hymn, a reading, the Lord's Prayer and announcements, sometimes a school telling-off. Miss Harries played the first couple of lines of the hymn and the school would join in fairly enthusiastically and quite musically. Miss Hudd read the appropriate passage from the Bible then said a prayer. All together we intoned the Lord's Prayer on automatic pilot, joining in from, "Who art in Heaven", apart from on Fridays when the service was in Welsh and a modicum of concentration was required to emit the right sounds in the right order. Then, apart from some normally innocuous communiques such as games results, names of girls winning essay competitions or gaining swimming certificates, that was it. Now and then we were harangued from the stage if someone had been guilty of un-Porth-County-like behaviour such as hanging out of a bus window waving one's scarf at a passing person, talking openly over the fence to boys in the Boys' School next door or clogging up the toilets with sweet wrappers.

One of the carnal school sins was Talking in Assembly, nearly as heinous a crime as not wearing your beret to and from the premises. This latter was almost an expulsion offence, but Talking in Assembly came a close second, with possibly wearing your school scarf when chatting to a boy in the street outside school hours, a third runner-up.

At the end of Assembly, the doors at either end of the Hall would be opened, Miss Harries would start to play the '*Marche aux Flambeaux*' or the 'Grand March', and each line of girls, following the Prefect at the end of their row, would march, in step to the lively music, to their room somewhere in the building. Although we were approximately only 350 girls in the school – decidedly mini compared with today's Comprehensives of a thousand and upwards – no-one could be expected to know which form each girl was in, and in which room that form was housed. Well, perhaps Miss Hudd and some staff did, but Prefects and especially the recently initiated Sixth formers of 6B didn't, and didn't really care to make the acquiring of this knowledge a major pre-occupation. I was one such. As a result, one morning, half-awake and possibly a month into my 6th form career, I found myself about to lead off a row of pink-cheeked, lively but innocent-looking schoolgirls into the relative unknown.

"What form are you?" I hissed out of the side of my mouth to the girl next to me, aware of the looming figure of Mrs Watkins nearby.

"3A," she hissed back.

"What room?" I wheezed, trying not to move my lips.

"New Block," came the whispered response. Seconds later it was our turn to march out to the music and I headed for the top door, the line of third formers trailing along behind. Turning into the corridor leading to the New Block, I abandoned them to wander on to their room and went to my locker to get organised for the first lesson.

"Mary, Mrs Watkins wants to see you," said a voice behind me, "Now, before first lesson."

"Oh God, what have I done now?" Pat Morris made a face.

"I dunno, jus' said to tell you to go to the Chem Lab now. She didn't seem too...er...overjoyed about something," she unconsolingly concluded.

Mrs Watkins, seated at her desk on the dais, was writing and didn't look up when I knocked and went in through the swing doors. Awkwardly I stood waiting for her to acknowledge my presence. I cleared my throat, attempted a smile and started casually, "You wanted to see me Mrs Watkins." A gaze I interpreted as full of loathing, contumely and disdain flashed from cold eyes in a flushed face. I noticed how very pink her mouth was without lipstick.

"You were speaking in Assembly." She didn't believe in beating about the bush.

"No, Miss...I wasn't." Anxiety made me forget my newly acquired 6th form sophistication to address her as 'Miss', reverting to a lower school mannerism. My mind raced to recollect Assembly. Oh God, she'd seen me whisper to that girl in 3B. I swallowed and went on, "I only...er..."

"Yes. Only...?" Her voice was frigid, manner brisk.

"Um, only asked a girl which form she was in to lead out."

"Nonetheless you were talking in Assembly which is strictly against the rules. Actually you spoke to her twice didn't you?"

I looked down defeated, biting my lip.

"Well?"

"Yes...I suppose...but only..." Fear of possibly the most cold-hearted, aloof person I'd ever encountered in my seventeen years, and guilt at my reprehensible crime caused me to tail off lamely, indefensibly.

"There's no 'but only' about it." her voice was rising, "Rules are rules and if anybody should abide by them, indeed help enforce them, it's the Sixth form. You had no business speaking in Assembly for whatever reason." Still seated, she had managed to assume gigantic proportions through utter distaste and indignation at my transgression. The pink face was now puce as her blood must have been coursing round her body with the 300mph speed of a sneeze, and she was all puffed up – at least that much of her that I could see.

"I'm sorry," I managed to put in as she paused to take breath, then to continue, completely ignoring my obviously irrelevant apology.

"And now you must face the consequences. Detention tonight, and until half-term you will stand two paces out from the rest of the form in Lines. I hope this will be a warning to you and everyone else in 6B not to overstep the mark. I will not stand for rule-breaking and improper behaviour."

However I was not quite finished yet. With the likelihood of incurring more wrath and censure, but emboldened by logic, "But how was I supposed to know which form I was leading out?"

She looked at me as though I was mentally deficient, raised her eyes patiently to gaze at the ceiling, sighed deliberately, tapped her pen on the desk and spoke to the near distance. "If that's what you were talking about, you should have waited and asked Pat Isaacs, out in the corridor. Please go to your lesson now. I have a class waiting to come in."

Stunned, confused by the feeling that I was not entirely guilty, I banged open the lab doors, fully expecting the Mephistophelian Bull to call me back for more haranguing. I got to the Geography room, trying hard to stop the tears spilling out, sat at the long desk and put my head in my hands wishing I was anywhere but in this wretched school. Concerned friends looked at me wonderingly, demonstrating quelled outrage when they knew the cause of my dejection.

At first, detention appeared the worse punishment. The humiliation of a Sixth former kept behind after school to sit for forty-five minutes in the company of naughty, talkative eleven year olds who'd forgotten to do their homework, middle school mitchers and Fifth form insolent and indolent rebels who only wanted to leave as soon as they officially could! Soon, however, come the end of a miserable recess, I discovered the malignant nature of what seemed initially as the lesser sentence.

Directly opposite the Hall against whose wall 6B stood in a row after breaks, were the First form classrooms. The Bull appeared and without a word beckoned to me to stand well out, in no man's land so to speak, and two paces in front of my form-mates. All eyes in that part of the corridor were on me, and the mouths of the little Form Oners gaped as they puzzled over what was going on. Had Mary Davies been elevated to the status of teacher? No, it couldn't be that, as she was facing the wrong way and wore no gown. Was she merely going crackers standing so much out of line with the rest of 6B? Perhaps she was the Sixth form captain, ready and at hand to help the form teacher, carry the register, fetch the chalk and board duster and note down the whisperers. But why was she looking so embarrassed and down-cast and on the point of crying? After an infinity of about two minutes the bell tinkled, denoting the end of Lines and my release from hell. Never brilliant at mental arithmetic, but spurred on by a suicidal despondency, I worked out in seconds that I would undergo this torture forty times until I had paid my dues. Half-term was two weeks away and we lined up four times a day. My heart sank and I could feel the lump in my throat ready to explode in tears. I wouldn't be able to stand it! I would leave school! What is more there were another two Lines to endure that day before I'd had time to come to terms with it. Perhaps tomorrow wouldn't be so bad after some home comforts and a night's sleep, if sleep were possible. It was a bit like going to the dentist – quite unbearable if he said come straight away because you needed time to panic. Then after the luxury of hours of worry the event didn't seem so fearful.

My friends were solicitous. "Don't worry, Mary," said Caryl, "We'll all stand out from the wall with you so you won't be noticed."

"Tell your mother to come up and complain to Miss Hudd," Jennifer Jones proposed forcefully, "That's what I'd do. The old cow, or bull rather, is making a spectacle of you and it's not fair. It's persecution. I'd have my mother up here tomorrow I would. That'd put a stop to the nonsense!" She was right of course, pink-faced in the faithful indignation of a friend. Miss Hudd was reasonable. She would have seen the cruel indignity and injustice of the situation, and sanity would have prevailed. The latter course appeared most sensible, but I was seventeen years old for goodness' sake! I couldn't trot my mother up to school at seventeen to speak up on my behalf. Most of my Trehafod seventeen year-old acquaintances had jobs, steady boy-friends or fiancés, some smoked, stayed out until midnight, were adults. One was even expecting a baby and had got married!

"Pretend you're feeling faint and can't come to Lines," suggested Hilary Evans, "She can't make you."

"You could always pretend to faint if she did," said Anne Morris, the actress who was one third of the Hamlet in the forth-coming school production. Scenes of even more attention-drawing drama flashed through my mind and I shuddered. Barbara Jones thought the best thing would be to treat the whole thing as a joke, handling it with the absurdity it deserved.

At the next lining-up, the rest of the form stood well out from the wall, almost level with me so that I was not particularly conspicuous. The Bull motioned them back but they surreptitiously slid forward, so my anguish was minimalised. This was repeated after afternoon recess.

In the security of home I told my horrified mother I was thinking of leaving school, that I'd realised I didn't want to do A levels and go to university, and burst into tears that had been threatening all day. Everything poured out. Minutes later Mam wanted to go up to the school there and then, at 5.30 in the afternoon. Lethal hat-pin in hand, supposedly intended to puncture the headgear, not the Bull, she was ready to go upstairs, put her hat on and catch the bus to Porth to confront the demons on my behalf. Fortunately my bewildered father's arrival from work, to a shopful of unserved, stoically patient customers, a tearful daughter, a wild wife with hat in place and a partially prepared dinner, calmed the situation and prevented hasty, possibly hapless, affray.

Eventually it was decided I would stay on at school, for the time being anyway ("Don't be silly, you can't let a foolish woman ruin the rest of your life!"), no-one would go up to complain which, my level-headed father pointed out, would be a retrograde step in my relationship with my form mistress, possibly with the school. With the support of my friends I should try to make the best of the predicament. If I couldn't handle it, my father would write a letter to the headmistress in his courteous, old-fashioned style in his elegant, copper-plate trained hand.

Mid-Autumn term 1953 was when I grew up. I stood out from the rest of 6B in Lines without the prompting of signals from the Bull, head held high not downcast, shoulders square not drooping. Towards the end of my period of correction I even felt confident enough to smile brazenly at the woman, wink at a Form Oner opposite, or turn slightly but openly to communicate silently with Caryl or one of the others, an eyebrow raised at something untoward. It was make or break and I took the first option which transformed me from an insipid, opinionless youngster into a self-assured Sixth Former. Looking back I prefer to think Mrs Watkins had decided to put some steel into my spine and that in her capacity as a professional educator of the young she knew what she was doing. It didn't endear her to me though, nor me to her I'm sure, when I cheekily stood prominently out, smiling broadly, after half-term, when she dismissively signalled me back into line. Fortunately this incident was my last real brush with her apart from being chosen by the form as the most appropriate person to hand over her Christmas present of a razor-edged carving knife.

Some years after this, I was a student at Aberystwyth, working during the summer holidays for the firm of Thomas & Evans, grocers and pop-makers, at their shop in Pontypridd on Fountain Square. One day to my initial but fleeting dismay, I saw a large, familiar figure in the shop. It was the Bull. She recognised me immediately and approached, smiling broadly, hand outstretched. "Mary Davies! How are you? What are you doing now? How nice to see you!"

Other pleasantries and chat followed with the promise she'd be in again to see me as she lived in Pontypridd. Before leaving she bought one of the shop's cream cakes which she gave me to eat at my break. I was struck dumb! True to her promise, she did come to the shop again, each time presenting me with some delectable, sugary morsel to help shorten the day. She was the essence of charm, friendliness, kindness and warm interest. She couldn't have mellowed to that extent in two or three years, so I presumed her out-of-school persona was her real self and that her severe discipline and mordant sarcasm was a front, developed for her pupils and their ultimate good. Rhondda officialdom was clearly impressed by her as she was later promoted to Headmistress of Porth County.

# 3. Geography and its Eccentricities

So, inauspiciously, began two years in the Sixth Form, mostly congenial, sometimes frustrating, occasionally exasperating, but never boring.

If you had decided to take A level Geography, it was deemed a wise move to also belong to the local Land Rangers. Not that Land Rangers had anything to do with contours, hanging valleys, alluvial plains and other geographical impedimenta. Not directly that is, but simply because Miss Orsman, Deputy Head of Porth County and Head of Geography was a Girl Guide Commissioner and Land Ranger chief executive. Since the Land Rangers were based in Porth, it was a bit inconvenient to be of their number if you lived north of Ynyshir in the Fach valley or Penygraig in the Fawr, as it was bothersome to be traipsing down to Porth on cold, wet, dark nights for meetings. But one felt one had an advantage in the A level Geography stakes by enrolling. So there we were, the southern Rhondda prospective Geographers, fresh-faced and bright-eyed in our grey blouses and navy, woggle-bound scarves, turning up on Tuesday evenings to learn the art of Land Rangering. At least the idea was that the teacher would get to know your name, might give you better marks for being one of her 'gels', and who knows what gems of geographical information might inadvertently fall from her lips when least expected, gems which, if hastily scribbled on an exam sheet, might mean the difference between pass and fail. Then again, it was a night out, a valid excuse for not doing Geog homework and an occasion for a reunion with Porth Sec Boys in Bacchetta's cafe before going home.

In actual fact I think joining the Rangers was a bad move. Not only did Miss Orsman get to know your name, but also your movements, parents, background, proclivities, abilities and possibilities. She expected more of you and was deeply mortified when you didn't come up to scratch, irretrievably mournful when you sinned.

We were seven or eight in the Geography group, so in reality Miss Orsman needed no more than sixty seconds to establish who was carrying on in the subject from Form 5. Our presence was required three afternoons a week in the Geography room, one of the largest subject rooms in the school, in the New Block. 'New' in this instance denoted recently constructed, with an uncertain future in mind, of cardboard and silver paper covered with pimply plaster instead of Pennant Sandstone like the rest of the school with its air of permanence. Amazingly it has survived to the present day though it is not the most eye-catching piece of architecture in the area other than for its look of tolerated distress. It was not damp however, being raised from the ground and supported by strategically placed bricks, often the attention of rebels who fancied themselves as Samson. Younger members of the school explored the underpinnings as a pastime.

In the company of Ianto Full Pelt, Miss Orsman's aged, shaggy, orange-coloured terrier which helped her keep order in turbulent junior forms by baring his ancient teeth at anything that moved, we studied Geography in all its guises. The sorry animal could scarcely budge on arthritic legs, apart from the regularly recurring occasions when he forgot about the polished lino in the corridor outside. Then he would skid and go whizzing along, missing the entrance, on legs pointing in all four major directions of the compass, a puzzled look of distant remembered pup-hood, speed and insouciance on his hoary face.

We took copious notes dictated by the teacher until our lifeless hands no longer felt as if they were part of our bodies. What was worse was that she proceeded at a certain speed, her own, fast, so that you were half-way through taking down a sentence when she was at the end of the next. This being 1953, before the era of pupil liberation, no-one even dared think of saying as they would now, "Hey, slow down will you? What do you think I am? A jet-propelled ink-missile or something?", or even asking "Would you mind going a bit slower Miss Orsman please?" as this would activate waves of patient, tolerated reproof upon the tortoise's head.

Consequently, girls were constantly leaning over to look at their neighbour's book, covert whispering was rife, heads clashed as they moved sideways, and sighs of despair, the noisiest unofficial sounds allowed, were numerous. If only we had a musical accompaniment as we swayed around more or less in unison, an unenlightened onlooker might think this was some newfangled exercise for the benefit of the desk-bound. A typical, hissed conversation would proceed as follows:

"Oh, A..Anne [Morris], get your 'ead out of my book!" Anne would plead,

"Pat [Morris – no relation], what she say after 'continental shelf'?"

"Oh, how can I keep up if you keep asking me things? 'The ocean basins are more than full'"

Thirty seconds of peace might follow then Anne would once more have her head over Pat's shoulder and, reading quietly but audibly, "and their overflow at present covers more than eleven million square...square...What's that word Pat? I can't make it out."

"Oh God, 'miles', you idiot!"

By this time Pat Morris would have fallen behind and would proceed to look at Margaret Algate's book, next along. Pat would write for a few seconds and turn the page causing whispered howls of anguish from her left and restraining fingers on the page. "Oh don't turn over yet Pat, I'm only on 'variations of density in the crust'."

"Oh look at Mary's book then!" and Pat would carry on, deserting her tardy friend in mid-phrase. The result of this would be a sudden leftwards head movement. I might well have been struggling by this time, move right to look at Anne's page and there would be a loud crack as our heads met with an accompanying "Ouch!" or "Aaww!" – in undertones, of course.

During one afternoon we arranged for the fastest writer, Florence Wilton, to sit on the extreme right of the bench and in descending order going left to the slowest, Anne. Heads would then only need to proceed in an easterly direction to catch up and hopefully there would be no more painful collisions. It was only marginally better though and the system fell into abeyance when a particularly virulent 'flu germ in December felled most of the class and we all had to copy up from Anne whose work was a succession of sentences with no endings and big gaps everywhere. She drew beautifully artistic sketch maps but with most of the explanatory notes missing.

Not all Sixth Form students could be taught all of the time so, of necessity, we occasionally had free lessons known by the more imposing name of 'study periods', those in authority not wanting girls to think they were 'free' to do as they wished. Good gracious, girls might conceivably bring in newspapers to read, or even worse, women's magazines, and fill their heads with all sorts of romantic rot. They might even think themselves at liberty to write letters, possibly, horror of horrors, to boyfriends, or file their nails, chat about last night's *Goon Show* on the radio or the latest hit record and its decadent singer. To complement the gravity of the study period, they were conducted in the august aura of the Library and supervised by a member of staff. Activity in the way of movement and talk was to be minimal.

These lessons were of course spent by the Geographers in copying up. Others might be able to get on with a language translation, English essay, Biological analysis, Mathematical configuration, Historical chart or simply day-dream (allowed because it was quiet and not glaringly illicit), but Geographers used the time in the detective work of tracking the unfinished sentence and missing, usually essential, word. In time the supervising staff got used to requests such as, "May I go and borrow Margaret's Geography book please?"

"Is it all right if I ask Evelyn what this says? It's her Geography book and I can't make these words out."

"Can I give Caryl her Geography book back please?"

The chief source of all the whispering and to-ing and fro-ing was therefore the Geography class but the staff soon recognised us and would resignedly wave us on to our port of call with a flourish of the hand or nod of the head. Other students though who might need to cross the room for a quick confab with a mate were thoroughly and suspiciously interrogated.

"Why do you want to speak to Margaret Evans?"

"Why haven't you got your own text book?"

"What are you copying up? Let me see please."

"Are you sure you need to speak to Jennifer? Be quick then so as not to disturb everyone. People are trying to work you know!" the supervisor erroneously assumed.

During the two years of the A level course, we filled approximately a dozen large, taupe-coloured exercise books impressively entitled, 'The Holborn Geographical Note Book. E.S.A. London' with extensive notes on and drawings of, among other topics, features of Physical Geography. Information about bits of rock around the world with mysterious foreign nomenclature – zeugen, yardangs, inselberge and dreikanter, and the life history of a river (all presumably having the same tale to tell), details of wind, water and ice erosion found their illustrated, albeit verbally truncated, way into our pages. These, together with data about earth movement including earthquakes and volcanoes we marked out on world maps for possible future reference *re* holidays and/or residency. Impressive world maps they were too, in a brown or black indent on thick, shiny paper, not only showing latitude and longitude lines, but contours, as well as information about the projection and scale. Not for the Sixth form the shaky, hand-rolled maps we had hitherto been given, with two or three coastlines and chunks of continent missing where the ink had dried. Oh no, these splendid specimens were from the stable, so they informed us in minute lettering at the bottom, of George Philip & Son Ltd., of the London Geographical Institute. It was an event when one landed on the desk in front of you, hearts missed a beat at its delicate beauty. It was a shame really to deface them with drawing and writing. You just wanted to slip your copy in your satchel and smuggle it out of school to put up on your bedroom wall at home, devoid of the information you felt must spoil it. So everyone took the utmost care. Place names were minutely and apologetically printed in pin-point sharpened 3B pencils, and rivers, towns, mountains and lowlands which required coloured pencils were first painstakingly and faintly traced in, in soft lead.

It was through one of these handsome creations I first discovered I had vision problems. We had been distributed with maps of eastern Scandinavia, notably Finland and I was dismayed to see mine was dirty with little spots. Out came my rubber and I gently attacked the offending area. Anne Morris, sitting on my right, was intrigued by my activity. "What you doing Mary?" she whispered.

"Ttt, she's given me a mucky map, look. It's got all black spots on it," I grumbled. Rapid inspection by Anne prompted a sharp nudge which dislodged my rubber out of my hand on to the floor, sending it bouncing inevitably and irretrievably off in the direction of the dog. "Oh, A-Anne! What you do that for?" I moaned, looking under the table to say farewell to another disappearing bit of equipment.

"They're not black spots, silly! They're islands! Look, see, they're islands! There's lots of little islands in Finland and you can't rub 'em out. They won't rub out. They're supposed to be there," Anne comprehensively explained.

"Oh. They looked like dirty marks to me they did," I countered lamely, then espying more inside the coastline, "And look at these! These can't be islands 'cos they're on land. My map *is* mucky. You'll have to lend me your rubber now. Mine's probably been devoured by Ianto."

"Oh, Mary, you dope! They're lakes they are! There's lots of lakes in Finland too. It's nearly all holes. Look, my map's exactly the same as yours. You need glasses you do!" Which I got.

We studied Wales and North America in all their glory, so much the better revealed to me after a couple of visits to Stewart Neviss, opticians in Hannah Street, Porth and furnished with a pair of their NHS glasses with specks of silver paper incorporated in the flesh pink frames. Map Projections which totally confused the innumerate among us and Ethnography, a study of simple societies around the world, hunting, fishing and collecting peoples, some of whom wore no clothes and drank blood drawn from veins in the necks of oxen, despite not being relations of

Dracula, were part of the syllabus. We studied Ethnography very late in the course and didn't appear to finish it, leaving the Borneo dayaks in G strings, lighting fires in their long houses perched on stilts in lakes. Our teacher seemed to have little enthusiasm for this part of the course. We suspected she recoiled from eccentric, possibly embarrassing revelations.

Personally, Miss Orsman remained singularly unencumbered by notions of abashment about her own body provided it was in the company of other females – or at least, having no evidence to the contrary I presumed that to be the case. In Guide and Ranger camps there were rather primitive, communal, cold water wash basins and some girls in those days couldn't even get used to the idea of cleaning their teeth if not in private, let alone the more intimate parts of their person. We were to surround ourselves with a *rideau morale* Miss Orsman said and all would be well. 'Premature blindness' is how it was translated by others.

Her lack of discomposure was illustrated one May morning at the Gorwelion Guide Camp, Porthcawl, where we were staying for the weekend. It being relatively warm with the rain clouds at least an hour away, Miss O decided that as there was a rising tide on Traeth y Mor, what option did we have but to sea bathe? Apprehensively but intrepidly we trooped after our tenacious leader over the dunes, in bathing costumes, clutching bathing caps, towels, a few clothes and a comb. Never one for hesitation, despite the dark grey sky, she rallied the troops to march bravely forth into the waves, no hanging back or shivering on the edge. To all, even the non-swimmers, "Plunge under the first breaker! That's the best way to get in" was her instruction – which she did – while we watched, slightly numb from the event, the unexpected command ordering prompt immersion, and the cold sea swishing around our toes. Numbness turned to horror, to amusement, to fascination, in seconds, as our leader emerged, not quite like Venus arising from the waves, but almost, as she had lost one side of her costume, and the left, not inconsequential bosom, billowed in the breeze. Initially she hadn't realised anything was amiss, but someone coughed in the group of goggling girls or perhaps she caught a glimpse of a vast expanse of creamy white out of the corner of her eye. "Oops!" she said, simultaneously gathering up the liberated appendage in both arms and popping it back inside its brown, straining, woollen fortification. She turned, plunged under the next breaker and swam off. No embarrassment, blushing or confusion as far as we could see. Her *rideau morale* was at work. But it provided those present with a life-long memory, at which some, now middle-aged ladies still shake their heads in wonder, and giggle.

# 4. Geography in the Field

The great thing about Geography were the outings, or Field Trips as they were officially called, rarely held in school time but fun all the same. The intention wasn't fun, but work, but how could we not enjoy ourselves marching around in the open air with like-minded, high-spirited, happy friends and possibly the most unconventional of the teachers in the school?

Since mud was usually involved, we had a dispensation to wear 'civvies' as Miss O put it, as school uniform might get damaged. "Be sure to wear old clothes," she would say. She would go on to explain that she herself would be wearing old, superfluous clothes – a skirt, for example that might have taken part in other expeditions and got torn on a stile or an unfriendly, protruding bramble. Once a garment had reached such a draggletailed state it was not worth mending other than with a piece of sellotape, or sticking plaster if no sellotape were available. Life was too short to spend time on needlework repairs when sticky tape was just as effective. The aforementioned time could then be profitably spent on the study of the earth and all its fascinating forms. "Also, wear sturdy, comfortable footwear," were her instructions, "As we shall be embarking on a short walk, and in places it might be muddy underfoot."

After the first Geography outing undertaken in Form 4 we were prepared for Miss Orsman's 'short walks'. We visited the northern edge of the coalfield where the Pennant Sandstone, Carboniferous Limestone, Coal Measures and Millstone Grit (probably not in that order) come to the surface just above Hirwaun. The land sweeps up to finish suddenly in a cut-off anticline and we went to examine this and the glaciated lake Llyn Fawr at its foot. This was our special geographical lake. The school had built up an affection for it over the years, every O level class having visited this watershed of the Neath and Taff valleys several times. The lake was especially close to the hearts of those girls in Craig y Llyn school house as it was the flagship, so to speak, of that mountain. We rarely went anywhere else on field trips and it was rumoured Miss Orsman had a special male friend in the area she was hoping to catch a glimpse of. Later we discovered she had studied the region in depth as part of her MA thesis and was personally acquainted with every rock outcrop, scree and stream of the mountain and hairpin bend of the road.

The bus stopped on the Rhigos mountain road from the Rhondda Fawr for us to view the area, the breathtaking panorama north to Penderyn and the Beacons, the Neath and Dulais valleys to the west and the Cynon and Taff to the east.

"This is all right," we thought as we, then uninitiated Fourth formers, thinking it was to be a day of pleasant sightseeing, trooped off the coach together with the O and A level classes, to admire the scenery.

"We're just going for a short walk first," announced Miss Orsman, cutting short our reverie. "Follow me! Stop and listen when I raise my hand and Form 6 can take notes." She marched off in her sellotaped-up skirt, at a cracking pace over the hummocky grass, ferns, moss, heather, stony and boggy patches, pointing at things with her walking stick which we barely saw as we strove to keep up. If you were not in the Athletics team you had no chance. Soon, the would-be Geographers were strung out over half a mile, a few red-faced, panting Sixth formers were racing on behind our tenacious leader, endeavouring to keep within earshot, paper flapping and pen poised to take notes but not having the puff, the vitality or the chance to write anything.

Some of the younger girls gave up and played hide and seek among the boulders; some just sat on a patch of grass and had a kip in the sun; others strolled in the general direction of the action but miles behind, geographical study being the last thing on their minds.

"Wha's the time?" from Mairona Parry.

"S' only 'a' past ten." Margaret Algate always wore a watch. ("See my watch? It's a good make this is. It's an Avia. An' it's gold as well.")

"Time for elevenses then," said Caryl, the brisk organiser. "Anybody got any biscuits?"

"Yeah, but they're in the bus."

"Oh, go and get them Margaret, will you? 'S not far, an' I'm starvin'. We can 'ave a little picnic here then." Mary Price looked back the mile or so to the road. "The bus isn' locked. Look, you can see the driver sitting on the step 'avin' a smoke."

Margaret looked anxiously in the direction of the by now, minute, figure of our teacher, some miles away, striding onwards, ever onwards to the OS trig point atop Craig y Llyn.

"Oh, I can't go back all that way. I'd never catch up. Ozzie'd probably be back here before me." She finished lamely, "Anyway I like a cup of tea with my biscuit. You can go if you like. I'll tell you where they are."

30

No-one keen to take a mile hike back to search for biscuits prompted disappointed looks and the ever optimistic Mairona to say, "Never mind! There's a town down there. Perhaps she'll let us stop and have a cup of coffee or somethin' in a café."

Several of the more realistic groaned. "You must be jokin'. If we stop there we'll be marched off to see the scree slope or the alluvial plain or the ox-bow lake or whatever."

"Anyway that's Hirwaun. Probably 'asn' got a caff," added Mary Price.

"'Asn't got an alluvial plain or an ox-bow either 'cos there's no river. An' it's flat so there's no scree slope," Florence Wilton advised.

"Oh shurrup about Geography will you Flor?" said her friend Jennifer.

"Well, this is supposed to be a Geography trip you know!"

Jennifer put an indignant look on her face. "I don't see you doin' much keepin' up with her and listenin' to her geographical explanations."

"Only 'cos I stepped in a bog and got a shoeful of mud. My sock's soaking look, as well as filthy. And it's all squelchy too," Florence commented ruefully.

"You'd 'ave to be an Olympic Gold Medallist to keep up with her in any case," observed Mairona.

Margaret Algate, no doubt still pondering on her coach-shackled biscuits to go with a cup of tea, changed the subject. "She won't let us go in a café anyway. We're too many. It'd be like the invasion of Normandy."

Mary Price quipped, "Gracious me, no! Even if we weren't many, she wouldn't let the sinful pleasures of coffee, biscuits an' choc'late deprave Porth County girls."

"Further deprave, you mean," added Caryl.

As we wandered in the general direction of the Irish Sea, we met a jaunty Miss Orsman and a few jaded Sixth Formers on the way back.

"You're a bit slow, girls, but never mind." She glanced at her watch, "We're in good time. Now I'd like you to walk to the Trig station and view the area from there. It's very important from the point of view of radial drainage. As you know full well," she continued hopefully and paused as though wanting confirmation of the fact.

"Yes, miss," someone obligingly said.

Then, pointing "The Afan, Dulais and Tawe rivers flow in a south easterly direction, and the Rhonddas, Cynon and Taff south westerly. It's an important spot that watershed which is the northern edge of the coalfield at the head of the Valleys. On the way have a look at the scree slope above Llyn Fawr, but don't go too close to the edge. Boulders at the top, fine scree at the bottom. Now, we're going back to the coach for a spot of early lunch. We're leaving at 12 on the dot. Don't be late!"

"No, miss," said the obliging voice.

She bounced off, clearly satisfied that her pupils were benefiting from the expedition and followed by the hot, exhausted Sixth Formers whose expressions indicated a clear desire to throttle their mentor. Needless to say, we were back on the bus eating our sandwiches well before the appointed departure time, not having made much effort to reach the designated OS station and not caring overmuch about the direction of flow of the various rivers.

So we knew what to expect when Miss Orsman announced a field trip with a short walk included, and turned up with rucksacks full of food, spare socks and plasters: the latter, not so much to mend skirts as blisters caused by the sturdy, comfortable, expedition-type shoes. The area of her expertise extended to the Ystradfellte locality in the south-east of the Brecon Beacons. Here we must have opened up the route along the Mellte river for miles downstream in true explorer style following the doughty dame. We hacked our way through undergrowth and overgrowth, clambered over fallen tree trunks and their jutting roots, sometimes having to balance on slimy, mossy stones in the water itself, slipped off eroded river-bank edges, got scratched, stung, poked and slapped by lurking brambles, nettles, branches, foliage and the odd, peeved wasp. When we reached the Falls where the Mellte meets the sunken Hepste river and plunges underground to join it for a few miles through the Limestone, we were a bedraggled, muddy, healthily-glowing bunch. In the triumph of the exploration, had she so demanded, we would probably have followed Miss O into the caving system before us. However, "We can't follow the river any longer. Although it runs through caves, some of these are small and filled with water so it requires swimming blind through short tunnels into the next cave," she explained. We were rather surprised that a minor consideration like 'swimming blind' should deter her, but she continued, "So we'll stroll along the former dry river-bed until the river emerges, which is quite a popular beauty spot where we'll have a spot of lunch." Which we did.

Miss Orsman gave up several Saturdays to take us girls on hikes or to the museum in Cardiff. She appeared to enjoy the occasions, and we certainly did, not so much because of newly acquired geographical knowledge but because of camaraderie. Her enjoyment was nullified however unless each individual girl made a personal speech of gratitude as she got off the bus. She always made it known beforehand that whatever happened she required to be thanked, (even if our true appreciation of her dedication to our cause only really evolved decades later). Consequently, disembarkation along the route and back in Porth took a long time, long enough for some to have their tea on the coach and others a quick nap before the exertions of the evening at the Tonypandy Library or Llwyncelyn Rink dance halls.

I distinctly recall one bitterly cold January afternoon when Geography was on the time-table. Although I went to the Geog room, it was with deceit, not study in mind. Geography lessons were constantly being peripherally disturbed by girls arriving to write their names on the signing-out sheet pinned to the back of the door. I suppose this sheet was in Miss Orsman's room as she was the Deputy Headmistress and it was within her realm of administration. No matter what the reason was, an excuse to avoid some bothersome lesson by going ride-about on the Valley buses, window-shopping in Pontygwaith, bird-watching on Penrhiwgwynt or singing with the Salvation Army, as long as you signed this sheet, everything appeared to be acceptable. Ninety-nine per cent of the reasons given for absence were 'dentist', 'doctor' and 'feeling ill' with the occasional 'going to meet cousin coming back from Africa'.

A young, Welsh, devastatingly handsome actor, for whom one would willingly give up chocolate, had just made the first film in which he had a starring role. This was Richard Burton, the film was *The Robe*, it was on in Cardiff and, like most of the female population of the enlightened world, Jennifer Jones, Mary Price, Caryl and I were incurably enamoured of him. What more natural then than to take a mid-week afternoon trip to the capital when the transport was cheaper, the queues shorter and the crowds thinner? We had school hockey matches on Saturdays our only free day, and we would miss those on serious threat of decapitation, shin bruises deliberately inflicted accidentally or forced exile. Jennifer wasn't a Geographer and had an afternoon free of lessons, Mary was a Scientist and an able circumventer of rules when necessary, Caryl decided she would have a head-ache and take the whole day off and I was possibly the most brazen sinner, missing the Geography class and, to boot, signing out with the lie 'Music Exam', which was partly true but which had taken place a week earlier after school in Pontypridd.

We had decided to meet up on the 1.55 Rhondda train to Cardiff, Mary boarding in Treorchy, Caryl getting on at Tonypandy, Jennifer in Porth and me in Trehafod. Jennifer, Mary and I signed out after morning school, taking care to perform this task separately, then went our own ways home to change out of school uniform.

Apart from the biting, easterly cold, the afternoon was a great success. There was no queue at the Capitol, Richard Burton's profile was more delicious than the strawberry ice-cream we consumed by the tubful, we all enviously loathed Jean Simmons, not so much for her beauty as her proximity to our hero, and we were proud to be Welsh like him. Heads full of images of sunny, ancient Roman scenes and comely masculine legs emerging from short togas, we happily made our way back to Queen Street station for the 5 o'clock Valleys train. It was reasonably empty when it arrived and we settled into a compartment which stopped opposite where we had been waiting. I was just passing round the last of the sweets I'd brought when I noticed Caryl's face, open-mouthed in horror. "Oh, my God!" she articulated. We turned to follow the direction of her gaze. There stumping up the platform, brief-case awkwardly held in arthritic hand was Bessie, our head-mistress. Evidently she had been to some kind of meeting or conference in Cardiff that day. Typical that we should have chosen that very afternoon for our escapade!

"Bloody Hell! Just our luck!" moaned Mary.

"What shall we do?" I panicked.

"Duck!" answered Jennifer.

"No! No! Don't duck!" urged Caryl, "She'll think the compartment's empty and come in here. Stand up, mill about, make it look full, but face the other way!"

Bessie clumped past. I couldn't resist a glance over my shoulder, paranoically feeling she'd recognised me as she looked in, seeking comparatively tranquil quarters. I was aware of someone trying to strangle me as a disembodied hand grabbed at the school scarf I'd forgotten I was wearing. A door nearby ground open and slammed shut. We held our breaths for several seconds, only eyes moving, before Jennifer confirmed, "She's in the next compartment!"

"D'you think she saw us?"

"No, I don't think so, but crikey, it was close!"

"She had a good look in!"

"What if she'd come in here? What would we have done?"

"Doesn't bear thinking about!"

34

In the mid-fifties, Valleys trains were, fortuitously, of the old-fashioned, soot-in-the-eye when face-out-of-the window type – no corridors. Whole carriage-compartment trains didn't exist then, only in Russia and uncomfortable places east which was fortunate for us as our Sixth form careers would probably have ceased to exist from the following day or at the least be blighted with eternal detention if not damnation.

Our next problem, basically mine, as I would be the first to face the predicament, was how and when to get off. Being towards the rear I would have to pass Bessie's compartment to reach the exit. She would most likely be disembarking in Porth where she lived in Cemetery Road, next door to the school. Trehafod was out, but was Porth safe? Could Jennifer and I linger behind at Porth and merge with the background, dawdle in doorways, cower behind platform benches? What if she and we were the only passengers? She'd be bound to see us! Fed-up and wanting my tea, I didn't make a move at Trehafod station. As the train began to set off I could see my house on the hill with the shop-door open and the lights invitingly on. I wanted to be there! My father would be home from work soon, my mother would be making dinner and I was feeling hungry, woebegone and cold. The train rattled merrily on, taking the long bend between the Lewis Merthyr colliery on the left and Llwyncelyn on the right as the welcoming lights of my village disappeared. "How long before I saw them again?" I wondered. Soon we were coming into Porth station.

Jennifer was hovering by the door. "We'll wait 'til she's going through the exit, then jump out at the last minute, Mary, OK?"

"Yes, OK," I agreed dispiritedly.

"And don't wear your scarf!" insisted Mary Price.

An action-less age seemed to pass as we peeped through the window. Jennifer began to panic. "She's not getting off! Why isn't she getting off? She lives in Porth! She must get off!" The train was starting up again to looks of all-round dismay.

"Oh God, I hope she gets off before Treorchy!" said Mary. "Perhaps we'll have to go to the end of the line."

"Where's that?" Jennifer wanted to know.

"Somewhere up near the North Pole," I grumbled, increasingly downcast and frustrated, feeling I was going to spend the rest of my life on this train.

"And we'll have to pay extra for all this riding around. Oh, this is not funny any more!" Jennifer complained.

"No you won't," consoled Caryl, who knew all about these things because her brother was in the Royal Navy, "because you won't be leaving the station. Just cross over the platform and catch the next train down."

"If there is another train down!" I moaned.

In the event, Bessie got off at Llwynypia, two stops after Porth. Did she see our anxious faces peering platform-wards into the gloom as the train overtook the disembarked passengers? The lights were on in the carriage, there were no blinds to pull down and we were as clearly visible as actors on a floodlit stage. No doubt we'd discover on the morrow! Relieved we could escape from our prison, but by now sick and tired of the outing, Jennifer and I got off with Caryl at Tonypandy and waved good-bye to the north-bound Mary.

I finally arrived home, travel-scarred, three hours after leaving Cardiff to a baked-dry dinner and a worried mother whose worry soon turned to annoyance on hearing my reluctant explanation. Dad pretended to be serious but the corner of his mouth was twitching with suppressed amusement. But I wasn't amused as I hungrily tried to dismember an ossified, black lamb chop covered in dry, cracked gravy lying sadly next to some curling, brownish cabbage and yellow, exfoliating potatoes with Mam going on, "Well, serve you right if you go mitching off school, even if you didn't have lessons" – I had told them I had a free afternoon in order not to compound the wrong-doing – "to go janting off to Cardiff to see some ol' film star! Oh, I don't know! I'd have thought you'd have better things to do with your time. Haven't you got any studying to do? And what about your homework? Don't expect sympathy from me, mind, if you fail your exams. And that nice dinner I made's gone all dry...." It went on. Dad had decamped to the shop to read the paper. I was waiting to hear about scrubbing floors in the Vaughan's Arms, my predicted fate at five years of age because I couldn't read. I'd heard it all before. Same sentences, different order.

School next day proceeded normally until French in mid-afternoon when a Fifth Former came in the room and spoke to Miss Llewelyn who said, "Miss Hudd wants to see you Mary," mischievously adding with a smile, "In trouble again! I don't know. You Sixth Formers!" whereupon my heart uttered one last, huge beat then stopped. On fast feet, the only part of me that seemed to possess any life, the blood in my body having drained south, I ran to her study to know my fate as soon as possible. A grey-faced Caryl was waiting outside.

"Oh well. This is it!" She drew a finger across her throat, "Curtains!"

After a timid knock, we entered at the Head's bidding. She didn't look up. "Just a minute please girls while I finish this letter to the Director." She must be writing to inform him of the expulsion she was about to give us! Mental, and by now fast approaching physical torment was prolonged until she was done. Then a long, searching look. "I was at a meeting in Cardiff yesterday," My eyes briefly met Caryl's, "so I couldn't see you then" – Oh yes she could have! – "Anyway I'm sorry this is a bit late, but I wanted to ask if you'd read in Assembly this week." She smiled pleasantly, "Don't look so worried, otherwise I might think you've got guilty consciences about something!"

# 5. Rangers in the Fairfield

On one occasion though, our heinous crime was detected and we lived in agonised suspense for several days expecting the worst for our misdemeanour. Miss Orsman, as leader of the Porth Rangers, had arranged a weekend away at Gorwelion, the Guide camp house on the dunes at Porthcawl together with the Pontypridd Rangers and their formidable leader Miss Mary Hunt. Miss Lloyd who shared a house with Miss O and who was also involved in some Guide Company somewhere, came along for good measure.

When we were younger these Guide camps were fun. We could play games in the field fronting the house, explore the woods behind, and practise our raw cooking skills in the big kitchen. No matter what inedible mish-mash was concocted, everything would be eaten up as everyone was constantly famished. At seventeen such childish pleasures no longer appealed. The older teenager needs something more exhilarating and exciting than singing 'Row, row, row your boat' in rounds around a camp-fire (or indoor hearth in this case) to end the day, with lights out at 10 o'clock, having spent most of it learning morse and flag codes, orienteering from maps, how to bandage up wounded people or erect tents so they don't collapse in a sylvan breeze.

A couple of miles west we couldn't fail to see the outline of the Big Wheel and Figure 8 ride of Coney Beach Fair and at dusk the bright lights attracted continual yearning glances. Finally it was too much for high-spirited Caryl who had devolved 'a plan for nocturnal entertainment' and wanted like-minded, mettlesome friends to meet for a confab after lunch (rest time) in the small, ground floor, back room with three bunk beds she shared with two others. The 'plan' was simple. We would retire, exhausted, at 9.30 but after the customary inspection and lights-out at 10, when all was quiet, we would dress in normal clothes, noiselessly make our way to Caryl's room, climb out through her window and be gone to the enticing delights of the Fair. Most knew of the proposed expedition but only six or seven were prepared to participate. Some were too fat or too awkward to get out of the narrow aperture, others didn't relish the long walk over the unlit dunes in the complete darkness while yet others, about as madcap as a piece of toast, thought they would be too tired. Some were too prim or fearful of discovery and the consequences. A clandestine practice of window exodus was undertaken on the spot to the accompaniment of tearing noises and yelps of pain as people became entangled with the window furniture. Personally I didn't like Fairs, being squeamish about violent movement inflicted on my person over which I had no control, but wanted to go along for the elation of the illicit outing.

At the appointed hour, waiting my turn to clamber out and no doubt feeling poetic in my excitement, I couldn't resist quoting Longfellow's lines someone had written in my autograph book when I was in Form 2 when autograph books were all the rage:

And the night shall be filled with music
And the cares that infest the day
Shall fold their tents like Arabs,
And as silently steal away.

"SShh!" said Caryl.

"Mmm. That's all very well," said Margaret Algate, who in the event gave up the escapade at the bottom of the field and went back, "but what if someone sees us going down to the lane? We'll be for it!"

"They won't," said little curly-haired Barbara Phillips, "Judith Clarke's keeping a look-out."

"SShh!" said Commander Caryl again. "There's too much nattering."

"Huh! A fat lot of use Judith's keeping a look-out is," Margaret complained, "She can't stop someone looking out of their window now, can she? And what if someone in charge is staring out of their window romantically looking at the pale moon over the shimmering sea?"

"Don't be so soft! They'll see something else other than moon," giggled Mary Price.

"No moon tonight," said Jennifer, clearly relishing the adventure.

"SShh! Will you be quiet!" ordered Caryl in a whisper. "They'll catch us before we're even out of the building." For a few seconds only squeaks and suppressed grunts were heard as the exit was underway.

"I just hope my sister doesn't find out about this, that's all," Rhiannon Jarman piped up. (Her older, responsible-looking and doubtless rule-obeying sister was an official and something important in the Rangers.) "Eileen'd kill me!"

Barbara Phillips joked, "Oh well, that's a better fate than if Ossie gets to know." We groaned.

"Oh, shurrup will you!" commanded our leader, "No-one will find out, but if you lot go on jabbering, they will, so no talking from now on. Right?"

Once out of the rear of the house we crept alongside the hedge to the bottom of the field and out into the lane, slightly anxious at seeing a light on in the Leaders' quarters at the far end of the building from ours. But then, it was only 10.10 and adults didn't go to bed until 11 or later.

"I hope Judith stays awake to open the window for us to get back in," I mused, not fancying a night bedding down in the already damp field.

"Oh well, we'll just have to tap on the window 'til she wakes," Caryl wasn't worried about anything.

Some people had a wonderful time at the Fair despite being constantly plagued by boys whose attentions we did not require on that particular occasion.

"Hiya girls! Looking for a good time are you?"

"Not the sort of good time you're offering, thank you!"

Typically, they persisted. "Fancy a ride on the Dodgems then, ladies?"

After disdainful, Girls'-Grammar-School looks and not deigning to reply, one said, "Hmm, obviously not ladies!"

Assailed by the greasy cooking, fairground smell and overwhelmed by the pop-culture sights and sounds, we merged with the background and bought an assortment of soft, twirly ice-cream, chips in little cardboard containers, sickly, sticky candyfloss, garish lollipops, chewing-gum, waffles piled high with synthetic, foamy cream, hot-dogs, hamburgers and ring donuts covered in runny icing. After the day's healthy, but spartan meals of boiled eggs, bread and butter with tea, cheese salad, bread and butter with water and finally sardines on toast (two pieces) with dry Madeira cake as a special treat and more tea we were more than ready to spoil our diet on a low-brow menu. Cholesterol hadn't been invented then, but on Fair food that night we must have wiped five years off the longevity of our arteries.

Not being a devotee of having myself tossed around like a brew in a cocktail-shaker, I tended to watch the capers of the others from behind a veil of pink, thinly-woven wadding on a stick tasting like sweetened cotton-wool. Screams and cries of joyous terror emanated from friends as they hung on for dear life to the trap-bar on the Swing Boat hurling them up towards the night sky. Dare-devil Caryl was the only one courageous enough to savour the doubtful delights of the Spinning Drum – a contraption which spun around so fast, the customer was left sticking, flattened to the wall while the floor dropped some twenty feet. The rest of us watched in fascinated horror and admiration for the dare-anything girl. A dubious pleasure indeed to my unadventurous disposition for which the Penny Falls represented extreme abandonment and the Prancing Horses Roundabout, foolhardiness beyond measure.

"Come in a Dodgem car with me Mary?" Jennifer proposed.

"No thanks. I'll hold your purse while you go."

"Oh, come on gul. You must go on something. I'll drive. I won't crash into anything. I'm good at this I am."

Against my instincts I reluctantly agreed to spend the next five minutes, face scrunched up, hands clenched, expecting my teeth to be shaken out of my head, blitzkrieged by shocks and shakes as Jennifer, either through total incompetence or bloody-mindedness bumped into every obstacle in sight including the metal rim when there was nothing else to ram.

The vilest machines were objects of desire to most of the others. The Octopus, in which brave people sat in little boxes at the end of mechanical arms which waved wildly in the air as the thing rotated; the Rocket which went upside down faster and faster through a 360 degree circumference and the Caterpillar contrivance which built up speed as it whirled around at a frightening pace up and down a slope while a cover descended to conceal the intemperate riders. Oh, what fun indeed! I'd willingly have paid not to submit to these experiences. After it was generally, teasingly agreed that Mary Davies was about as daring as a baby's rubber duck and drunk with jarring and jolting, not to mention flushed with the escapade's success, we began the long trek back to Gorwelion. Jollity became caution as, past midnight, we got near, but all was still, dark and quiet on the house front, the back window was open although its guardian Judith was fast asleep. We climbed in with not a few giggles, waking her up and then were soon all bunked down along the length of the corridor.

The warning bell for next day's breakfast was ringing in no time and eventually, bleary-eyed Rangers were washed, dressed and seated before their hard-boiled egg. No-one took much notice of the Officials until Miss Orsman marched brusquely out of the room, followed by her right-hand man, Miss Lloyd, without her usual 'Good morning, Rangers', and instructions for the day. The feeling something was afoot was confirmed when Miss Hunt rose to announce that Miss Orsman wished to interview certain people in the 'flat' reserved for Authority at the western end of the building. The game was up. Officialdom knew of the escapade and was clearly angry despite the harmlessness of the occasion. It would probably require vengeance to be wreaked. But how had we been found out? Who had told on us? How did they know who had gone?

The escapees, ashen-faced now as well as bleary-eyed were summoned individually. My turn wasn't long in coming. The misses Orsman, Lloyd and Hunt sat, in full regalia, at a desk under a window, and the hot seat faced them. The court-martial began.

"You were absent from the building last evening from approximately 10 o'clock to 12.15, Mary." There was no point in denying the obvious.

"Yes Captain."

"Have you anything to say for yourself?"

"No Captain...I mean I'm sorry Captain."

"Where did you go? And what did you do to be sorry for?" Things were already looking bad and we'd hardly begun. Clearly, apologies were not expected at the beginning of the interrogation. Quickly realising my incompetence at this sort of cunning, courtroom approach to investigation I'd seen in films where the clever lawyer soon makes the defendant look an utter fool as far as wits are concerned, I decided only to answer the question and not give any supplementary information. So, with head lowered as three pairs of eyes probed my impure soul.

"Well, we went to the Fair. And I had some candy floss, and candy floss is bad for your teeth." I looked up apologetically to gauge any adverse reaction, only to see Miss Hunt look away. hand over mouth as though trying to suppress a smile. Miss Orsman and Lloyd continued to be implacable in their displeasure however.

"Were there any others with you, that is, people from outside the company?" I was puzzled. Nobody knew anyone in Porthcawl. She must be alluding to the opposite sex. Yes, that was it! Boys! What did she think we were? Boy mad? Didn't she realise boys were a nuisance? I answered indignantly, "No miss!"

"Did you go on any of the attractions in the Fair?"

"Yes. I went for a ride on the Dodgems. But I can't say I liked it much."

"Why not?" Miss Lloyd took over the interlocutor's reins. "Did anybody try to intervene when you were on this ride?"

What was she talking about now? My reply seemed incredibly naive even to me.

"No, it's just that I don't like being bumped and jerked about much. I don't really like Fairs all that much."

"Well, why did you go at all, you silly girl?" Miss Orsman wanted to know.

"I suppose I wasn't feeling tired at lights-out. I didn't think I could go to sleep. I was wide-awake."

"Well Mary, we're very disappointed in you – thought you were altogether a more responsible sort of girl. Your parents would be upset to know you'd been cavorting around Porthcawl at the dead of night, wouldn't they?" Miss Orsman didn't wait for a reply so I hurriedly nodded to be on the right track and she continued, "Is there anything else you want to tell us?" I thought I'd better admit to my other vice to clear my conscience.

"Well, I did have a few goes on the Penny Falls."

Miss Lloyd turned sharply to the other two, "What's that?" she hissed. Miss Hunt answered quietly, sucking in her cheeks, "Oh, it's a sort of gambling thing. You roll a penny down a slot to knock other coins off a ledge which you then win."

Miss Lloyd looked bewildered, then shocked as she heard the word, "gambling", which she repeated. Her horrified gaze fell on me, deeming me henceforth decidedly a lost cause and totally beyond redemption.

Finally, all the escapees were interviewed. Control must have come to the conclusion we were still 'virgo intacta' so we were thoroughly lectured about responsibility, accountability and culpability, not to mention duty and some even managed to weep which was good for effect. We were bafflingly called 'loose women' – a term which no-one understood. Hitherto the only irregular application of the term, apart from reference to an absconded prisoner or bolted wild animal from zoo or circus, was to the volatile state of one's bowels – something we'd prefer not to dwell on unnecessarily anyway. Punishment was in the form of cleaning the place in every nook and cranny for the rest of the stay and confinement to rooms after supper until breakfast. A hard fate for a few mouthfuls of sickly, pink fluff, a monetary loss of approximately 4d and a set of jarred bones!

Sometime during our career in Rangers, there was awed excitement among the Power-Wielders of the Movement as Olave Baden-Powell, widow of the Lord himself, the legend who had started this whole outdoor romp on the little island of Brownsea, off Poole, Dorset, was coming to town – Cardiff town that is –

for a weekend conference. No doubt she would bestow wisdom and benignancy on us and simply being in her presence would make us better human beings, which, especially after the Fair affair, some of us needed badly. Ranger wires all over south Wales were buzzing, organising the weekend and as girls from miles away had to be accommodated, it was the lot of the Cardiff Rangers to provide the lodgings. The conference was to be held in the Main Hall of Cardiff High School for Boys in Newport Road which we were well acquainted with as this was also the venue for classical French play performances we had to go and see now and then.

Unlike Porth, Cardiff is a big place so in order to be within reasonable walking distance of the location, it was principally the Rangers of south east Cardiff who were called upon to provide a bed for the Saturday night, or beds, probably in some cases if they were allocated two of their travelling brethren. I was in harness with Margaret Algate and we were to stay with Brenda Morris in Splott. Although we weren't keen on the sound of the place – we'd have preferred to have been staying in a Manor Park, or Woodland Court or Queensway for example, we were encouraged by the address – in Topaz Street which sounded bright and well, rich.

My parents had naturally enquired where I was to lay my head on the night absent from home and when I said Splott, Dad had smiled briefly in that sardonic, teasing way of his which Mam noticed, causing her to look a bit anxious. "Oh, I don't know that I like the sound of that much. Is it all right Jack?" she asked.

"Well," answered Dad who knew something about Cardiff, having worked there, "it's not exactly one of the er...posh parts of Cardiff, but yes, it's all right. Down there behind the Infirmary it is."

"Oh,well, it's only for one night anyway," mused Mam. "D'you think you'll be all right Mary? You'd better take a vest and your thick winceyette pyjamas and an extra cardigan." To Mam, if anywhere sounded a bit dubious, it meant that, more than likely, the bed arrangements would not be up to her scratch and you had to arm yourself against the unlikely, in my view, invasion of chill/bugs/other humans or all three.

"Oh no Mam, it's only September! Don't fuss! I'll be OK. I'm sharing with Margaret anyway." Mam had great faith in Margaret Algate as she had passed O level Maths, liked poking our fire and her father worked for the Gas Board. And Mam cooked with gas which she trusted more than electricity.

"Oh dear, are you sure? I won't have no sleep that night, worrying. Splott..." she ruminated uneasily.

Dad provided a little more information, "Some of the streets in Splott are named after jewels – Diamond, Emerald, Topaz, Sapphire, Pearl, and others after metals – Silver, Gold, Tin, Zinc, Lead, etc. Quite a good idea really. Very helpful to taxi drivers."

"Yes, that's right. We're staying in a girl's house in Topaz street."

Apart from Tin, Zinc and Lead, it sounded an affluent place to me, but I wasn't over-bothered and set off for Cardiff and my first visual encounter with a noble lady. I had sent Christmas cards for some years to Lady Rhys Williams at Miskin Manor on behalf of my auntie Rach over in Tydraw but never met the grande dame in person. Auntie Rach gave me the instructions, "To Lady Rhys Williams," she would say, "signed Rachel and Dick Richards." I wrote exactly what she said so the Lady for years received Tydraw cards, "To Lady Rhys Williams, signed Rachel and Dick Richards." She must have thought us an odd lot!

I don't remember much about the conference itself and the undoubtedly uplifting words of the long, long talk on the sunny Saturday afternoon by Lady Olave, only the part about how Sir Robert had been inspired to start the Scout movement, most of which I knew already. The fine, early autumn day streamed in through the long, multi-paned window and I could see bright blue bits of sky between fluffy clouds as I sat cross-legged on the unyielding parquet floor. My attention wandered constantly as I thought how much more interesting it would be to be at Ynysangharad Park watching Pontypridd RFC playing whoever they were playing on such a nice afternoon. However, there were always the delights of Topaz street to look forward to.

Margaret and I were allocated to Brenda Morris after tea. She seemed congenial enough if a bit vague and lethargic, and had attractive, long, thick plaits secured in brown elastic bands even if her hair was slightly on the mousey side. We had our paste sandwiches, Chelsea bun and pale orange squash together and attempted some conversation.

"Do you live far from here?"

"No, not really. Only a couple of streets."

"That's good, because we've got to be back here by 9 tomorrow."

"Yes."

"Does it take long to walk?"

"No, not really, I suppose."

"Oh, good. Not that we've got much luggage to carry. I've got a small rucksack. 'S' not very heavy."

"An' I've got a holdall. 'S' not very heavy either," I chipped in.

"Exactly how long d'you think it'd take us to walk?" persisted Margaret. Brenda Morris looked slightly baffled, then after a few moments reflection, "It depends if you walk fast or slow really."

Margaret looked briefly at me, raising an eyebrow as if to say, "We've got a right one here," then, "Well I was thinking about normal speed actually."

"Oh well, about five minutes, perhaps ten."

"Did it take you long to get here today?" I enquired.

"I don't know. I didn't look at my watch."

Margaret tried another tack. "Have you got any brothers or sisters?" This was beginning to sound like O level French conversation.

"A brother and a sister."

"Are they at home now then?"

"Well, my brother isn't because he's married, but my sister lives there."

"How old is she then?"

"Three."

Margaret and I glanced at each other non-plussed. Even if there boded something inauspicious in this disinclination to impart some background information, communicatively-speaking we were in for a difficult weekend.

"Oh, that's nice. I like little kids. I've got a younger sister," Margaret went on brightly, but Brenda, this time voluntarily offered some information

"She won't be there. My mother and her have gone to stay with my auntie."

"Ah! What about your father then? Will he be there?"

"I haven't got a father. He went away," was the pathetic, but not sad reply. Again, looks were exchanged as the accommodation situation dawned on us. "D'you mean that...that it'll only be us three in your house then, all night?" Margaret asked, a slight note of anxiety creeping into her voice.

"Mmm," Brenda Morris was quite unconcerned. "But it doesn't matter. I'm often alone there at night."

I reflected briefly on what a good thing it was Mam wasn't apprised of the situation. She'd have sent for the taxi down in Powell's garage next to the station in a trice or a 'winkie' as she said, and come to fetch me with much palaver. Margaret too would have been whisked away from what Mam would consider life-threatening circumstances. In the event, it took us twenty minutes to get to Brenda's house, by the time we'd crossed Newport road and trudged through the bleak jewel and precious metal streets to Topaz. No doubt they had been given these names as a target to live up to, because nothing in the appearance of the place seemed remotely prosperous – just street after dusty street of grey houses facing each other. No trees, no front gardens. It was true my house in Trehafod had nothing between the doorstep and the pavement, but at least we had a superb view across the railway in the valley, past the football field to the waterfall, rolling green fields and wooded hills beyond with white farms dotted here and there. In Splott there was nothing to relieve the general depression and lacklustre – only the occasional ambulance screeching to the nearby Infirmary.

Brenda showed us to our room where we were to sleep in a double bed, then in the small, lino-floored kitchen made a cup of tea which assumed the colour of the condensed milk when that was added. No biscuits were forthcoming – probably didn't have any in Splott.

"Make sure you lock and bolt all the doors," Margaret said after bidding our hostess good night and attempting a cheery smile which developed into a nervous grimace.

The night wasn't the most restful we'd ever experienced. The bed was high, the mattress squashy and the springs played a wailing toccata and fugue every time one of us breathed. If you turned over, this became a protesting, protracted, wheezing hornpipe and jig. At least with the truculent bed leading a noisy life of its own, the other night-time, scary sounds were drowned out. I saw every hour of that night pass by on my luminous Ingersol watch, carefully inching my right arm towards my face so as not to disturb the dormant bed into more discordant twangings. True to the Scout motto, I was 'Prepared' all night long. My body was numb, my legs were stiff and my neck ached with trying to maintain an unmoving position.

Never was I so glad to see day-light creep around the room. Margaret had found it impossible to sleep too. Around 6.30a.m., "Gracious", she said, loudly, to be heard above the bad-tempered bed springs, "With a bed like this, they don't need gramophone records."

"No," was my reply, "And it's no wonder the mother goes off to stay with the auntie."

"I wonder if we'll have a decent breakfast. I'm starving!"

"Me too. At home we always have a cooked breakfast with

black pudding on Sundays".

Needless to say, no cooked breakfast was tendered. Brenda Morris did have some cornflakes though, but no milk, only the tinned, thick, sweetened stuff that David Thomas my neighbour in Trehafod liked to eat in sandwiches.

"I norm'ly have hot water on mine," said Brenda. "D'you want some hot water on yours?" Margaret, eyes round with incredulity, giggled in disbelief. Brenda took this to be an affirmative and Margaret found herself staring at a mushy, tan sludge in her bowl. "Put some sugar on it. It's OK with sugar," advised Brenda, tucking in. I was presented with hot water too but decided on that occasion to eat dry. As our hostess went to make us a slice of toast each, Margaret hissed, "What next? Boiled grass? Fried worms?" In fact it was another cup of the beige tea.

Weak with hunger, exhausted and aching from no sleep and bed-springs and irritated with discussions on how to be good, cheerful and useful on every occasion, we were more than happy to leave the prospective, smart capital of Wales for the humdrum, uneventful Rhondda valley where life was very different. We did feel sorry for Brenda Morris, though!

# 6. The Seduction of A Level English

Denise Ormond came to RCSG to teach English in 1951. She came, not so much like a much needed breath of fresh air as a gale force wind and showed the school what the twentieth century was.

Although a near namesake to our Head of Geography, Miss Orsman, they had little else in common. Denise Ormond was of our generation, only half a dozen years, or thereabouts, older than us, whereas Miss Orsman was of the parental era. All of the 350 or so girls in the school admired her, many had a 'crush' on her, some were infatuated with her. After university she had trained at RADA but, it was rumoured, had been too short to get parts on the London stage. Added to her mystique was the fact that she had been born in Canada – rather on another planet than on another continent in those days. She walked around school like a whirlwind, academic gown billowing behind in the breeze she created; she smoked, tossed her head, laughed full-throatedly, swore mildly under her breath, but swore nevertheless, words that probably invaded Porth County's portals for the first time in its history. She was exciting. English lessons took on a new significance. Suddenly dry-as-dust adverbial clauses and the like became interesting and for the first time ever you wanted to know how they worked. Girls took more care over essay-writing to get a good mark and a few words of praise from this contemporary icon. Chapters of set texts were actually read for homework, instead of conjectured as previously so one could put forward sensible views and possibly shine in discussion.

For the first time ever, pupils were interested in finding out something of the background of a teacher. Her family lived in Tenby, and she wore an engagement ring – for the first year anyway of her several decades at the school. Speculation was rife and wildly romantic about the intended. He was a Shakespearean actor, someone she'd met at RADA, about to burst forth on the world's screens and become the nation's heart-throb. A second Richard Burton perhaps? He was a jet pilot, living in such a fast lane as was unimaginable, rushing all over the globe, object of admiration to all female eyes but seeing no-one other than his loved one to whose side he was ever impatient to return. He was a successful, enormously wealthy London businessman who had a chauffeured Rolls Royce to take him to his City offices and the Stock Exchange, arrogant and ruthless in his pin-stripe suit and bowler hat, but jelly in our teacher's arms. Someone as charismatic as our Miss Ormond surely would not have chosen anyone but the most glamorous of men? In the event, she never married her fiancé, the ring disappeared and it was decided that the unlucky, disengaged man was after all someone she'd met while a student at Aberystwyth University and was deemed not worthy of her.

Porth County girls were not sorry to discover she had an ex husband-to-be. When teachers got married they either had to go and join their spouses whose careers took them off to some other place, or they started having babies, attention-demanding creatures if ever there were any! At least that is what happened to the nice ones. Whatever, marriage usually signalled the end of their residency at Porth County and what we wanted was for the fascinating Denise Ormond to stay and captivate us. She so captivated us in fact, that after we discovered she lived in Aberrhondda Road, (where she gave occasional, free coaching lessons to grammar-dense girls, lucky things!) her southern Rhondda pupils would often take a walk in that district, hoping to catch a glimpse of their heroine leading her fascinating life. If she ever glanced out of the window she must have thought she'd come to live in the most thickly pupil-populated road in the world.

My relationship with her when she arrived, in my second Fifth form year, didn't kick off on a very harmonious start. Each new, young teacher was welcomed with interest, enthusiasm and affection, only for these sentiments to be tragically dashed on the rocks when they got married and subsequently left to trot after their consort or to have offspring. Surely the same thing would happen with the delightful Denise who was already bespoken for?

Lower down the school was a lively group of reprobates, with few, if any inhibitions, led by a Pat Rowlands. Pam Nicholls, Marjorie and I were friendly with this crowd of younger girls, a friendship stemming initially from seeing them waddling hilariously off in their long, stiff Penguin coats and coronets for their Cookery lesson. They were similarly entranced by the new English teacher.

"Don't get too keen on her! She'll be leaving soon," I warned Pat.

"Aw, she won't will she? How d'you know that?" she demanded.

"Well, none of the nice young teachers stay long, 'specially if they're pretty. They get married and leave," I explained.

"Oh, p'raps she won't," Pat responded hopefully. "Anyway she told us she liked it here."

"Yes, she will, she will go," interceded Marjorie, "She's engaged already, so it makes no difference if she likes it or not. She'll be off soon."

There was a pool of little concerned upturned faces with downturned mouths.

"You ask her," I said, "You ask her next lesson when she's leaving. I bet it'll be soon."

"All right. I will then. I'll ask her next lesson when she's leaving an' I'll say you said she was leaving soon."

"No, don't say that, silly. Don't say I said. I'm only guessing from past experience."

Two days later, Miss Ormond asked to see me after the lesson. I'd been getting some creditable marks for essays after lavishing ten times the effort of previously on them to be in her good books. She'd referred a few times to the school magazine and I assumed she wanted to talk about that.

"Do you have anything you'd like to say to me Mary?" she began.

I blinked in slight surprise and scanned my thoughts briefly.

"Er...er...no, I er...don't think so Miss Ormond."

"Because I'd far prefer that if anything is bothering you, you'd come to me direct rather than go through the intermediary of a Second Former."

Realization of what she was getting at dawned as I understood the concatenation with 'Second Former'. Oh God, that silly little kid had gone and told her I said she was leaving! I blushed, bit my lip.

"Ah, I can see you obviously do know something about this. Well, for your information, I'm not leaving the school, and I'm only sorry you wish I were. Fortunately I don't think the majority share your view."

My confusion and abashment were total. Never one to comfortably discuss personal emotions with others, specially adults and particularly teachers, I couldn't open my mouth. I just stood, beetroot-faced, not knowing on what to focus, wishing God would wave his magic wand and let me melt away. This was awful! She'd got completely the wrong end of the stick. I didn't want her to leave! I adored her. But I could hardly explain this. In effect I couldn't explain anything, and if I could, my recurring stammer in stress would make me sound like a gibbering idiot. My whole being was paralysed in horror, apart from a few fleeting thoughts of murdering a certain Second Former.

She went on, "So, in future, if you have any problems with being in my class, please come and discuss them with me personally and save me the embarrassment of having my private life aired in front of the Second form. All right?"

Her normally friendly blue eyes were cold as icebergs as, not waiting for a reply, she turned and flounced with her energetic stride into the staffroom opposite our Fifth form-room, leaving me with tears in my eyes, leaning against the brown tiled wall of the corridor, weak with anguish.

The incident was never again mentioned. I doubled my already decadupled efforts at English, kept my head down and my mouth shut. But at least she intended staying. That was some consolation even if, henceforth, I was to be persona non grata in the class as far as she was concerned. In the event she was at the school for at least a quarter of a century so my early fears were well off target.

The A level English classes blossomed in numbers under Denise Ormond and I was accepted without demur into the dozen strong group despite my horrendous, but misconstrued gaffe in Form 5. And, although not pursuing English as my principal study in tertiary education, thus began a course of instruction which has had more influence on my life than any other. Hundreds of students, including men who were at the school years later when the Girls' Grammar became Comprehensive Mixed, and who came under the guidance of this remarkable woman, will say the same thing.

English lessons disclosed a whole new vista of experience, and of all the subjects studied, it was in this one that the immature chrysalis gradually fell away to reveal the emerging young women. Invigoratingly, the mood of the lesson was under constant change. We were submitted to the gamut of seriousness, humour, anger, sympathy, teasing, formality, friendliness, comedy, flair, subtlety, wittiness, craftiness, resourcefulness, originality, drollness and inspiration, all within the hour 'til our senses reeled. What was so different in Denise Ormond's approach was that she treated us, not quite as equals, but as intelligent people able to cope with any contingency. We weren't and couldn't, but that didn't matter.

Poets, novelists, playwrights and their fictitious characters all came to life as though they lived around the corner and might walk into the room at any moment. So realistic did she make *Paradise Lost* that we wouldn't have batted an eyelid had the door opened and a greenish-coloured Satan, complete with little horns and scaly underpants and wielding some sort of pronged trident vaulted into the room to smarmingly present his point of view and smilingly bare his teeth at our disapproval of his evil ways.

Chaucer's thirteenth century Pilgrims with their individual foibles, charms and duplicity paraded before us as though they were trooping along a catwalk in a fashion display. Middle English gave us few problems, expertly read and explained as it was by our Thespian Miss Ormond. "And if there's any part of it you are not sure about, get Neville Coghill's translation into modern English", which everyone did, not because of failure to get the drift, but involvement.

The seventeenth century poet John Donne we worshipped like a pop-star and in several girls' minds he was on a par with Frankie Laine, the then pop-idol. Indeed some girls who had previously walked around quietly singing or humming *Rawhide* as they clicked their fingers and rhythmically hunched their shoulders, now went around declaiming, especially to lawless but uncomprehending juniors, "Goe and catch a falling starre! Get with childe a mandrake root!". The usual response from this source was, "She's nuts, she is!"

Jennifer, who had a histrionic bent, might march up to Margaret Evans in the corridor and demand, "I wonder by my troth what thou and I did 'til we loved?" Margaret would immediately start to play the game, responding intently, "Were we not wean'd 'til then? But suck'd on country pleasures childishly?"

Jennifer, to the interest and raised eyebrows of halting passers-by, unperturbed by their attention, would continue, "Or snorted we in the seven sleepers den?", to which Margaret would answer sagely in her clipped, distinct voice, nodding her dark head and waving a hand, "T'was so; But this, all pleasures fancies bee. If ever any beauty I did see, Which I desir'd and got, t'was but a dreame of thee."

Attendant girls would look at each other with a slight frown, twirling a finger into the side of their forehead to denote derangement whereupon Jennifer and Margaret would peal with gleeful laughter at their unrehearsed dialogue and bounce off arm in arm.

Donne's love poetry revealed to us attitudes and sentiments hitherto undisclosed and arcane and although we couldn't imagine ourselves in similar situations with the Valleys boys we knew in school next door, life clearly held promise. We emerged dreamy-eyed and reflective from these lessons, feeling we'd been privileged members almost of a secret society initiated into the spiritual wonders of life, while the chemists, mathematicians and biologists only learned about insensate things like molecules, atoms and cells. If not exactly feeling superior to these scientists, we felt decidedly maturer and cosmopolitan, as we knew about love. Donne's later transformation into a religious poet and Dean of St Paul's Cathedral rendered his earlier, uninhibited verse perfectly respectable in our estimation. Really a bit like being a naughty Catholic and going to confession. Ormond's splendid reading of 'Death be not Proud' generated goose pimples like hailstones among her students, while after her rendition of 'Hymne to God in my Sicknesse', there was not a dry eye in the house.

Her success with Wordsworth was not quite as titanic and to tell the truth there were class rumblings of insubordination with the super-virtuous Luke and Michael and the maiden lost in the snow but ever striving for Godliness. However if our teacher said it was good poetry, and she stressed Wordsworth was fallible, we took her at her word, such was our trust in her judgment and captivation by her personality.

Although we took it in turns to read around the class. everyone best liked Denise Ormond to be narrator. She had skills we'd never acquire. Her accent was refined and polished compared to our Rhondda pronunciation. Then, sophisticated as we had become under the influence of English, we were not above self-consciousness, awkwardness and blushing, obvious to all the class at parts in the text particularly tender or sexually allusive whereas our teacher showed not one iota of embarrassment. She would sail through these and all other passages, illuminating them with modulations of voice attained through drama training and we would be left breathless with delight like young children enraptured with their first experience of story-telling.

*Vanity Fair* was the prescribed A level novel. Denise Ormond would arrange a chapter's end to coincide with the end-of-lesson bell, because as she explained, Thackeray wrote the novel for a weekly literary magazine and the final words of the chapter left you in suspense for the following week's revelations. We could hardly wait for a free moment to read on!

Although the History of English Literature wasn't an integral part of the syllabus, Miss Ormond decided we needed an over-all perspective of it to broaden our perceptions, so several lessons were delegated to talking about the literary Greats through the centuries. Snippets, undoubtedly the most exciting or stirring, were read to us, stimulating our taste-buds for more, which she refused to impart, implying we were to read the work ourselves.

Pens ran out of ink and pencil points were reduced to the wood as we strove to note down these gems of the written word. Libraries throughout the Valleys were nightly besieged by RCSG Sixth Formers demanding dusty tomes which hadn't been moved from their shelves for decades.

"Oh, excuse me, I'm looking for a copy of *Roderick Random* by Tobias Smollett and it's not on the shelves."

"Wha'?"

The request would be repeated.

"Oh, I've never 'eard of tha' book. Is it new then?"

"No, it's very old – eighteenth century. I need to read it for my A levels."

"I don' think we got any eighteenth century books 'ere. We don' keep antique books."

No, no. It was written in the eighteenth century, but there must be a version printed in the twentieth century. You know, like Shakespeare."

"Oh, 'ang on. I'll look it up in the file for you. Whassit called again?"

Book name and author would be repeated, *Roderick Random*, Tobias Smollett."

"Yes love, but what's the name of the book?"

The student patiently explains, "The book is called *Roderick Random* and it was written by a man called Tobias Smollett."

"Oh! Funny sort of name!" The clerk would rifle through the shelf file, then, "No, it's not 'ere. Can't be much demand for it. Wait a minute, I'll look to see if it's in the Stacks." More plundering of the catalogue files would take place, then a pair of frustrated eyes would look up accusingly over half frames, "No, it's not 'ere either. You better try Pentre. P'raps they got a copy up there."

"Oh, all right. Thanks. Um...you 'aven't got *Tristram Shandy* by Laurence Sterne by any chance, 'ave you?"

"Oh, God. Wha'?"

"*Tristram Shandy*, by Laurence Sterne."

The clerk would give the fervid, would-be reader of English Literature a mock-patient, suspicious gaze.

"You not 'avin' me on 'ere are you?"

"No, of course not. Honest now, these are books we're supposed to read for our English A levels."

"Well, 'aven' they got 'em in your school?"

"Well, they're sort of extra to the syllabus really. But very important."

With a resigned sigh the clerk would continue,

"Is this another seventeenth century book?"

"Um...eighteenth century."

"Oh well, whatever..."

During this time a line of book returners would be building up behind the spurious enthusiast of ancient, forgotten literature, causing much sighing, eye-rolling, conspicuous fidgeting and mutterings, "It's ridiculous there's only one clerk on duty here, isn't it?" until the flustered man would plead for assistance

"Oh, Berwyn, Beryl, come an' 'elp over 'ere will you? I gorra look for these ancient ol' books see."

Miss Ormond had to answer for much exasperation and long queues in libraries throughout the Rhondda from her transference of enthusiasm for literature to her pupils.

Perhaps the most electrifying of Ormond's lessons was after she had marked a set of essays which didn't reach her first class honours, skyscraper standards. She would stride into the room or stamp up the stairs to 6A room, gown trailing off one shoulder, one arm cradling green exercise books, lips tight and unusually unsmiling, blue eyes frosty and face rather pink with the build-up to rage. As soon as we saw her we shivered with intoxicating anticipation. We knew we were in for a performance. A terse "sit", would be the response to our perfunctory, self-conscious shuffling to our feet. The exercise books would be deposited in disgust on the table followed by a cool ten second gaze around. And ten seconds is a long time in strife. Then, leaning forward on both hands placed on the table and encompassing the sorry pile of books, "I have *never*, repeat *never*, before had to sit and waste my time reading such a farrago of abject nonsense and appalling fabrication as I found in these essays. There was no evidence of your having followed my guidelines, or done any research on the topic at all!" Then, banging the table, making everyone jump, "Some of you can't even be bothered to quote the author correctly!"

At this point, breathing hot smoke, she might abandon the confines of the table for a walk-about, pausing in her tirade to gather breath and possibly to avoid a heart attack. We'd pretend to covertly grimace at each other while really enjoying the whole drama. She'd turn suddenly, hauling her slipping, billowing gown back up on to her shoulder and demand, "Have you anything to say for yourselves? Caryl, Margaret, Pat?"

Nobody ever did.

"Well, if you harbour any hopes of passing this exam, your thoroughness of approach and dedication to the task in hand must improve fifty per cent, because at the moment, no-one here has a cat in hell's chance of anything other than a fail grade!" Another pause, pacing around, white-knuckled hands clasped in histrionic anguish behind her back while we waited, breathless in excitement for the attack to resume and possibly some daring words into the bargain.

"Personally, I don't give a damn whether the lot of you fail! On this evidence no-one deserves to pass! Far from it! Some might even wonder why you've embarked on a course of A level study. All I know is, I will not have my time wasted in this manner again!" these last words accompanied by another bang on the table and the expected twitch from the class. "I will not accept such egregiously bad work. DO YOU UNDERSTAND?"

We would lower our eyes in maidenly shame as her temporarily furious blue eyes razed the room, then look up smartly in the attempt to catch an exercise book accurately but contemptuously flung in the owner's direction. In ten minutes she'd reduced us sophisticated Sixth Formers to shame-faced kids.

"Now then, let's approach the topic, 'The use of the Pastoral in *As You Like It*'." Immediately she'd resume her normal, witty persona and would shortly even be smiling at us. She was friends with us again and the performance would be over for another week or so.

# 7. Treading the Boards

Performances of another kind were also in store for us. Besides *As You Like It, Hamlet* was the other Shakespeare play spanning our A level period. As well as reading them in class, Denise Ormond with her background of stage training, was firmly of the opinion that plays were for acting and what better for students, than to perform them as the annual school production? She had probably not forgotten, but chose to overlook my misinterpreted peccadillo of Form 5, had accommodated me like any other in the English class, and, casting *Hamlet*, had given me the role of Osric, fop, to be delivered with a French accent. In the event, the French accent never materialised and the part was delivered in an upper class English, well Welsh, accent.

*Hamlet* must be a difficult play for even the RSC to perform, let alone a Welsh Valleys girls' school, what with a ghost popping up now and then, a madwoman, duels, rampant strife and the long, long role of the eponymous character with three soliloquies. But we did it, to many plaudits from parents – even those of girls not taking part – pupils from other schools and the local press. The school Hall/Gym extending into the Library via folding doors was packed out every night with enthusiastically clapping audiences. Sixth formers and their teachers from schools all around came to watch our efforts with this set text. So enthused were we, so seduced by the acting bug that three quarters of the cast decided their futures lay facing the footlights. Ormond judiciously abridged the five acts to three, thus reducing it to a manageable three hours, abolished Rosencrantz and Guildenstern and three girls, Carol Bunn, Mair Hughes and Anne Morris were Hamlet in each act, individually having one soliloquy to handle. My friend Hope Higgs, rattling around behind a gauze curtain with staring eyes, a grey beard and a white nightie, was the ghost. Never had she been so scary and the afternoon of the school performance, really the dress rehearsal, instead of the usual, typically Shakespearean cat-calls, hisses and boos (throwing mature fruit and rotting veg was not allowed as the cleaners would complain!), an eerie, rare hush accompanied her every spectral appearance on stage.

During the fights, especially when Mary Price as Laertes acci-dentally lost her already wonky moustache off her face, together with the multifarious deaths, there was much laughter from the juvenile audience. Hurrahs greeted the deaths of the King, (the head-girl, Margaret Howells) and Queen, (Anne Towers) and Laertes, but the Third Form, most of whom anyway had the concentration powers of a gnat, became rather mutinous at Hamlet's moribund procrastination, no doubt aware of the approach of home-time, fear of missing the bus and dismay at the thought of a delayed tea.

"I am dead Horatio" is followed by another twenty-four lines before he actually performs the deed and in between interpolates, "But let it be. Horatio I am dead" and, "O, I die Horatio". Needless to say, comments like "Well get on with it then!", "You're taking a bloomin' long time over it" could clearly be heard on stage plus a hissed observation, "Cor, they're all kicking the bucket. There'll be nobody left soon!" which received an unequivocal reply of, "Good, 'cos I've 'ad enough of this now! I wanna go 'ome and 'ave my tea."

Slightly out of control after three hours concentrated sitting in the Hall with only a brief toilet break and following the unintentionally comic build-up of the assorted deaths, amusement turned to outright hilarity and unwarranted applause on the stiff appearance of Margaret James, the First XI goalkeeper, as Fortinbras, so fortified with shiny armour she could barely move.

"Cor, look, it's the school goalie!"

"She should wear that to play hockey. They'd never score any goals against her!"

"She can 'ardly move in that outfit. They'll 'ave to wheel her off."

In my final Sixth Form year – 6A in Porth County – I was more involved in dramatic proceedings. This time the annual play was to be *As You Like It*, and I had a bigger part, starting off as Touchstone the jester, and ending up as Jaques. The reason for this was that Mair Hughes, Hamlet no.2 and first choice Jaques was so smitten by the acting bug after her triumph with 'To be or not to be', she decided she couldn't waste any more time treading the creaky, temporary boards erected once a year by the school caretaker but had to leave straightaway to train for the real thing at some London Drama School. So there was a gap to be filled. Miss Ormond wasn't sure who to choose to play the rather enigmatic part of Jaques so, one afternoon, summoned a few possibles, provisionally cast in other roles, to the Hall after lessons for a kind of audition I suppose. These included Jennifer Jones (Rosalind the heroine), Caryl Williams (Silvius the love-sick shepherd) and me (Touchstone, the fool).

"I want you to listen and watch," was her instruction, and we did watch as she put on so stunning a performance for our impressionable seventeen year old senses as she enacted 'All the world's a stage', that after a moment's awestruck pause when she'd finished, we exploded into involuntary applause, much to her embarrassment.

"Now then, I want each of you to read that speech in turn for me," she said. We looked at each other, irresolute and faintly grimacing.

"Oh yes. Follow that! Easy peasy," Caryl muttered as she bravely attempted the first of three sad imitations of Ormond's acting. In the event Jennifer stayed as Rosalind, a role she had no intention of giving up and which she'd had her eye on from the outset anyway ("I've worked hard for the part of Rosalind. I don' wanna be Jaques. Ugh! Boring ol' character!"). Caryl became Touchstone and I was given the dubitable treat of Jaques's portrayal. This meant I had to shoulder the responsibility of putting across one of the best known of Shakespeare's speeches. The more I thought about it the less I wanted it and even tried to persuade Mair Hughes that an acting career was a real shot in the dark.

"Actors and especially actresses are out of work fifty per cent of the time you know, actresses probably more like sixty-five per cent," I said, vaguely choosing a random figure to denote the female variant's hapless plight.

"How do you know that?" she demanded.

"Well, I...er... I read it somewhere."

"Huh, that's a load of moronic pabulum!" she retorted.

"Crikey!" was my surprised response, and still in the encouragement mode, "Using words like that you should be going for a degree in Oxford."

"Oh God, I've had a gutsful of school and homework. That's partly why I want to go really." So she couldn't be persuaded. Perusing the part of Jaques, I discovered to my initial consternation, that he had to sing. However it occurred to me that perhaps here was the glimmer of an escape route. Summoning up my courage I casually approached Miss Ormond.

"Er, Miss Ormond, I er... I um... don't think I'll be able to be Jaques after all."

She blinked and shook her head momentarily in surprise as though coming back down to this planet from some elevated plane of thought.

"Good gracious me! Why ever not Mary?"

"Well, you see, he has to sing, and," shaking my head with a despondent look, "I'm absolutely no good at singing."

She looked at me, eyes wide open as a grin spread across her face erupting in a laugh.

"Oh Mary, don't be so silly. It's better actually if you can't sing. Much more in keeping with the character. Is that all? Any other problems?"

"No, I suppose not," I replied glumly as she smiled and carried on up the corridor. Thwarted again, I wasn't smart enough to think up any more negative reasons forthwith, but was determined to work on it.

Come what may, it was pointless. Denise Ormond had cast her production and that was it. I was handed a record of the actor Anthony Quayle reciting Jaques's speeches and told to absorb his delivery.

Rehearsals took place at lunch times, after school and for the last fortnight on Saturdays. It was just as well that Miss Ormond and Mrs Hopkins Games were good friends as hockey practices suffered. At least the cast, which included most of the team weren't as prone to bruises and other minor injuries as usual. As far as possible, rehearsals were organised with cast rotation and were good fun even if the emphasis was on work. Redundant actors would watch whichever act or scene was being rehearsed from a vantage point sitting on the buck, box or pommel horse in the Gym so that everyone more or less knew the whole play. Ormond would stand as far away as she could from the action. Speeches and dialogue were initially, then less and less punctuated with shouts from her of, "I can't hear you", "You must speak up! People will be paying to hear you!" or, "No, no Adam, not 'masster'! It's 'marster, marster' – 'What! My young marster? O, my gentle marster'. Right, carry on from beginning of speech then." "Celia, I know you're supposed to be weak and tired running away in the forest but not so weak that you can't deliver your lines. Better to shout, 'I cannot go no further' than lose them by whispering. OK?"

She had terrible trouble with one Anne Oliver, cast as Adam the old shepherd. Anne was a brilliant girl who quoted Latin and Greek in her essays, had earlier in her school career created a great impression and won much respect by winning a prize in a World Art competition, and had travelled in the USSR with her unconventional family. Minor aberrations such as forgetting to put her shoes on to come to school or begging permission to eat her sandwiches in an afternoon lesson because she hadn't remembered to have them for lunch, were readily forgiven and ascribed

61

to innate eccentricity. It seemed there was nothing she couldn't do, that is except speak. She was articulate enough, far more so than the rest of us, but she simply couldn't be heard. Pearls of wisdom and original announcements would fall from her lips and carry about three centimetres. Fortunately she had a close ally in Jennifer whose ear would practically be touching Anne's face to hear and pass on her pronunciamentos.

"What did Anne say Jennifer?"

"What did you say again Anne?" Jennifer would move her ear up close to Anne's mouth then with a puzzled look say "Um, she said Dover Wilson in his book on *Hamlet* insists that Shakespeare intended Hamlet to hear Polonius's plotting and that's why he goes mad." Perhaps Jen would sometimes mishear and so misunderstand, then Avo (Anne Veronica Oliver) would shake her head with a delicate frown, touch Jennifer's arm and she would listen again.

"Oh, sorry, I got it slightly wrong... and that's why he *pretends* to go mad, but he isn't really."

Denise Ormond, never the shrinking violet or blushing bluebell-type to circumvent obstacles especially in the speech department, no doubt decided to confront the challenge of rendering Anne audible and thus, gave her a part in the play. Rehearsals with Adam scenes were painful, punctuated with, "Adam, the audience must be able to hear what you're saying", "Please speak up Adam" – a request having the ring more of a command than a plea, "Adam, Rosalind's missed her entrance cue because she can't hear you". Ultimately, Anne won, Ormond retreated defeated and disappointed, gave pretty Pat Jones the part and the play was back on a more or less even keel. Avo ended up at Swansea University to read English, forgot to attend a few lectures, was politely asked to go and do something else, chose the French degree course and not unexpectedly got a first.

Excitement, apprehension and incipient stage-fright began to affect those involved with the arrival of the costumes. The first performance was under a week away! There was glee and horror as each saw what she had to wear. Nervously, and with clumsy stitches that would have given Miss Griffiths apoplexy, the cast sewed under-arm protecters in their doublet or dress to safeguard the expensively lined costume from the wearer's tense perspiration.

That Saturday at costume fitting, Mary Price as Orlando strutted around in a very fetching yellow and red, richly embroidered ensemble with a dashing, short silky cloak that swung stylishly around her shoulders. Even the floppy cap with its jaunty feather sat so well on her short fair hair that it was not only Rosalind who fancied her. Jennifer as Rosalind had two costumes, one an ugly, dun-coloured, but attractively figure-hugging garment for the forest, and a vibrant, low-cut decolleté dress for the court scenes. Unfortunately, the latter was so well-padded and amply materialled that it made her look thirteen stone.

"Oh, look at me in this!" she said in great disappointment before the one long, jostled-for mirror, "I look like Henry VIII in skirts! You could take six yards of stuff out of this and there'd still be enough material for half a dozen costumes. Oh, I'm not thrilled with this I'm not!" she understated, "What will Robert" – handsome boy-friend – "think? Look at me! I look pregnant all round! I wonder if Miss Griffiths can take it in. Oh, it's not fair it's not."

Pat Morris as Celia was in the same situation with similar dresses. But at least Jennifer as Rosalind was tall and could carry off the frilly yardage to a certain extent, whereas Pat who was small, looked like Mrs Tiggy Winkle on wheels as no feet were visible. She was also required to wear a helmet-style tiara with spikes which further added to the impression of a bewildered hedgehog.

Caryl had a silly red and yellow quartered Fool's outfit with a close fitting hood and side horns but didn't care one jot and my suit was entirely black, boring and a bit on the small side. I wasn't too enamoured of the form-fitting hose topped by bulbous, pleated knickerbockers either, but by now I was too scared to worry much about my appearance. The next time I put on these clothes I'd have a cartload of lines to remember and deliver audibly to the far recesses of the library through a moustache and beard stuck on to my face, stiff and colourful with stage make-up probably melting in the heat from the arc-lamps blazing down on the stage.

Everybody had nightmare-type acting dreams of being unable to move, with all memory of the text having decamped.

"Gosh! I woke up scared stiff this morning," Jennifer said, the morning of the dress rehearsal, "I had this awful dream about being on stage and when I opened my mouth nothing would come out. I knew my lines but I just couldn't speak. I was just making gargling noises and the audience were laughing like anything. It was awful. Frightened me it did."

"You're lucky," quipped Mary Price, "In my dream, I was rooted to the spot and couldn't remember any of my lines. Someone in the wings had to say them while I mouthed something and waved my arms around."

"If you were rooted to the spot, did you have to stay on stage for every scene?" thoughtfully asked someone who only had a small part and aspirations to stardom.

"I don't know! I didn't dream about all the play, only a bit, silly," answered Mary.

Performing before the school in the dress rehearsal was probably the cast's favourite worst experience. Tension beforehand caused temporary aphonic, not to mention bladder problems, and people came out in nervous rashes and various allergic responses. The calmness and re-assuring encouragement of our producer, however, ensured the play progressed on fairly smooth wheels. Some face make-up ran in the heat of the arcs giving people a stripey appearance, beards became stragglier and lopsided as time went by. Le Beau's hat fell off at one point dislodging one side of her moustache which then had to be searched for in the interval among the Forest of Arden, and once Rosalind was having a cup of tea in the Dining Hall when she should have been making an entrance so Celia and Touchstone had to replicate half a page of play.

Two incidents particularly, stand out in my mind concerning that production, perhaps four if you count the partial cutting off of my left ear one night as I was having my beard trimmed in make-up, and being booed on every appearance after the first in the school performance as the boring old Jaques. On the second night, the First Lord, Barbara Rogers was taken ill half an hour before curtain-up. Since Jaques's first entrance was shortly after his speech at the beginning of Act II, I had usually sat through the scene perched up on the vaulting horse in the Gym, so I knew the lines by heart. Denise Ormond was preparing to send a replacement on to read the part when, impetuously and rashly, I volunteered.

"I think I know the First Lord's speeches. Perhaps I could go on instead of Barbara."

Miss Ormond looked at me thoughtfully. "Do you think you could Mary?"

"Well, I'm not sure of the movements but perhaps I could just stand in one place."

"Oh, never mind about the positioning. If you're sure you could handle the speeches?"

I was sure. They set to work to alter my appearance, sticking my Jaques's beard up under my chin (the painful unsticking was to follow later!), plonking a green satin cap on my head, draping a colourful short cloak around me and fastening a belt around my waist to which they attached a sword which I fell over at my exit, somewhat converting the comedy into a farce.

My earlier conviction of knowing the lines did not prove to be so accurate when I was actually face to face with the audience. My memory failed at one point to the extent of confusing the First Lord's two speeches. Getting muddled with the 'quoth he' and 'quoth Jaques', I realised at a certain stage I'd just said 'Sweep on you fat and greasy citizens," for the third time. I fleetingly wondered whether I'd ever manage to reach the end of the speech or whether the rest of my life would be spent on stage at RCSG being the First Lord in *As You Like It*.

The other memory is of the apple I had to throw up in the air after Mary Price's sudden, aggressive entrance on to the forest feast of the exiled duke and his faithful courtiers when Orlando says, "Forbear and eat no more!" Jaques's response, "Why, I have eat none yet" was to be followed by the apple being tossed in the air, expertly caught and defiantly bitten in front of this upstart intruder. My worry was that I might not catch the apple in its descent. After initially only throwing it up a few inches, Miss Ormond had said, "No, not like that! Chuck it up in the air. Like you do a tennis ball when you serve!"

"But what if I miss it?"

"You mustn't miss it. You can't let it drop on the stage. Someone might tread on it and slip. It could even roll off stage and hit someone in the audience. You must make sure you catch it."

Fine words indeed. In rehearsal we'd practised with a ball which I'd missed occasionally after a mis-directed throw up. Needless to say the bite was mimed. It was a worrying moment though. Not as worrying however, as the last night performance when, arriving on stage and scanning the rustic log table for the prop for the scene, my heart sank on seeing no apples anywhere. They'd probably only bought a pound and after my one bite, the apple had been gobbled up by the ever-hungry backstage crew. There wasn't much time before the 'A fool in the forest' speech.

"No apples!" I hissed to the First Lord, now Sheila Fitzpatrick, who subsequently took a casual stroll towards the wings. Halfway through my first speech, my attention was distracted by the sight of the rehearsal rubber ball rolling on to the stage directed by an unseen hand. It was expertly dribbled by the Duke then neatly gathered up by the First Lord who placed it in the bowl on the log. My bite wasn't as enthusiastic that night. I managed to suppress a grimace while all around were broadly grinning and watching with more attention than usual. Fortunately the 'apple' didn't come apart on contact with my teeth so I didn't have to spit out any rubbery sponge on stage which would have been preferable to swallowing it for the sake of the art.

# 8. Melancholy Francophiles

Up to the Fifth Form, French had been an emotional subject for me. I'd had a crush on my French teacher, pretty, dark-haired Miss Mary I. Davies in Form 3, probably because of her name and some sort of hopeful cross-identification. I'd worked hard for her approval and for my efforts had heart-brokenly been promoted out of her class into a higher set. Then in Form 5 on the school visit to Paris I'd fallen head over heels in love with Charles Trenet, and his song 'La Mer' and any picture of Paris still made my stomach quiver and my heart flutter. What excitements then would I encounter studying French at A level? I could hardly wait to begin.

Miss Alice Llewellyn from Morriston, Swansea was the old-fashioned type of teacher who brooked no nonsense and got on with the job. Typically Welsh in build, small, dark and rounded with a retroussé nose and a flashing smile when pleased, she was the soul of steadiness and reasonableness. Even her modest sense of adventure was thwarted when for her university year as *assistante* in France, she was despatched no further than Calais, the doorstep, so to speak, of that country. This didn't seem to have adversely affected her capabilities in the language though and as time wore on all eight of us in the French class realised she was a first-rate teacher – bland, prosaic and solemn, but solid. Her lessons were decidedly the least wacky of the three that I took. Perhaps it was this solidity, making you feel you were having a thorough grounding in something, that persuaded me to opt for a career involving the subject. French classes were not as crazy as Geography and less unpredictable than English.

"We are going to study the Romantics" announced Llew in our first week of A level French, "that is, the poets of the French Romantic movement, namely Alphonse de Lamartine, Alfred de Vigny and Victor Hugo. The class looked at one another in pleased anticipation. Jennifer nudged me, "Good," she said, "We're going to study love and romance. Perhaps she'll give us a few tips."

Poised as we were at seventeen to learn the great mysteries of life via these Romantics while wallowing in a warm aura of torrid fantasy, and hopefully, on the way, we thought, discover how to deal with that strange race, the opposite sex, we were unutterably disappointed. To our great dismay, what these Romantics were mainly concerned with was not so much love, as death and misery; Lamartine's lover Elvire dying of consumption and his going alone the following year to 'Le Lac' where they'd consummated their passion, whatever that was, to mourn her passing; Hugo yearning for the old days when he and his now faithless wife were happy in their now crumbling country house; Vigny to whom life was one long torment to be borne stoically until the final, welcome release in death.

We emerged downcast and depressed from French lessons to be greeted with hilarity and exuberance from those who'd just had for example, History. No doubt they'd been learning about kings running riot, politicians being cunning and all sorts of exciting things involving plots, mistresses and duels. Caryl would bounce up, "Hi, fancy a hockey knock-about up the field before lunch?"

"No."

"Oh. [Taken aback.] OK then, what about going down to the basement to get some crisps? We're second lunch today and I'm starving."

I might answer half-heartedly and with a deep sigh, "Aye...all right then."

"Cor, what's the matter with you? Lost two bob and found a penny?"

"No, just feel a bit glum that's all"

Jennifer and Florence also in the French group, would approach with long faces.

"Oh Lord, here's another pair. You'd better watch out. Your knees will be knocking your teeth in a minute." Jennifer, never one to ignore a reproach responded immediately.

"Huh, it's all right for you Caryl Williams. You don't do French you don't, so you don't understand, see."

"What don't I understand? Did you get a telling off from Llew? Have you got to stay in or something then?"

"Don't be silly. We don't get tellings-off and detention now. We're not juniors. No, in French we've been reading about a wolf and his family and they get attacked by some men and to save his family he faces these men and dies slowly in agony without making a fuss. And it's made us sad, so there!"

Her matter-of-fact résumé of *La Mort du Loup*, avoiding all the poetic tricks of stoic philosophy and man's inhumanity, made us smile and Caryl splutter.

"You're kidding! It sounds nutty to me. Is that what you do in French? Read kid's stories about animals? I would have thought

A level French would be more advanced than that!"

"Oh Caryl!" Florence reasoned, "It's classical nineteenth century literature. And it's poetry in any case. It's about stoicism and the wolf is only an analogy for...."

"OK, OK, I believe you, many wouldn't," Caryl waved her hands in the air for a truce, "I don't want a lesson on classical French wolves or whatever now. Anyone coming to get some crisps?"

"Oh, let's go'n have a knock-about up the field," I'd say, "Got a ball? I'll just go'n get my hockey stick and change my daps."

"No need, don't need hockey boots, s'not muddy."

The mopes would be forgotten until the next lesson on the brooding Romantics and we'd go and have a run around and a breath of fresh air.

Nineteenth century poetry did improve. After Margaret Evans was heard to comment ironically in a stage-whisper, "Oh, good! French Romantic poetry this lesson girls. We're in for another barrel of laughs," Miss Llewellyn assured us that one appreciated and sympathised more with these early Romantics as one got older which was true, but no re-assurance at the time and that next, we were going on to the Parnassians, only one of whom, Baudelaire, was a bit on the lugubrious side now and then. So things perked up especially when we read in the notes at the back of the book that the afore-mentioned believed that virtue was artificial and vice natural to man, plus "undesirable acquaintances and certain lapses in conduct, with disastrous consequences for the health of body and mind, led to violent scenes at home". We looked forward to Baudelaire and his lapses in conduct but I never got to the bottom of them until well into my university days by which time I had become quite blasé about such things.

Doubtless had Denise Ormond been teaching us French we'd also have learned about Verlaine's homosexual leanings and even discovered what a homosexual was and did, but Miss Llewellyn concentrated on the musicality of the verse and delicately side-stepped the sexual proclivities.

Gloom was temporarily relieved by reading Beaumarchais's *Le Barbier de Séville*, the play for study that year. Miss Llewellyn, grinning broadly enticingly announced, "Now girls, a bit of relief from the seriousness and intensity of the poets. You'll enjoy this play. It's a comedy of intrigue which we'll read aloud around the class." So, with frequent carollings of mirth from Llew who was clearly determined to enjoy herself enormously, we followed the antics of Figaro, servant-cum-barber-cum-surgeon-cum-musician to the Count Almaviva as he tries to win for his master, the hand of the innocent, beautiful Rosine who is kept isolated by her soulless guardian Bartholo. Llew chirruped merrily as they dodged in and out of cupboards and rooms to hide from unwelcome visitors or dressed up incognito to gain the upper hand. The trouble with reading roles in class in a foreign language is that sometimes, or mostly, you don't understand what is going on, so you don't know what to do with your voice. People mis-pronounce and stutter through a word three or four times until they get it right which renders the whole process bovine and snail-like. Sixth Form girls are not wildly eager to make fools of themselves enthusiastically acting. If Avo was reading you wouldn't have been able to hear anything anyway, so really the jollification we derived from this comedy was muted to say the least. But Llew smiled bravely on through her periodic impatience with us.

Then came *Jacques Thibault* to finish us off. No doubt, the study of *Le Barbier de Séville* between the poets and the novel was Miss Llew's version of the Shakespearean device of sandwiching a comic scene between the bitter tragedy fore and aft. *Jacques Thibault* in terms of happiness was like spending a holiday on Devil's Island, a forced march through Death Valley in August or being left to survive in the Brazilian Jungle with only a fork as an aid. To boot, this book had ghoulish illustrations to all its ninety seven chapters except Chapitre L which had a nice little cat looking out of a window. Its chapters were enumerated *à la romaine* so when Llew would instruct us to turn to Chapter 48 which was Chapitre XLVII, it'd take us half the lesson to find it. Some never did.

Basically this pre-First World War tale of woe starts with the eponymous figure, the teenage Jacques running away from home in Paris to Marseille with his friend because it has been discovered in his Catholic school, horror of horrors, that he reads novels, Romantic poetry voluntarily and his friend is a Protestant! His philanthropist father Oscar, has endowed a male children's prison, whither Jacques is sent when retrieved from the south, where he endures isolation in a cell together with bread, water and refrigeration. We could hardly believe what we were, with difficulty, translating. Dickens without the humour in the twentieth century! After a year, the absconder is rescued from these dire (to put it mildly) straits by his scandalised doctor brother who evidently has a bit of the warmth of human kindness in his veins and elects to be responsible for him. Although lobotomised by his experience, Jacques manages to pass some exams but only coming third, to his father's disgust. Then unsurprisingly he disappears for three years. Meanwhile we are treated to the multi chapter account of the demise of Oscar surrounded by nuns. Here we have the episode of the death rattle, an event which appears to fascinate French writers more than English as we'd never previously heard of it.

"What exactly is this death rattle then Miss Llewellyn?" asked Gillian Morgan, spokeswoman for an intrigued class.

"Well Gillian, it's the noise that a dying person makes with the last exhalation of air from the lungs."

A few gargling noises of different speeds and tones could be heard around the room, to be silenced at Miss Llew's peripatetic frown and "Sshh girls! Don't be facetious!"

"Well what does it sound like Miss Llewellyn?" asked Hilary Evans reasonably, "We've not come across it before."

"I can't exactly say I've had personal experience of it either, but I imagine it to be like a gentle, swishy noise in the throat. Certainly not like the strangulation noises some of you were just making. This is not noisy supporting of some football team but Death remember."

How could we possibly forget? The French psyche was clearly obsessed with The Crossing of the Great Divide and no doubt it would be on the menu until we'd read all the books on the course. However, there was always the relief of Grammar and Translation. For the rest of that day, groaning noises of the throat could be heard from time to time followed by, "I wonder if it sounds like that?"

Now and then we were invited to despatch ourselves to Cardiff for the south Wales performances of classic drama by members of *La Comédie Française* – a misleading identification if ever there was one. These performances took place in the familiar Main Hall of the grand and celebrated Cardiff High School for Boys in Newport Road, usually on a Friday evening. We enjoyed these outings immensely and after the first, wouldn't have missed one for the world, not because of the play, but because the place was full of Sixth Formers from all over south Wales eyeing one another up like mad. After the first we all wore make-up too. The best time was at the beginning, choosing seats near the most promising-looking group of young men. One's view of the stage was the least consideration. The keenest student Florence Wilton would automatically, rather short-sightedly march towards the front to be restrained by one of us, "Oy, Flor, where are you off to?"

"Well down there. There's plenty of seats near the front, look."

"Oh, we don't want to go there Flor. All the teachers'll be sitting at the front. We'll sit back up here. Won't be able to rustle sweet papers down there." Florence, much addicted to sweets would comply eventually,

"Well as long as I can see the stage."

Little Pat Morris standing on tip-toe and craning her neck would espy a group of handsome, square-jawed, chunky young men in blazers.

"Oh, there's enough seats over there, look, on the left, in front of that row of pupils in black blazers."

So we'd settle obviously in front of the handsome young men with much fuss, girlish laughter and sidelong glances in their direction without trying to seem too forward. Hilary Evans might yank her chair back to touch the outstretched legs of a boy draped languidly over his seat. She'd turn, gushing mock horror, "Oh, I'm so sorry. I hope I didn't hurt you."

"No, not at all," he'd predictably reply without moving and with a steady gaze. Then his friend next to him, nudging him rather obviously might say in a stage whisper, "He was hoping you'd end up in his lap actually", whereupon Long Legs would stir slightly and grin making several female hearts flutter. Oh these city boys were so urbane and sophisticated! Loud whispering, quiet banter, coy looks and giggles and sweet passing would go on all through the performance. And the play itself? Always something three hours long by Racine or Corneille. Curtain-up would be greeted with polite applause from the front and impolite groans from the back. Actors would arrive, the men always dressed in togas or short skirted armour and the women in long, plain dresses. Then one of them would proceed to look into the middle distance, spouting reams of French rhyming couplets that few could understand. When they were exhausted, someone else would take up the cudgels and reel off pages of anguished, revenge poetry. Now and then Florence would have a grumble, "This is a poor old seat. I can't see very well from here," so someone would pass her a toffee to take her mind off it.

Occasionally someone on stage would drop dead for a bit of a change and they would all more or less die around 10.15 in time for us to catch the train home. By this time though and with the help of the interval, new friendships had been made, new names learned and some even had rendezvous planned for the Saturday afternoon.

And to Llew's enquiry, "What did you think of the play?" the answer was always, "Oh, great Miss. When's the next one?"

Lower down the school it was French films we sometimes went to see in Cardiff. These were special schools' programmes on a Saturday morning in the Park Hall cinema, almost opposite the New Theatre. That part of Cardiff resembled a rugby international morning with thousands of youngsters, most in school uniform, milling around the entrance in a mainly navy blue scrum. Fortunately, tickets had previously been distributed in school otherwise so great was the throng, some would still have been queuing to get in when the film was over. Inside the huge cinema it was difficult to find a single unoccupied seat, let alone two together, not so much because they were all taken, but because of the bedlam going on. Pupils were dashing hither and thither on some urgent mission, skipping along the rows of seats bumping into knees, stumbling over feet, waving scarves and arms as they located acquaintances on the far side or upstairs. Some people were standing looking around bewildered or wandering absent-mindedly down the central aisle pointing to friends in the gallery who were leaning precariously over the guard rail watching the antics of the groundlings and surreptitiously dropping toffee wrappers on their heads. Most seats seemed to be taken, if not by a body, then by a scarf, cap, belt or bag placed proprietorially thereon. Hope Higgs might say "Aha, quick over there, there's a couple of places," so we'd push our way urgently through the pack to reach the seats and see triumph turn to dismay at a claimant hand appearing from nowhere and a disembodied voice trilling, "Sorry, these are taken."

We'd usually end up somewhere very close to the front underneath the screen so we'd have cricked necks for the rest of the week-end. Harrassed usherettes, ten times as many as in the Central and Empire in Porth, wielding torches more as weapons than givers of light would try to settle kids in seats, a man would give a whistle blast and the film would start to great cheers, only surpassed in decibels by those at the end.

One film we saw was *Nous les Gosses* which was basically about a troop of ragged children devastating the undevastated parts of some unfortunate war-damaged town, similar to what was happening off-screen in the Park Hall. Another was *Mon Oncle* with the funny, straight-faced, beanpole actor Jacques Tati getting into scrapes. He was also the chief person of Jour de Fète in which as a postman, he unwittingly wrecked the French postal service for miles around and constantly missed a turning on his bike, riding straight into the river to great cheering and whistling.

We liked the Tati films as he didn't speak much – his expression and bodily stance said it all – so there wasn't so much reading to do of sub-titles. Even if we could have understood the French we could hardly have heard what was being said as the initial pandemonium was only marginally abated in deference to the action. There was also a continuous noisy stream of arguing people going for ice-cream or to the toilet so you were up and down in your seat letting them pass all film long. Apart from that, the sub-titles were in white, hard to read and disappeared altogether on roads, houses, white cows and flowers. It was a relief when it was over as your head could resume its normal position on your neck even if you had to battle your way to the exit. I never saw any teachers watching these films. I wonder why not?

# 9. Hockey Trials, Triumphs and Tribulations

RCSG had a good reputation for Games. Admittedly we had difficulty in winning the Rhondda Schools Sports year in year out
like RCSB, whose all-round Sports renown was formidable. We
couldn't measure up to them, turning out Sports Stars,
International players in Football and Rugby and Olympic and
Commonwealth (Empire in those days) Games Athletes with cal-
culated regularity, but at least our First XI hockey team was more
than a match for the other Rhondda Valleys Secondary Schools'
teams – with the exception of Pentre that is. For some reason the
white-shirted Pentre girls who always seemed so big and fast,
worried us. We practised at lunchtimes with less fooling around
during the week preceding the Pentre game, and the match itself
was often a tense, close-fought, bruising affair. Luck and the
moderate balance of skill was usually with us, but on those occasions when we lost by the odd goal, we felt utterly miserable and
humiliated for days. It was no good mothers saying, "Oh, don't
worry, it's only a game!" to us it was a major set-back, like being
a wallflower at the Rink dance hall on a Saturday night, getting
3/10 for an essay you'd spent a fortnight writing or expecting
chips for dinner and getting boiled rice.

Mary Price, centre-half, who lived in Treorchy in close proximity to the Pentre girls, would be particularly glum. She'd have
a good old moan, "Aw, I wish I could move I do! All I heard
every time I put my nose outside this week-end was, 'We won!
We won! We beat you!' or, 'County 1, Pentre 2. We're better
than you, we are, see.' I'm fed up I am, and I got a huge bruise
on my ankle where their mad left-inner took a swipe at the ball
an' missed an' hit me instead. An' it was 'sticks' an' all, an' their
teacher didn't award us a free hit."

"Oh, I know what it's like," Margaret Jones from Pentre would
chip in mournfully, "In St. Peter's last night, a boy in the choir
saw me, pointed to himself and put up two fingers then pointed
at me and put up one. He was grinning so much he couldn't sing!
In the first psalm," she added informatively and irrelevantly.

Margaret Howells, centre-forward and captain would try to re-
assure the woebegone bunch, "Come on now girls! There's no
point being down in the dumps. We'll get them next time in the

75

home game. We nearly equalized anyway and their second goal was a bit on the dubious side to say the least. Mrs Hopkins would never have awarded it. It was struck miles outside the circle. We've got to look on the bright side 'cos the Whitchurch match is coming up in a couple of weeks." And Whitchurch was altogether another kettle of fish!

At the beginning of the school year in September, hockey trials were held during lunchtimes. Half the upper school turned up as being in the First XI held some *cachet* and interest was rife. Would there be any new stars this year? Would any of the former stars be replaced? Would any of the younger girls in Form 5 be selected? The outcome was more or less predictable and generally, up-and-coming players had to cut (sometimes lose) their teeth in the Second XI first. When the teams were picked, the captains, vice-captains and a secretary had to be elected. Secretary was the unpopular job as the victim had to draw up a fixture list for both teams, a nigh-on impossible task unless you were an Oxbridge Senior Wrangler and Soothsayer combined. The elected unfortunate had to send postcards to the other hockey playing schools in Glamorgan suggesting dates for the home and away matches. You had to be prompt at the start of term to get your dates fixed or several postcards-full of negotiations had subsequently to be despatched for alternative dates if you were not quick off the mark. In some instances replies were slow or altogether unforthcoming, although other secs. swore they'd sent them; schools suggested dates already taken; postcards got lost in the post; some were illegible, some positively illiterate. My first grey hairs began to appear in 6A and I remain convinced they were due to these protracted and worrying hockey negotiations. Yes, I was the hapless player elected to the 1954-55 post, agonizing over whether the season would proceed without us, losing sleep on a Friday night trying to remember whether I'd absent-mindedly put AWAY for the next day's home match on the pc. I imagined Ferndale, for example, and their team coming down-valley to Porth while we made our way in the opposite direction, up-valley, waving to them from passing buses.

Fortunately Mrs Hopkins, an RCS Old Girl herself and our PE and Games teacher organised the half-time orange quarters and post-match paste sandwiches and squash, but travel arrangements for getting the team to the away venue on time was the onerous duty of the secretary, adding more worry to her already over-loaded brain. The night before a match you were either having nightmares or tossing restlessly in bed, so rarely was the secretary in any condition to play anything the following day more innocuous than Snakes and Ladders. For a sport-loving girl but luckless School Hockey Sec, incongruously the best weekends were those when it had been raining torrentially for the last few days and the pitches were water-logged and unplayable. However during my reign the winter was extraordinarily fine...

It was an eerie experience making one's way to school for a 10 o'clock match on a Saturday morning. There was not the bustle and rush of the weekday mornings, the bus was virtually empty and the streets almost deserted. One noticed the light mist hanging over the valley under the grey-white sky, the damp pavement flagstones and the stillness in Porth; little traffic apart from a crawling milk float or a stationary delivery van outside the Co-op. A team-mate or two might be encountered en route for school and greetings and subsequent conversation would ring out unnaturally loudly in the air free of the normal competitive vehicle noises. One needed almost to whisper to contain the mounting adrenalin and conserve energy for the approaching game. Skin felt shivery, and longing for the cosiness of a leisurely morning at home you pondered on whether the rewards of being a Games player equalled the comforts of a warm Saturday morning bed where you might have been dozing or reading the latest James Thurber. Usually, Games lost in these cogitations. The empty shool building would be cold and cheerless and again the approaching voices of unseen people would resonate strangely transforming artless bystanders into guilty spies forced to overhear others' conversations.

The arrival of Mrs Hopkins, smiling, rosy-cheeked and brisk, usually with Ferndale headmaster husband Ken and three year old daughter Janet warmly wrapped up in a Porth County scarf, would concentrate our minds and bring us back to routine.

"Morning girls. Everyone here?" she'd ask unoptimistically in her husky tones, speaking to everybody but generally addressing the captain Margaret Howells who'd answer, "Yes, well...er...all except Caryl and one of the reserves. I... er, don't think the 'Pandy bus has got here yet Mrs Hopkins."

The latter would raise her eyes to God in mild frustration. The 'Pandy bus never got to school on time on a Saturday morning because the journey took twenty minutes and Caryl only allowed ten from first hearing the alarm clock. Our right wing had been known to sidle on to the field, trying to look invisible, five minutes after the bully-off and that against Tonypandy Sec, half a mile from her house and the player living nearest to the ground! Curly-haired, jolly and resourceful Barbara Phillips who played right-half and myself at right back nursed the inconvenienced reserve expected to speed along the wing until the team's ten o'clock scholar arrived still only half-awake.

"Right then. I'll go and meet the Mountain Ash team who should be arriving shortly. Um, now, let me see. The Gym is unlocked, Margaret. Here's the key to the cupboard for the goalie pads. Mr John's cutting up the oranges and I've got the corner flags. Is there anything else now?"

We'd go and change into our green aertex shirts, navy divided skirts and hockey boots. Some would don shin pads, bulky but effective protectors which strapped up behind the calves unlike the neat guards of today which tuck inside a sports sock. Margaret James, our brilliant goalie usually put the pads, kickers and several sweaters on in the Gym then waddled up to the field looking a fearsome sight. The tallest and biggest girl in the side, she looked a true descendant of the Amazonian women with her swarthy complexion, short dark hair, high cheek bones, strong features and athletic build. We always hoped the opposing team would see her making her way to the pitch as this gave us a moral advantage before even a ball was struck. Opponents would stop in their tracks, jaws dropping and eyes staring in despair as she passed. Her nature belied her appearance. Moderately shy, with a gentle sense of humour, thoughtful and modest, she was not an ebullient character. But opposing teams weren't to know that, and in any case she was a fine athlete and a magnificent keeper of the hockey goal which she occupied with distinction, saving us from many defeats. Smaller girls like Hope Higgs, who played very competently, were often hot-blooded, impulsive and temperamental, noisily urging on the rest in difficult situations, almost taking over from the calm, cool resolution of Margaret Howells.

Someone would carry up a canvas bucket bag with a rope handle, full of whitish, used hockey balls, and, with breath evaporating in the Troedyrhiw mountain air, we'd knock them around the field to each other to take the sting out of our hands. Despite rubber springing in the top of the stick, the first hard contact with the ball would send sensations resembling electric shocks into your hand, wrist and lower arm. Girls would grimace, utter an 'Aouw', abandon the stick to the left hand and shake the right, paining limb.

There were few spectators apart from the ever-faithful Mr Hopkins and baby daughter sporting County colours. Occasionally, a long-suffering father pressed into service as chauffeur; Denise Ormond who was a close friend of the Hopkinses; a new, eager boyfriend of one of the team supporting his love; the reserves of both sides and the opposing team's teacher.

Then Mrs Hopkins would arrive with shiny new ball and whistle, chatting to her counterpart and followed by the opponents in red shirts and green shorts if they were Mountain Ash. Both teams would furtively size up the other, each player hoping her opposite number wouldn't be the one wearing the Glamorgan School XI's badge on her breast or the six footer with legs up to her armpits. After captains' handshakes and the toss of a coin, we'd take up our positions, Mrs Hopkins would glance around the field, put whistle to mouth for the familiar clack of wood against cork to echo around in the morning air.

Once the game was underway you were unaware of anything but the chase after the ball, the tackle, the dodge around an opponent, the receiving or giving of a pass with the joy of one successfully taken or chagrin of seeing the ball intercepted by an opposing player or roll into touch. Gradually, perhaps after a dribble up-field, you would be aware of dampness along the hairline or a searing calefaction in the chest after a sprint back as you strove to fill your lungs with air. You knew you must look a frightful sight with a perspiring, beetroot face, gasping vapour into the cool ether, but who cared (unless of course a boyfriend was watching)? The exhilaration of the game was uppermost with the warm sensation that you were part of a whole. Inside this whole existed another unique relationship dependent on your location on the field of play, so that when I at right-back had the ball, I'd mostly pass it to Barbara Phillips at right-half who, after a dodge or two would then get Caryl on a run up the right wing. Such repeated inter-dependence and trust in work or play situations creates a distinct, unforgettable bond of friendship and thus it was with our triumvirate on the right hand side.

Along one edge of the Porth County field was an abrupt, grassy slope down to the tennis courts and it was a favourite jape to lure opponents into cascading down this slope. Pat Williams at left-half was particularly good at this, as also was Barbara Jones on the wing. Dribbling along the touch line and aware of a defender racing diagonally across the field, Pat would choose the exact moment to stop suddenly, pull back the ball and run infield. The defender, unable to stop and with a yell and a momentary unbalanced pause, then a waving of arms and stick, would topple over the side, disappearing from view. One player less for a minute or two and barely perceptible grins on County faces. Play would continue with the spectators' interest now focussed on the courts. Then a sheepish-looking head would re-appear, followed by a damp, grassy body which would disconsolately assume its playing position.

Another surprise for opposing teams was when one of our team shot at goal and missed wildly. Someone would chant, "One, two, three" and the rest of the team joined in to yell, "Four eyes!" usually to the irritation of the other side. One-upmanship indeed!

Away games, while being more of a worry for the secretary who was responsible for getting the team there, were more enjoyable for the others. There was the journey to unknown places, the warm welcome and the after-match refreshments. Aberdare Grammar School was probably our preferred away venue as they fed us sausages and mash after the game and they were Valley girls like ourselves with no pretensions and posh accents. Their pitch, at the front of the school was unpretentious too. While the ground for the building had been levelled and terraced out of the mountain-side, they seemed to have forgotten about the playing field which had clearly been left to its own devices, still retaining its original mini-anticlines and synclines. It was grassy enough but some players partially disappeared down hollows while others appeared to be perched on hills. Only the right wing's head and shoulders bobbing along were visible from the left wing and the half back disappeared altogether bending down to take a roll-in. As a result of this irregular terrain, the ball had a disconcerting way of suddenly appearing from no-where, hurtling over a hillock so you never knew what to expect, where to be or who you'd find over the next knoll. I wouldn't have been surprised to discover a player having a surreptitious read or a cup of tea in one of the craters. And the odour of sausages cooking wafted over us from half-time making mouths water, stomachs rumble and concentration impossible. I was never sure whether we went to Aberdare for the hockey or the hospitality.

Whitchurch away was another matter. They were easily the best of our opponents and as their Games teacher was Miss Jennett who had been ours and much admired at RCSG a few years earlier, we wanted to beat them just to show her. Their playing fields were extensive and immaculate which was why the Glamorgan Schools Hockey trials were always held there. One of the problems with playing Whitchurch was that you couldn't visualise the game beforehand as you never knew where in their unblemished acres you'd be performing. Another was their bands of enthusiastic supporters wearing orange and brown striped scarves, many of them boys in the co-ed school, through whose ranks you'd have to run the gauntlet on the long trek from changing room to pitch. Comments like, "Ah, nice legs on that blonde one," prompting a reply, "Yeah, but she's got a big nose", and "Cor, look at the size of that one! She could play second row for us in rugby", could clearly be heard which didn't do much for our confidence. Then there were the Luxton twins who had become famous in schoolgirl hockey folk-lore. These were tall, athletic, large-framed, identical twins chosen to play for Glamorgan Schools when they were in the fifth form, who in the sixth played for South Wales and were no doubt destined to play for Wales, Great Britain, Europe and the Northern Hemisphere.

On the Cardiff bus down, Margaret Jones broached the subject. "Are the Luxton twins still in Whitchurch, or have they left?"

Pat Williams, who knew most of the hockey gossip answered. "Hmmm. I'm afraid not. Still there, still playing better than ever and even huger than last time."

"Oh God!" from Margaret Jones, "The one who plays right-inner, Julia is it? dwarfed me last time. She's impossible to tackle, she's so strong. It's like taking on a brick wall," she wailed. "Oh, I feel sick." She looked across at Dorothy Jones, reserve that day. "Fancy a game Dorothy? I'm not feeling very well."

Dorothy replied with a cynical snort, "Huh, you must be joking. I'm here to watch and bring on the bandages," Groans all round.

Anne Towers, one of the new team members warily asked, "Er...what position does the other twin play?" The rest of us gazed pityingly at the innocent newcomer about to face a fiery baptism. Mary Price assumed the counselling, "Oh Lord! Don't mention Susan Luxton. Right or left-back. I tell you Anne, if she goes to hit the ball, get out of the way. Never mind the game, just get out of the way if you value your life. She hits the ball harder than a man. It goes the length of the field at 100 mph. If you tried to stop it, it'd take your arm off. I feel faint thinking about it."

Even the re-assuring presence of Mrs Hopkins who came by car to away matches failed to encourage us. We were a hesitant, pale-faced troop to be greeted by the hale and hearty, hockey stick-wielding Luxton twins, already changed in gold-coloured shirt and brown short skirt, clearly, unlike us, looking forward to the contest. They were excellent hockey players, but as in many things reputation exceeded prowess and two brilliant sportswomen don't constitute a team, though the other nine were no fools. The usual outcome was close. They'd win narrowly at Whitchurch and we in Porth. Rarely was any bodily damage done apart from the expected few bruises around the lower legs, and the post-match tea and sandwiches were consumed in friendly chat.

The other unforgettable location for playing hockey was Quaker's Yard. Firstly they appeared to have no buses in that valley so it was the only away match we travelled to by train. This was a much more relaxing mode of transport as far as I, the secretary, was concerned. Trehafod station was not far from my house and Mr Jones, station-master, ticket-seller, collector and porter could give me the times of the train at each stop down the valley, so after passing on the information, if anyone missed the train, that was their fault. Secondly we played on a flattened, grassed-over, disused tip and occasionally dug up and sprayed small coal with an energetic swipe. This tip overlooked the river so we got through at least half a dozen balls per match sending them irretrievably to freedom, bobbing and dancing in the frothy waters of the Taff as it gushed along over its rocky bed south to the sea. At the end of the game the question was not so much, "Who won?" or "What was the result?" as "How many balls were lost?" I once heard a late arrival supporter ask what the score was to be told quite spontaneously by the captain, "Only nine balls lost today." The result was unimportant. Hockey for Quaker's Yard must have been an expensive business in replacement balls. At least the homeward load of equipment was lighter to carry than the outward.

Once a year, at the end of the Easter term, house matches were held. There was much excitement and all manner of unenthusiastic games players pressed into reluctant service "for the sake of the House". Moans such as, "If the ball hits me I'm off mind!" or, "For God's sake keep the ball away from me. I won't know what to do with it!" and, "Don't blame me if I mess up. I don't know the rules" and the latter after at least five years of hockey in Games lessons! These were put to occupy the wing position where they were out of the way or could hide or take cover amongst the vast ranks of vociferous supporters who never turned up to watch a proper match. It was virtually impossible to play along the field edges, so encumbered were they by the eager hordes yelling, "Come on Penrhiwgwynt!", "Foul, ref, foul against Craig-y-llyn" by girls who had little inkling of the rules of hockey. As a result, house matches were played along a gradually narrowing band down the middle of the field as the encroaching support became more heated. Rival house-supporting pests though could be momentarily subdued by a well-aimed, hard shot in their direction, forcing them to a bit of physical as opposed to vocal exercise by having to perform an unanticipated standing high jump.

Occasionally the staff bravely consented to play the First XI as part of the Christmas frolics. And as a frolic the match exceeded all expectations. We were warned the staff had to win by at least ten goals and it didn't matter if we scored them. They took the field in baggy gymslips, creased blouses, ties draped in Just-William fashion around their necks, hair where it was long enough done up in plaits or side bunches tied with exaggeratedly over-sized ribbons. Some had put blobs of lipstick on their faces to resemble rosy-cheeked schoolgirls. Miss Orsman, who had kept goal for Wales in the thirties, had a chair placed in the goal upon which she sat, mummified in pads, several jumpers, cardigans, scarves, a blazer and a hat. Hockey sticks and other paraphernalia formed a hedge in the goal-mouth beyond which it would have been impossible to propel a ball of any sort. St. Trinians had been born before its time, in Porth! Miss Ormond took off her glasses, presumably fearing the worst, and wandered around blindly, not knowing which way she was supposed to be playing, and needing directional pushes now and then to set her on course and Miss Long was so short in hockey boots she was lost in the grass. The whole school came to watch this performance – there was no-one left to teach anyway – and cheered wildly when a teacher hit the ball or the ball hit a teacher. Some, such as the young and glamorous Miss Frances Davies, didn't touch the ball at all, but made their way, squealing in horror in the other direction when it came anywhere near them. Miss Llewellyn, clearly embarrassed by the whole thing approached the stationary ball once, took a little skip, prodded it three inches, beamed around at the spectators and, deeming her contribution made, retired to a far, safe corner of the field to have a chat with the non-participating Misses Pennington, Griffiths and Simon who were organising the half-time tea. Miss Sandys stood on the same unmuddy, grassy tuft all match, even after the change-over at half-time. Mrs Hopkins, who was adjudicating rather than refereeing was carrying a stick herself and was not above pushing the ball in the right direction or accidentally scoring a few goals herself. Margaret James in the school goal made no attempt whatsoever to stop anything so at half-time the score was already 8-0. The school side could hardly play anyway for laughing. Biscuits, cake and cups of tea were provided for the staff and a whole form of little girls was needed to move Miss Orsman and tackle to the other goal.

The affair was hugely enjoyable, probably the best event, including parties and dances that Christmas. There were lots of groans next day from stiff staff as they sat down, got up or staggered round the school. But what a sporting bunch and unforgettable occasion!

# 10. Across the Great Divide

Starting at around Form 4 or fifteen years of age, girls would use the exit at the dining room end of the school at recess and stroll up to the playing field past the new Biology Lab, maidenly eyes constantly flicking sideways. Once on the grassy acres, innocently unaware little girls would be blithesomely playing at the Cemetery end while groups of older girls would stand chatting and laughing at the other end always facing down-valley towards Porth. The reason for this was the Boys School next door, separated only by green (of course) metal railings. Some bold girls actually talked to boys through the iron bars, conversations which ended abruptly when a teacher 'on duty', or just having a breath of air hove in sight. Scores of marriages were the eventual outcome of illicit chats through that barrier and hundreds of 'dates' resulted.

Living in Trehafod, I was at a disadvantage as far as boys were concerned as approximately half of them, depending on home location *vis à vis* the borough boundary at the Trehafod hotel, went to the Pontypridd schools and I never saw those. I envied girls who came down from Treorchy or Tonypandy where all the glamorous boys, the good-looking Romeos and the sportsmen seemed to live. Perhaps it was the old story of familiarity breeding contempt, but the lower valley boys simply didn't appear to be as urbane, girl-aware, sophisticated, desirable or as many, as those living higher up the Rhondda. Friends and acquaintances arrived daily in school, beatific expressions on their faces, not only having spoken to these delightful persons, but sometimes having sat next to them on the school transport. Myself, I caught the service bus to Porth and walked chastely from there, so could never look forward to any post-prandial breakfast excitement, other than perhaps a letter from a pen-pal in Australia which is not at all the same thing.

Once in school, Margaret Jones from Pentre, a grin stretching across her face would sigh, "Oh, I sat near Philip Padfield on the bus this morning and he kept smiling at me."

Mary Price would join in. "Oh, lucky you! But no chance there I'm afraid. He's been going out with a girl from Pandy Sec for ages."

"Oh, don't remind me. But you never know! He could get fed-up with her. Stranger things have happened. He's got a lovely smile." Margaret would say dreamily.

Mary again. "I like Derek Brooks I do. He's so good-looking."

Mary Collins, another lucky Upper Valleys girl would join in, "Well, I'm going out with Peter Lewis on Saturday. Walked part of the way home with me from the bus-stop yesterday and asked me. How about that then?" she'd ask with obvious delight. The others would gather round for more details and we Lower Valley girls would look on enviously, yearning for similar assignations.

Although during their breaks, the vast majority of boys seemed to be chasing footballs in innumerable games on their asphalt yard, there were evidently some who, while whizzing round, still apparently had enough time to mentally register the female potential on the other side of the railings. Balls were often kicked out of play towards the fence and had to be retrieved by a lad who might merit a mild cheer as he approached, red-faced with embarrassment. If the ball sailed over to our side, the cheer from the boys for a girl attempting a punt would reverberate around.

If you saw a boy you fancied, the first course of action would obviously be to find out his name, then, of utmost importance, was where he lived. Sometimes a girl living, for example, in Ferndale might be discouraged on finding the object of her admiration lived in Treherbert as distance would more than likely be an obstacle to romance. She might well seek out a young man from Wattstown or even Porth to transfer her affections to. Then the next step was to find a girl who lived in the same village and tell her. Conversations went something like this.

"Oh, Rhiannon. You live in Ystrad, don't you? D'you know Bernard Edwards? Y'know – blonde wavy hair, brown eyes, always going around with Wynn Thomas."

"Yeah, lives a few streets away from me. Why?"

"Oh, I dunno. Looks nice that's all, 's got nice hair. Er... is he going out with anybody at the moment?"

"Aha, you fancy him don't you?"

"Well..." with a shrug of the shoulders, "He's not bad, is he? Anyway, I could be askin' for a friend."

"Well, as far as I know, he's not going out with anybody at the moment. I could find out for you though Joan."

"OK then."

"OK. I'll ask my friend tonight. She'll know."

After feeling hopeful for twenty-four hours, Joan would engineer an encounter with the intended go-between the next day.

"Oh, hi Rhiannon." Then, proffering a bag of sweets, "Wanna toffee?...Oh, by the way, did you..."

"Yes, yes I found out. No, he's not got a girlfriend at the moment, but my friend says he's keen on a girl in Pentre Sec."

"Oh," somewhat downcast.

"Oh, don't let that put you off. D'you want me to mention you fancy him?"

"Well, I s'pose so. What's he like? Is he fast?"

"How d'you think I know? I shouldn't think so. Doesn't go out with many girls as far as I know."

This business of boys being fast was generally a worrying one to most girls who were prepared for kissing, which seemed harmless enough if rather boring. Mouth activity was acceptable up to a point. Some girls though had 'love-bite' marks on their necks which needed covering-up at home and in lessons, but which they revealed in private, showing them off proudly like trophies. To me they looked sore, ugly and painfully acquired and went through a rainbow colour scheme of angry-red, dirty brown to bruise yellow before they disappeared.

'Fast', however, had to do with male hands seeking out soft, warm places where they weren't welcome. And evidently some boys wouldn't even desist when told to stop. Then other things would happen. Exactly what I wasn't sure, but I did know it gave you a bad reputation.

Hitherto, my experience of love and romance had been confined to accepting a horrible wet kiss from a smelly boy in Trehafod school in exchange for a chocolate cream. I suppose finding a yellowish balloon-type object when I was seven, secreted away in my father's trunk on the landing together with medical things, bandages, finger stalls and an eye-patch, and which I unsuccessfully tried to blow up also comes into this category, though I didn't realise it at the time. I also remember coming across a box containing small grey torpedo jellies, which, although I didn't much fancy the colour, tasted quite nice and which all got eaten within the week. 'Contraceptive Pessaries' it said on the box and since it was in the cupboard behind a jar of calves' foot jelly, I assumed it aided recuperation. I couldn't help wondering though why my parents kept sweets hidden away when they had easy access to them in the shop. I never mentioned these sweets or the balloon, thinking I might get told off for poking around where I wasn't supposed to.

After a few more convoluted arrangements in school, including allowing yourself to be seen on the field, and a shy smile in the direction of the inamorato, you would receive either a letter from the persuaded party, or a message to meet him at a certain venue, usually outside a cinema on Saturday.

Similar 'fancyings' went on from the other side of the railings, but were, so it seems, more direct.

"Who's that brunette on the left?"

"Barbara Rogers."

"D'you know her?"

"Yeah, sort of."

"Get her to go out with me, will you?"

"OK."

And it was usually set up, at least for the one date.

Parties were a good excuse to meet boys, and from the Fourth year, no Christmas was allowed to escape without a form party being arranged. Preparations, normally instigated by Caryl, the Organiser par excellence, began in October, as an outside venue – St John's Church Hall, the Scout Hut in Cymmer or Penygraig, or the Guide Hut in Porth – had to be booked and fees collected in class. These Form Christmas parties were always initiated by the girls. I never heard of one organised, extra-murally as it were, by the boys. And why not I wondered? Is it because at an equivalent age boys allegedly less mature, really are, and lack assurance and confidence? This I could scarcely believe, witnessing the self-possession of boys like Noel Jones from Tonypandy, Alan Goodwin who ended up working with jazz musician Johnny Dankworth, athlete Des Barnett, built like a rabbit, future lawyers Colin Samuel and monocled Graham Julian Jones, tall, dark and handsome Graham Shephard, David Herbert and Robert Davies and tall, fair and handsome Mike Stephens (Stumpo) and Jeff Davies, footballer Everard Kerslake (Tiss) and the renowned Marcus Morgan, to name but a few. I assumed they were just lazy or sated with female adoration.

The plan of course was for each girl to invite a boy. Easy, if you had a regular boy-friend, such as Mair Morgan who was known as one of a pair with Haydn Scourfield. Comparatively trouble-free if you travelled on the school bus from up Treorchy way where all the lovely boys came from. They were packed together on those buses for a good half hour twice a day so had ample time to get acquainted. But what if you were like me from the bottom of the valley where there were scarcely *any* boys, let alone lovely ones? The solution was for a group of these demure young ladies to ask a corresponding group of bashful young men via the less timorous, more practised, afore-mentioned Upper

Valleys intermediaries. Whatever happened, numbers on each side of the sex divide had to match.

On party night, the boys, self-conscious in suits, would turn up at the appointed place where the girls, freezing in taffeta party frocks and nylon stockings which laddered if they so much as passed a nail or splinter, would have been shiveringly and anxiously arranging food – trifles, sandwiches and cake – for an hour beforehand. The food was the most important part as everyone knew that the route to a male heart was via his innards. Some attempt was normally made to transform the drab wooden hut with its one-bar electric wall-heater into an enchanting, inviting, Aladdin's cave of delight with coloured balloons, streamers, paper chains and strategically placed twigs of mistletoe.

The invitees would hover in a group, uncertainly at one end of the room near the entrance, hands thrust in pockets, deep in light-hearted conversation with each other, seemingly unaware they were being appraised by many pairs of virginal eyes from the other end. Even the ever-ebullient Marjorie Woosnam would be unnaturally subdued.

"Oh look, some boys have arrived! What shall we do now? Somebody'd better go and speak to them."

"Go on then Marjorie. You go," Pamela would suggest

"Me! Oh no, I'm not going! I don' know 'em. They're boys from up the Valley they are."

"Well, never mind," I'd say realistically, "Somebody's got to go and speak to them. They must've been invited."

Jennifer would put in her suggestion, "You go then Mary. That boy you like, Gerald something or other, is in that group."

"Yeah, I know, but I didn't invite him. I said I'd invite Ben Edwards, and he's not there."

"Well, it doesn't matter. Oh, go on gul, pluck up your courage!"

"Well, what about you Jennifer? You've norm'ly got plenty to say."

"Oh no, I'm not gonna be the first I'm not!"

Then someone, usually Caryl, would go and ask if they'd like some tea and biscuits, always a reliable ice-breaker, while the rest of us looked on in admiration at her bravery and panache.

At the start these parties smacked of some sectarian convention of nuns and monks with a no-go middle area, then someone would remember the records and music would animate the ambiance. A bunch of girls, less intimidated by the second, would skittishly conspire to ask a corresponding bunch of boys to dance so that no embarrassed couple was alone on the floor, sole object of all envious gazes.

After the food at 7.30, people would be chatting and intermingling, if not exactly freely, at least with a supporting friend at their side and by 8.30 the atmosphere would have been sufficiently thawed – it had to be as the caretaker was coming with his lock-up key at 9.30 – to play romantic games. These, Winking, Postman's Knock and Musical Chairs on Boys' Laps, involved kissing, or rather, pecking. Any party game remotely involving contact of the lips, or easily converted into such, we played. No sensual excitement was ever generated as you were under your peers' close scrutiny. If a kiss lasted longer than five seconds, howls of approval, baying support and applause for one's audaciousness would resonate. However, these games were a useful indication as to the lie of the amorous land, as if a boy continually contrived to land you in a pecking situation, it was a fair bet he was smitten and life then held all sorts of interesting possibilities.

These parties wound up with a Paul Jones and spot-prize dances, eventually becoming drooly dancing, by which time everyone was partnered off – if not always with the desired partner – and in the dimmed lights it would be untrue to say pecking did not become kissing. Once dispersed, we could hardly wait to get back to school to compare notes, although compared with later decades, experiences were totally innocent – no alcohol, drugs (drugs? What were they?) or fornication.

Some friends were allowed to hold mixed parties in their houses, and while the food, prepared by mothers and aunts, was always far superior, the sense of freedom was somewhat diminished. Although adults had promised to stay in the kitchen, you never knew when one might intrude under the pretext of offering coffee/ seeking a particular pen they thought (falsely) mislaid under a chair/ fetching the daughter of the house to say goodbye to a visiting next-door neighbour, while in reality just wanting to see what was going on. At these parties though, particularly Margaret Algate's, you would be offered a glass of cherry brandy. Wild living indeed! In the relationships stakes you simply gazed and smiled at the object of your passion, hoping the penny would drop before your face muscles congealed.

Invitations to some parties, especially those held in a boy's house, arrived and with them a certain status. Most had a small addendum to the necessary info. about time and place, such as "Bring a bottle", "Presents not requisite (but acceptable) – no-one's birthday" or "Possibility of transport home if father in cups." It was rumoured that the rather glamorous Alan Goodwin was holding a party and invitations were coveted. Girls waited anxiously. However, when they were distributed, the brief PS stated, "Girls required to wear a blouse or dress buttoning up the front."!!! Many girls invited suddenly found they had urgent appointments on the designated date so although a class-mate might ask, "Did you get an invitation to Alan Goodwin's party?", and to the positive answer, enviously reply, "Oh, you lucky thing!", she didn't know you had absolutely no intention of going anywhere within five miles of the celebrations.

The Library dance-hall in Tonypandy was a favourite place for a Saturday evening outing. At one time the majority of the 6th forms from both County schools plus the other Rhondda Secs twirled on its sprung floor, sat as wallflowers on its upright chairs or clustered in groups at one end, glass containing dandelion and burdock pop (looking like beer) in hand, eyeing the 'talent'. Occasionally one would find oneself dancing with a non-pupil.

"What's your job then?"

"Oh, I'm not working. I'm still in school. Porth County."

"Going to college are you?"

"Hopefully."

Then after a pause for a think,

"I'm in college."

"Oh really! Which college is that?"

Another pause when you could see your dance partner desperately searching for inspiration,

"Um, um...Oxford."

"Oxford! Oxford University?"

"Yeah."

"Gosh! You must be clever! Which college?"

"Well I told you. Oxford."

At this stage one begins to smell a rat.

"Yes, but Oxford University is divided up into colleges like Exeter and Brasenose and Queen's."

The partner, if uninformed, is quick on the uptake.

"Oh, I'm in King's."

"Oh, King's eh! I've not heard of that one at Oxford."

"Well, that's where I go."

In the Rink dance-hall in Porth, the situation was reversed as more of the local working, rather than the local student, citizenry frequented the corrugated-iron-roofed building. Students were considered snobs.

"Dance love?"

Then if the fellow appeared sober, "Yes, OK."

"'Aven' seen you 'ere before. Only come in the matin' season do you?" Ha, ha, ancient joke, no longer very funny.

"'Aven' been living 'ere long." (I'd lived one and a quarter miles downstream all my eighteen years).

"Oh, where d'you live now then?"

"Trehafod."

"Ah, that's not far. Can I take you 'ome?"

"No. I'm with my friend. She's over there."

"Where d'you work then?"

"Marks, in Ponty."

"Oh, there's posh! I'm working in Steiner's on the Estate I am."

"Oh aye."

"Good job is it, like, in Marks. Good prospects?"

"Yeah, great. I'm in the Ladies Underwear Department."

"Oh, I'll pop in and see you sometime."

If he did, he would have had a fruitless search.

Some suffragette-type members of staff weren't keen on girls having anything to do with boys. One fine, cold spring evening, I was innocuously walking home from Porth with the then boy-friend Brian Deere. We weren't even holding hands, just chatting amiably. Suddenly I was aware of a disapproving, haughty face with pursed lips staring at me from a familiar, green, slightly battered car slowly driving by. It was Minnie the Morris with Miss Orsman at the helm. She must have noticed a Porth County girl by the school scarf I was wearing, but had she recognised me? Next morning I was summoned to the Geography Room.

"Mary, I was dismayed to see you out mid-week when surely you should have been at home working. Didn't you have any homework last night? However, I was even more dismayed to see you displaying to all and sundry when fraternizing with the opposite sex that you are a pupil here. If you must go out with boys, please don't wear your school scarf."

On the ultimate Christmas of one's progression through school, 6A were allowed an official party with the corresponding class in the Boys' School. No doubt the powers-that-be had decided that we be made aware of another species of humanity before we left for the big, bad world. To many, this party was a bigger incentive than future work prospects to struggle through the two years to A levels. These festivities were held in alternate schools each Christmas. I was in 6B and party day had arrived cold and fine. That year, it was to be held in the Girls' School.

There was much talk and speculation about what 6A girls would be wearing, which staff would attend, which girls were keen on which boys and vice versa, altogether much interest in the approaching bacchanalia, not without smugness on the part of 6A who were going, towards envious 6B, who were not.

Doing some patrolling as a sub-prefect outside, Caryl, ever vigilant as to favourable opportunities, spotted a ladder in the rear yard, tucked away neatly against the old toilets wall. No sooner spotted than mental plans were afoot to profit from this unexpected donation to the cause of curiosity.

"We'll meet tonight in Bacchetta's, have a cup of coffee, then come up here to see what's going on. OK?"

So, around 8 pm (official parties in those days finished at 10 pm), Caryl, me, Jennifer, Florence, Anne Morris who'd come down from Trealaw, and Gillian Morgan whom we'd called for in Cemetery Road on the way up, stealthily sneaked into school past the lit-up boiler room under the Chem Lab where the caretaker lived in school hours. With much giggling and "Ssssh's" we manoeuvred the ladder into position against the Hall windows and took it in turn to climb up and see what was going on. Nothing very much in fact. Only sedate dancing was reported by Caryl, the first to look as she'd found the ladder. Snippets of gossip came down from above.

"Cor, look at Bessie! Very glam! She's wearing a long, black skirt and a green blouse. Talking to Andy Williams, Games."

Jennifer remarked, "Well we can't very well look Caryl, 'cos you're up the ladder and we're down here in the dark. We can't see anything! And who's Rob dancing with anyway?" Robert Davies was Jennifer's current beau.

"OK, OK. I'll come down now in a minute and you can have a look. Can't see him Jen. Oh, yes I can. He's over there by the piano with Margaret Booker. Cor, Ormond is dancing with Graham Julian Jones and giving him some very funny looks. He's not wearing his monocle though. P'raps he's made some lewd suggestions. Jeff Davies is dancing with Miss Davies Biology." Caryl squeaked, "He's got his hand on her bottom."

"No! He hasn't!" from a shocked Florence.

"Oh, I like Jeff Davies I do," said Anne Morris.

"Bernice Lewis has got a gorgeous dress. 'S black with a full skirt and a slashed neck." At this point Caryl in her enthusiasm demonstrated a slashed neck and the ladder creaked and wobbled about.

"Oh, watch out Caryl, the ladder's moving! Don't jump about

on it! Keep still!" were various concerned shouts from ground level.

"Sssshh! Don't shout! You'll attract attention. Mr John will hear. I'm all right. Just hold the ladder steady!"

"Aw, come on down Caryl! It's someone else's turn now," complained Jennifer. "I want to see what Rob's doing," she said to no-one in particular.

Caryl was replaced by Jennifer who was upset to see her boyfriend with the same girl. "I bet she's after him. Oh, I'll tell him when I see him next I will," she grumbled.

"Anything interesting happening Jen?" asked Gillian, bored with Jennifer's commentary

"No. Robert's still with Margaret Booker."

Groans emanated from below. "We know that Jennifer! We don't want to hear about Robert all the time. Who's Llew dancing with? Any of the staff dancing with anyone interesting?"

"Llew's talking to Mrs Hopkins an' I'm coming down now 'cos I'm fed up. Wish I hadn't come," she said petulantly.

Florence didn't want to go on the teetering ladder but the rest of us duly ascended. However when it was my turn, the partygoers were all streaming out of the Hall doors. "Cor, it must have finished. They're all leaving, an' it's only ha' past eight."

"Naw," piped up Gillian, "They're going to have some food. They've gone to the Dining Hall I expect. It won't finish for another hour at least."

Caryl investigated while we hovered uncertainly in the yard outside the Hall. She wasn't long.

"C'mon, we'll take the ladder and prop it up by the Dining Room. If they come out for some fresh air or whatever, we'll be seen."

"Rob had better not come out for some whatever with Margaret Booker!" Jennifer asserted, "If he does, he'll have a surprise, 'cos I'll...I'll accost him!"

We laughed. "Yes, you accost him Jen, and make it cost him too!" advised Anne.

Half a dozen Sixth Formers creeping around the back of the school carrying a ladder must have been quite a surprise for Mr John, the caretaker, as he rounded a corner on his beat to ensure no hanky-panky was taking place outside. It was quite a surprise for us too.

"What the devil...?" was what I heard as I yelped in shock, in unison with the other miscreants before dropping the ladder and scarpering. He didn't set off in pursuit of us, just yelled, "I saw you! I know who you are! I'm reporting you tomorrow!" Lights seemed to come on all over the school as we ran out through the gates for the haven of Gill Morgan's nearby house.

The ladder was back in its usual place the next day and six Sixth Formers apprehensively waited for a call that, happily, didn't materialise.

And our Christmas party the following year in the Boys' School? Not half as interesting as the one we'd been to the year before.

# 11. On Homeground

Although my life revolved around school, I did have relatives I saw from time to time and interesting they were too. Some might even say bordering on the eccentric.

I'd never known my maternal grandparents, my grandmother, also Mary Davies, pre-marriage, having died before my birth, and my grandfather, William Richards, following her to the grave when I was in my first months on earth. My mother's brothers and sisters all still lived on farms however. The nearest one to us and within reasonable walking distance (which is how my father came across my mother in the first place) was Tydraw, a mile and a half beyond the top of the mountain. This was Gelliwion mountain which towered protectively above our little village and behind our house in the bottom of the three rows of miners' terraced cottages of upper Trehafod, commonly known as the Tump.

Two bachelor uncles and a cousin farmed Tydraw with some hired help and they were looked after by my maiden aunt Rachel. In those days my uncle's sheep grazed Gelliwion mountain, unlike now, adopted as it is by the Forestry Commission and covered with Christmas trees. My mother would often look up out of the kitchen window and utter a cry of pleasure on seeing a fast moving speck on four legs galloping in some direction or other followed by two smaller specks.

"Oh, there's Dick, look, after the sheep. I wonder if he'll come down and have a cup of tea?"

He frequently did, tethering the horse to the lamp-post just outside our shop to the great delight of the smaller, scruffy inhabitants of the three Tump streets who, in seconds, would accumulate in hordes to gaze awesomely and admiringly at the animal. They saw plenty of sheep ambling around the Valley streets, some of whom were such regular visitors they had been given names. These would respond to a call, especially if you had bread in your hand and were so tame you could stroke them. Some daft kids even tried to ride them, largely unsuccessfully. They were also used to seeing weary horses pulling carts, but not a spirited hunter that somebody actually rode and tied up to a post à la cowboy film. It was as though Gene Autry had come to town!

"Is it a real 'orse, mister?" some urchin would ask.

"Will 'e bite you?"

"Will 'e kick you?"

"Can I stroke 'im?"

"No!" my uncle would boom for he had an enormously powerful voice, no doubt developed over the years with shouting to his sheep dogs on the mountains. "He won't bite me or kick me. But he might eat you. So you'd better stay well away from him."

The children would utter a collective "Oooh", and hastily shuffle backwards as one. Uncle Dick would stride through the shop and into the house followed by his nervous-looking dogs Bonnie and Clyde, tails and bodies low, unaccustomed to streets, people, noise and fuss.

"Sal! Where are you Sal?" he'd yell to my mother, who, aware of his arrival was putting the kettle to boil. "Let's 'ave a cup 'a tea. I 'aven' got long. I gotta go and see to those sheep that've strayed over the Western Tip. One's broken a leg so Gwyn Tylawinder says."

When younger, if I was lucky enough to be home when he dropped in, he'd take me for a ride on the horse, back up to the lower mountain slopes. I was the envy of all childish eyes as I sat on the saddle in front of him with one of his arms firmly clutching me after my mother's exhortation, "Oh, for God's sake Dick, take care she don' fall off!" We'd set off to a raucous cheer from the assembled juveniles who'd follow us up the hill. Once off the road and on the grass, Uncle Dick would make a chirruping noise and spur the horse to a gallop. The animal would lunge sure-footed and effortlessly up the steep, rough terrain, then race, mane streaming once on the flat, followed closely by the two eager dogs now in their element. I never felt unsafe on these occasions, a bit scared initially, then exhilarated. Fame and envy were short-lived though as I had to walk back.

Coming as she did from a family of ten children, five boys and five girls, my mother had brothers and sisters to visit on farms in the area other than Tydraw, the original family home. There was Gellilwch, a half mile or so off the road at the top of Graigwen Hill where it begins to flatten out, where Aunty Polly lived. This four hundred year old farm whose name means Dusty Grove, probably something to do with its stone slate roof and nearby quarry rather than dryness, nestles under the brow of a gentle slope and has a panoramic view over the lower end of Ynysybwl and the Taff Valley.

The trouble with Gellilwch was getting there. Not only did you have to negotiate the endless steepness of Graigwen Hill, but once off the Llanwonno road at the top and on to the cart track, there were more problems afoot, literally. First you were greeted by a mini waterfall coming off the high grass bank except in a summer drought which was not often. This demanded a wary sidling along the track edge and was a good preparation for the ordeals ahead. The track was very rough, rutted by carts and the very occasional car brave enough to venture its exhaust and undercarriage along it. Slabs of rock and stones sticking out of it lay in wait to trap the unwary town shoe or twist the unsuspecting, uninitiated ankle. After rain, and it usually was, by the time a hundred yards of track had been negotiated, stockings and legs looked as though they had a bad knee-high dose of a brown brand of measles. An onlooker from a distance seeing my mother and me making our way along this road would think they were witnessing some sort of tribal dance. Arms held aloft for balance and proceeding gingerly, we would traverse muddy ridges, balancing on unstable stones which often spitefully gave way landing us in muck or puddle. We would creep forward, searching for drier, more solid looking clumps of grass on the verge, only to end up for our pains with water squelching over our shoes. For every yard of forward motion, at least half a dozen of zig-zag had to be performed. Conversation went a bit like this:

"Look Mam, there's a dry bit on this side."

"No, watch out Mary, there's cow dung by that long grass!"

There'd be a slight pause then, "Oh jawl, look at my shoe now!"

Mam, watching out for my footing had stepped in a cow pat herself.

"Never mind. A bit of spit will get it off when it's dry. We ought to wear wellies to come up here."

"Wellies! You can't wear wellies to go visiting, silly. Anyway I haven't got any wellies."

"You could wear Dad's."

She would tut and sometimes, though she smoked very little, always carried cigarettes and matches in her handbag, would get so exasperated she'd have to have a smoke and a 'little spell' perched on an oasis of a flat slab in the middle of the murk before continuing the battle with nature.

"If you can jump on to that stone, see, you'll be OK."

"Jump indeed! I'm having enough trouble trying to walk. Oh, why don't they do something about this damn road?"

"Yes, blow it up'd be the best thing."

Laughter, giggles and mild swearing accompanied us this half mile from the road to the farm. Even if we'd had a drought and arrived with dusty, dry feet and shoes with the heels intact and a vestige of polish remaining, by the time we'd traversed the farm-yard, we looked as though we had personally built the Aswan dam in any case.

There was little passing traffic in those days, which was a good thing as far as we were concerned as we'd have to scamper away from the track through dung, the odd stray sheep and goodness knows what other pitfalls and unmentionables to avoid being spat-tered all over and arrive looking even less presentable than usual.

It was fortunate Auntie Polly was an excellent cook as the food you were plied with there made the awful journey worthwhile. She always had a plentiful supply of farmhouse cake and fruit tarts of all sorts. She could slice bread the thinnest of anyone I knew to make mouth-watering salmon, scrambled egg or sweet-cured ham sandwiches with a generous layer of butter. Wielding a honed-hollow bread knife, she would grasp the loaf against her bounti-ful bosom and saw rapidly towards her body. I watched, fasci-nated at this expertise, but there were never any mishaps, never a blood red tinge colouring the sandwich fillings, not even any crumbs, so perfected was the slicing to produce the lacy piece of bread soon to be spread with pale yellow farm butter. Re-fuelling with delicious food however, was necessary to fortify visitors prior to their return journey through the ruts, puddles, dung, loose stones and boulders otherwise they might have stayed forever.

Another of my mother's brothers lived in the Lan farm with his eldest sister until she died, when I was seven years old. These were John and Maggie. The Lan was a couple of fields south of Gellilwch and is historically famous because, as its Welsh name suggests, was the site of a church. Some maintain it was the first church in the area of Aber-rhondda as Pontypridd, according to the Margam parchments of 1215 was then called. Since the Welsh name for Brecon is also Aber-rhonddu, to avoid confusion, Pontypridd's name was changed to Ffordd Taf (Taff Ford). In 1815, this became Newbridge and probably to avoid more con-fusion with the other Newbridges about Wales, the name was changed in 1856 to Pontypridd, home of the Old Bridge, Evan and William James composers of the Welsh National Anthem, a famous market and a fine rugby team.

The ancient church at the Lan was situated in the sometime barn, sometime wash-house at the edge of the field fronting the house and overlooking Lan Wood. Although of course a Christian, not a Pagan church, in my childhood, I and it wit-nessed many massacres. With a huge fire burning in the grate, the

Christmas chickens and geese were killed, plucked, dressed and trussed there. Paradoxically, my happiest times spent at the Lan were amongst the killing of scores of birds in the former place of worship. But then, who or what could wish for a better send-off to the happy hunting grounds? Next to the barn and attached to it was the smaller building, the implement shed – undoubtedly the former church vestry. A low, dry stone wall at the edge of the field separated the buildings from the steep descent of Lan wood. At the base of the wall where it runs along the side of the barn, was a solid path of flat paving stones. In the summer the congregation would sit on the wall outside with their feet on the stone slabs and the preacher would conduct an open-air service. The view from the Lan over Pontypridd is as panoramic as that from Gellilwch over the eastern valley, so it is to be hoped that this didn't distract the worshippers' concentration. On the other hand, it might help to explain why a church flourished in such an elevated, isolated spot.

Elevated and isolated in the extreme the Lan seemed to me when a small child. My mother and I, and occasionally my father when he wasn't at work, would get off the bus from Trehafod at the Welsh Harp at the bottom of Graigwen Hill at the start of our epic journey. It was the same if we were visiting Gellilwch. The Hill towered disconcertingly above like an Alp and was so steep it seemed to me that if you took one step you would hit your knee on the road in front of you. Mam was always at her most cheerful and most talkative going up Graigwen Hill, not that she was ever miserable or silent, but on these occasions she was particularly merry and talked faster than usual. I gradually realised this was to jolly me along and counteract moans and grumbles on my part at having to climb the sheer incline.

"Oh Mam, can't we catch the bus up this ol' 'ill. It's too far an' my legs are tired."

"No love, there's only one bus a day up and one down."

"Ooh, why just one Mam?"

"I dunno. 'Cos it's so steep I 'xpect."

"Can we catch it Mam?"

"Well, it doesn't go until this afternoon when all the people have finished their shopping in town see. You don't want to wait hours for a bus do you?"

"Ye-e-e-s," uttered very wearily.

Suppressing a sigh and, no doubt, thoughts of, "awkward little brat", she'd cajole, "Look! We're nearly up to the Post Office. You shall have some nice sweets if it's open."

Apart from on annual holidays when we were far from our shop, the Post Office near the bottom of Graigwen Hill was the only other place my mother would offer to buy me sweets and chocolate as she was rightly worried about my intake of sweet things, both licit and otherwise. When she was fetching coal for the fire, or putting out the washing, I'd nip into the shop and secrete a horde of goodies into my bedroom. I think she discovered the implicating wrappers in vases and under my mattress.

"Look what I found in your room today!" she'd say triumphantly, catching me unawares as she flourished silver and purple chocolate paper. But equally cunning I would smartly change the subject and say something like, "Miss Bird was pleased with me today, 9 out of 10 for Algebra. D'you want to see my book?" hoping, if the answer was an affirmative one, I could somewhere find a 9 out of 10 in it and put my thumb over the date. A bit of local gossip, not that I knew much, would instantly make Mam forget my wrong-doings, "Joycey Bevan told me today that those people living next door to her have fights in their 'ouse. She can hear 'em through the wall an' she said the wife's leaving."

"No-o, not Billy and Vanno James?"

"Yes," then adding a bit of embroidery to extend the story until Mam had absent-mindedly thrown the incriminating piece of chocolate paper in the fire, "'An she said las' night Vanno locked 'im out when he went to the Vaughan's, but she 'ad to let 'im in 'cos he was 'ammering on the door an' shoutin' an' wakin' everybody up."

"Well well! They 'aven' been married long either. When's she leaving?"

"I dunno." By this time the misdemeanour would clearly have been forgotten so I'd cut the conversation short with, "I'm goin' out to play for a bit now Mam. Tara!"

But I digress, deliberately though, as digression was the order of the day during the ascent of Graigwen Hill. My mother told me who lived in which house – not that I cared a jot – and told stories about them. We frequently stopped to look at the tremendous view back up the valley to Trehafod and the Rhondda, across the river to Maesycoed and the winding road above the houses to Tydraw, then back down at the western part of Pontypridd with the square, white flat-roofed County cinema dominant and Ponty station opposite with the longest platform in Britain. Half way up, where the road levels out at Pant-y-Graigwen – aptly named because people were panting if not

101

wheezing by the time they'd climbed this far – was a seat where mam was willing to have a quick sit down. I used to run to this seat to have a longer sit because although placatory, Mam was firm and insisted there was no time for hanging around. Having had a farm upbringing, my mother was fit and strong and never baulked at the prospect of hikes and treks and never wavered during them.

The view became more extensive the higher you went, and to take my, by now, numbed, mind off my equally numbed legs, Mam would quietly sing Welsh songs and encourage me to join in. We always had Dafydd y Garreg-wen, appropriate as our goal was the White Rock atop Graigwen. She would tell me happy stories of her childhood and point out things of interest in the amazing landscape below us and above, such as the Rock sticking out over the valley like a huge chin. Our route swung right off the main road but before engaging this we would call on my mother's welcoming friend Auntie Cissie in her house called Pentwyn. She greeted us with a beaming face and cries of delight and hugs even though our last visit might only have been a week ago.

"Sal! Sal and Mary! There's glad I am to see you! How are you today? Come in, come in! I'll just put the kettle on. Oh, you must be tired after that ol' hill. We'll have a nice cup of tea now. Oh, there's nice to see you!" More hugs and kisses followed this pronouncement. "Sit down on that comfy chair Sal! Here, let me get you some more cushions. There you are! That's better! D'you want to sit on my little stool Mary, or are you coming to the kitchen with me to get some marshmallows?"

Tiredness miraculously vanished, legs wondrously recovered, I'd go with Auntie Cissie, who, winking and shushing, would stow away a few wrapped marshmallow cakes and sweets in my pockets, whispering conspiratorially, "There you are! A few sweets for you 'cos they don't have any up the Lan. Don't tell Mam! It's our secret, mind!" Usually she'd slip me a shilling as well.

"Oh, I bet you'd like to live up here with me, wouldn't you Mary?" she'd say.

"Well, I'd like to live with you, but I wouldn't like to live up here so much."

"Why ever not?"

"Because if you were playing ball an' it tamped out of reach, you'd have to run all the way down to Ponty to get it back."

She'd roar with laughter and on every visit it was identical. Same procedure, same conversation, same jollity. We'd be seen off with more overt affection and much waving and Mam would say, "I suppose she gave you some money and sweets did she? Oh, she's kind, so kind. She's a lovely lady. She'd be missed mind." This part about missing always gave rise to a daft bit of conversation. I could converse now, as after the Hill the lane was reasonably level.

"Where she goin' then?"

"Going? I dunno. She's not going anywhere."

"Well why will she be missed then?"

"Oh, you know, one day..."

"No I don't. What day?"

"Well, when she...passes over."

"Is she bad then?"

"No, not as far as I know, but we all got to go one day, see."

Two hundred yards up the lane was Gellifynaches farm – another historical place, the most historical in fact. Perhaps its illustrious aura was slightly deflated when the White Rock Estate was built around it in the sixties and its address became 8, Nun's Crescent. The farm was mentioned in the early thirteenth century Margam Monastic Deeds when Pontypridd was Aber-rhond-da. Gellifynaches was an old Welsh long house, where the animals lived next door to the family, separated by a wall. The name might mean Pretty Place and it might also mean Nunnery which is the more likely as there was a small nunnery or possibly a cell inhabited by a few nuns adjacent to the farm which took its name from them. When the town of Pontypridd had its first name change to Ffordd-Taf, it was sometimes referred to as Gelli Fonaches Isaf (the lower slopes of the nunnery). The nunnery was the female branch of the important monastery of Mynachdy or Llanwonno as it is today a few miles further on in the direction of Ynysybwl. Whatever, the building is the first known residence in Pontypridd.

There was nothing historical about the people living in Gellifynaches, as they were the younger branch of the family – my cousins in fact. We didn't stop here if we had called at Auntie Cissie's or we would have spent all day visiting in different places, would never have got to the Lan and been bursting with tea. Gellifynaches stood isolated and sprawling in the middle of a meadow at the base of Lan Wood – a paradise area of play and adventure for youngsters. Indeed a younger cousin with a Walter Mitty imagination, deciding to become a Red Indian for the afternoon, removed all his clothes and, hiding them in the bracken, daubed himself all over with mud. He undoubtedly ran around freely and unhindered among the trees, ululating as Indians do, and tracking wild animals – in this case the family dog and cat and the farm pigs and chickens rooting around in the fields. Looking for his clothes later in the afternoon when hunger struck and it was time for the Indian to return home for his tea, the hidden clothes, despite desperate searches were not to be found and the muddy Brave had furtively to get back to the house, naked, to his mother's wrath and an immediate bath. The same Red Indian, having access to plenty of wood and space to build, started in September to construct a magnificent bonfire for November 5th. Its fame spread and neighbouring, envious marauders under cover of darkness, would steal bits off it for their own paltry erections in small back gardens. Our enterprising young warrior, no doubt thinking in terms of wigwams, then hollowed out the centre of the pile to form a chamber. Borrowing blankets, a torch and with enough sandwiches to feed a school at midday, he spent the night warmly ensconced therein, keeping guard and frightening prospective thieves and arsonists out of their skins by pursuing them with weird noises and wrapped in a white sheet.

The final haul to the Lan was 150 yards up a gentle slope through the wood. This was pleasant enough as it was cool beneath the trees – a panacea to the heat engendered by the climb up Graigwen. Also, you never knew what you might see, apart from small naked Red Indians – a fox, stealthily sliding through the undergrowth, the sudden movement of a rabbit scurrying into a hole with a white flash of tail or a long-eared hare racing as fast as possible to nowhere in particular, going off at a tangent every so often for good measure but no apparent reason. Steep straight or curved gentler wooden steps finally led up to the field in front of the house, with the wash house and former church at its perimeter.

Uncle John was the eldest of my mother's five brothers, who at the age of thirteen left the paternal home to go and live with a childless aunt and uncle, Leah and David Rowlands, at Llwynperdid farm just off the Llanwonno road. In his late twenties, John was about to marry so took the tenancy of the Lan farm from the Tredegar estate. However the marriage did not materialise and John's eldest sister, Maggie, went to help run the farm with him, as his housekeeper and companion.

The Lan was rather a gloomy, formal house of grey rendering, unlike the other relatives' squat, white-washed, friendly-looking farms. To my mind it didn't look like a farm at all – more the country residence of some squire who spends his time fox-hunting, shooting game, being condescending to his tenants. The inside wasn't much more cheerful either. The rooms were large, dark, cold and high-ceilinged with big, mahogany furniture and hard settees. A flagstone-floored corridor completely surrounded the sitting room to emerge on its far side after having passed the larder and the rarely used, heavily bolted back door. This corridor was quite useful for games. The only trouble was that once you had brought a friend to visit the Lan, they wouldn't come again, not wanting a re-conquest of Graigwen Hill, and there wasn't much point running around it on your own. My friend Hope Higgs visited the Lan with me on one occasion, and although she didn't say much during the ascent – indeed all but Mam had to conserve their breath climbing the Hill – and I had great hopes for future visits, I was disappointed. We had a lovely time running around Lan Wood exploring in holes and caves, rolling in the hay, playing hide and seek in the house where I even showed her some secret magazines with nude people in. We had a warm welcome, plenty of chips for dinner from my cousin who was there at the time and Hope was given a bagful of gooseberries to take home for her mother. Then when I confidently asked her later in school if she would come to the Lan with me again, her response was, "No fear! I've still got a bruised chin from where my knees were knocking against it going up that hill. What do you think I am? Dopey?"

A door in the corner of the sitting room opened on to the dark, narrow back stairs which led up to one end of the landing, while from the hall. the main staircase with its oak bannister took you up to the other end. Two more rooms, dank and dismal, one with a secret larder off and in which I, at seven, was taken to see the corpse of Auntie Maggie after she had been laid out, completed the downstairs geography. The bedrooms, as is usually the case, being nearer the sky, were lighter than the living rooms, but no less intimidating with their huge, high beds and dark wood head and foot boards. I discovered when I stayed there overnight that the beds were very soft – so soft in fact that if you accidentally strayed to the middle. you disappeared down a depression in the feather mattress and it was a struggle to get out again. So worried was I about being lost or suffocated I tried to keep awake at night to stay perched on the side. Better to fall out and survive bruised than fall in and be lost, smothered in down.

There were five bedrooms, one at the top of each staircase and three off the landing. The three middle ones all had dressing rooms and long windows almost to the floor. At one stage I spent a lot of time upstairs, having come across a pile of magazines in one of these dressing rooms called *Health and Efficiency*. To my eye-popping, shocked, interested amazement, they were full of naked people cavorting in lakes and meadows, playing games, or ladies standing in rows being judged for something or other, as bereft of cloth as the day they were born but with a number on a plaque around their neck or waist. Sometimes it was a line-up of men. Whatever were they being judged for I wondered? They were all laughing and enjoying themselves tremendously. I assumed they were mad – running around naked and grinning like fools – until I came across a notice informing that this was the magazine of the nudist society.

"Well," I said to myself, "if that's the way they carry on, that's one society I won't be joining!"

Then slowly, other thoughts assailed me....Surely, none of my relatives belonged to such a sect? I couldn't even imagine Uncle John in his underclothes let alone in no clothes. Up until then I had thought people were only ever naked in their bath. Apart from it being rude to display parts of the body normally kept under wraps, what about the cold? I perused the magazines closely and wondered whether I could legitimately borrow the magnifying glass Uncle John used to read the newspaper. The nudists didn't look cold and I certainly couldn't spot any goose flesh. I could have done with that magnifying glass as branches, hedges and tennis nets got in the way to hide bits of people in the foreground and although in the background the happy figures weren't concealed, they were too distant to see properly.

The other main interest for a bored child in the Lan house was the china. My aunt loved trinkets and baubles and there were dressers and glass-fronted cupboards full of them – small porcelain animals, lots of dogs, some supine, some watchful, some standing proudly, of different breeds and colours. There were china pigs and a little flock of four geese all alike with lurid yellow beaks and feet, graduating in size from a gosling to a gander. One red and white cow resting in some bright green grass had a removable top half and could be used as a butter dish. A few small china houses with flowers lapping the front door stood looking out at the room, and a shepherd gazed adoringly up at a cross-eyed shepherdess with blond ringlets and an enormous blue bustle. Level with my eyes was a brick garden wall overgrown with roses and with a small pink door set into it. Only this was a little porcelain soup bowl resting on a plate, with a lid to keep the contents warm, depicting a sun-dial with Roman numerals around the edge. On arriving at the Lan, welcomes over, I would go to look at this bowl and imagine the scene through the pink door in the wall. One day, Auntie Maggie, coming across me with my face in close proximity to the glass, said, "You are fond of that little bowl, aren't you?"

"Oh yes, I think it's lovely. Is there a garden in the middle?"

She took it out of the case to show me. Disappointingly there was only a smooth, white glaze. Disappointment however, quickly turned to delight.

"Well, since you like it, you shall have it to keep. We'll take it to give it a wash and wrap it up so Mam can put it in her basket to take home for you tonight with the eggs."

More than half a century later it still bears pride of place on my shelves.

Vases of all shapes, sizes, materials and colours abounded: fine little statuettes and figurines: jam dishes, one in the shape of a leaf painted dark blue and white with gold membranes: egg cups, singly as waddling ducks and chicks, or in a quartet on a plate with holes to accommodate them together with a salt cellar and pepper pot. There were endless delicate small jugs with coats of arms declaring they had come from Bognor Regis, Llandrindod Wells, St Annes on Sea, Weston-super-Mare, Leamington Spa and Barry Island. Similarly, ashtrays, some with little perimeter curved dents to rest the cigarettes while others were simply dishes perhaps with a map of Scotland or a picture of a Cornish fishing village painted on. There were larger jugs too, in sets of three or four, white with deep blue patterns, dull grey pewter next to shiny lustre which changed hue depending where you stood, and brightly painted Toby jugs – jolly, smiling men in breeches, lace jabots and riding coats, all with red cheeks and enormous noses – brothers no doubt. I wasn't so interested in the huge, willow patterned turkey plates out of reach on the top shelf of the dresser, but was fascinated by one of its mates kept in the secret larder. This pathetic object had lost a lot of its willow and parts of the surface glaze had been gouged out down to the rough pottery.

"That poor old thing came from Clawr-y-Plwyf," my aunt would tell me. Clawr-y-Plwyf was the original family farm on the mountain above Pontllanffraith.

"One of my father's cows had foot and mouth disease so it had to be destroyed. For some reason they put the cow's tongue on that plate. For the vet'rin'ry to examine I suppose. Then when they went to burn it a few days later, the disease had eaten away most of the pattern and part of the plate as well."

I loved her telling this horrific story and each time as I accompanied her around the house, if we happened to go into the secret larder, I would gaze at the plate anew and innocently say, "Look at this dish Auntie Maggie. Whatever happened to that I wonder?" She must have told the gory story twenty times, probably thinking her niece was not blessed with the keenest of memories.

If the house was gloomy, the occupants were not. I didn't see much of Uncle John as farm work is demanding and the hours long. A reserved man, he was always cheerful without being ostentatiously so. Auntie Maggie was like her neighbour a hundred or so feet further down towards Ponty, Auntie Cissie – a demonstrative, generous, spontaneous person. Perhaps the rarer air in those elevated parts had something to do with this type of personality. Our arrival at the Lan was similar to that undergone thirty minutes before in Pentwyn, except this time I would be gathered up in my aunt's arms, smothered with kisses and swung round in a hug before being replaced, dizzy, on the floor. Auntie Maggie was unmarried, probably lonely in her eyrie atop Lan Wood and was glad to have visitors, especially my mother who loved to chat which is what they did all day in between cooking, tidying and inspecting the huge house, doing things to the garden and making *creision* if a pig had recently been killed. *Crwsin* were crunchy things rather like thick, salty, meaty crisps. They had no connection with potatoes though, as far as I knew. In the nineties they would be outlawed as most unhealthy to eat as they were basically the fatty lining of the pig's stomach, oven-roasted until all the white, ripply fat had been released and collected in an earthenware bowl. They were then salted and cooled on greaseproof paper. I liked them and Auntie Maggie would put some in a brown paper bag which became very greasy, for me to take home.

One day when I was seven, Mam went to the Lan alone. Auntie Maggie was not well and couldn't tolerate the excitement of a visiting child and I was to be spared her pain. I was being bathed in the tin tub in front of the fire by our neighbour Mrs Brittain when my mother returned looking sad and drawn.

"Is Auntie Maggie better?" I asked, "Did she send some *creision* for me?" There was a pause.

"Oh love," Mam said slowly, looking tearful, "Auntie Maggie's gone to Jesus."

It took some minutes to dawn on me exactly what this meant – that I wouldn't be seeing this kind person again. Often in life at a certain significant time, the moment when one receives perhaps an exam result, specially good, or bad, news, information about a raffle win or a prize awarded, is later associated with something extraneous, completely banal and completely divorced from the event – a bluebottle buzzing at a window, a pencil peeping out from under the dresser, a piece of coal falling from the fire. Then when the momentous event is recalled, the other lesser memory is also evoked. The moment is associated in my mind with two plops forming circles in the bath water as a tear fell from each of my eyes. No more was said. There was no further discussion of death although it was the first time it had consciously affected me.

We went up to the Lan, gloomier than ever, before the funeral and I was asked if I would like to see my aunt for the last time to say goodbye. She was on a bed, specially brought down, in the room off which was the secret larder. Apart from a yellowish-grey face she looked as if she were asleep and I wished she'd open her eyes and smile at me. I touched her ice-cold hand and wondered if the story of the willow plate in the larder so close by was now exclusively mine.

My first sleepless night was that one, spent at the Lan in a big soft bed with my mother, not because I was afraid of smothering in the middle of the mattress but because the dead Auntie Maggie was downstairs. I think I was overcome with a mixture of grief at her departure and awe that she was no longer the same as the rest of us – just an inert body whose spirit had gone somewhere unknown and left her with a yellow face. Also the strange bed waiting to envelop you in its deep recesses didn't help although Mam was there to rescue and cuddle me if needs be.

Uncle John was left on his own and clearly had to have a housekeeper. After some worrying discussion about whether we should uproot from our little valley shop and go to this isolated place high above Pontypridd to live, another relative was found who was ready to live at the Lan and housekeep. This was Gladys, the daughter of another sister, Anne. Gladys was a young woman in her thirties, unmarried and, fortunately, jolly like Auntie Maggie. She had an oval, shiny, smiling face with pale blue, round eyes. There was a surprised look about her, probably because her sparse eyebrows were a long way above her eyes. While not plump, she was ample. Although a cousin, I had never met her before. I took to her immediately and we got on from the start. She would abandon her tasks when you arrived to make tea and chat and entertain and was even prepared to come for walks and play ball!

She was very fond of sausages – at least there always seemed to be a good supply of them during Gladys's time and we always had them for dinner with chips and a fried egg. Eggs caused her some problems however. If she espied a globule of blood in a fertilised egg when she cracked it open, she would peer into the bowl, then her face would crease in horror. "Ugh!" she'd say indignantly, "There's blood in this egg!" then run to the door and throw it into the garden, usually over the apple tree just outside the kitchen door. She liked unbloodied eggs though and taught me how to make a fluffy omelette by beating up the white first until it was stiff. If I burnt the omelette or messed it up in the pan, no matter, over the apple tree it went.

Gladys loved visitors too and wasn't at all cross when the rather noisy and unkempt Morgan children from Graigwen farm came up for the day to play with me and ran all over the place rampaging. Gladys introduced me to the delights of icing sugar. For some reason, although I never saw iced cake at the Lan, there were several packets of it on the larder shelves. My mother was very keen on my being healthy and was a great believer in the health maintaining qualities of red capsules called Adexolin containing horrible tasting oil. I had to take one of these Adexolins three times a day after meals. On one post-prandial occasion at the Lan, one of these little bombs, catching the edge of an unaligned tooth, burst open before making its descent to where no doubt its goodness operated. The foul tasting experience was vocally and histrionically shared with all present. I made loud, indignant noises and a lot of fuss with hand fluttering and jumping up and down.

"Have a spoonful of icing sugar," Gladys suggested helpfully, "That'll take the nasty taste away," and she duly fetched a packet from the larder, thus introducing me to its palatable delights but dubious health imparting properties.

There was a marvellous loft above the cowshed in the Lan. It was reached via a wooden ladder going straight up the wall through a square hole in one corner of the cowshed ceiling. At one end a doorway open to the elements allowed the hay to be forked in from the gambo in August after haymaking. The loft was always generously supplied with fragrant, soft hay so the floor was never visible. Since anyone rarely went there you could rely on privacy and peace. I would occasionally sneak out some 'Health and Efficiency' booklets to peruse there sitting on a makeshift swing Uncle John had rigged up for me – a cushion on some rope thrown over a rafter. There were nests in the roof and the occasional small bird flying around among the rafters and coming and going through the hay entrance. At this time in my life, no doubt through a keenly developing gastronomic awareness, the Lan became associated in my mind with icing sugar and eggs – with a very cavalier attitude to the latter. No sooner arriving at the farm I would abduct a packet of icing sugar from the dairy, carefully stuff some eggs into my pockets and climb up into the loft. There, lying in abandoned pose in the hay like a decadent Roman, I'd indulge in an orgy of icing sugar consumption, licked from a wet finger stuck into the packet and lob eggs at the central rafter. If my aim was on target, there was a satisfying crack and the albumen and yolk slid down the rough wood leaving a viscous, snaily trail before oozing like a tailed comet into the dried grass below. If I missed, the egg would land unbroken in the hay and I could have another go. At the time I had no conscience whatsoever about this wasteful extravagance and unauthorised 'borrowing'. If I did think about it I simply mused on what a nice surprise some cow would have getting an omelette in his hay instead of the usual boring old grass. And I never ate all the icing sugar, replacing the packet with the level perhaps half an inch lower than the last time it had sat on the larder shelf. Goodness knows what Uncle John thought were the shiny streaks on the rafters if he ever noticed them and I don't think he was given the trouble of puzzling over the broken eggs in the hay.

Over dinner of sausages, loads of chips and an unfertilised fried egg, Gladys, who had a multitude of brothers and sisters would talk non-stop about them and to my delight at my ever increasing connections, discovered relatives I never knew I had. Two sisters lived in Norfolk, one a midwife and another married to a farmer holding the tenancy of Marsh farm on the Sandringham estate at Woolverton.

"They know the Royal Family well, see. All the tenants of the farms get invited to Sandringham for drinks after Christmas. They tell me the Queen can't half knock back the cocktails."

"What do they call them Gladys?"

"Well the King calls the farmers and their wives by their first names and they call him Sir and her Ma'am, short for Madam. I suppose they can call him Your Majesty, but it's a bit of a mouthful."

"Does the King go to their farm then?"

"Oh yes. Whenever they're at Sandringham they go round their farms in their Land Rover. And the Queen wears wellies and a scarf around her head. Looks just like an ordinary person she does. They got rabbits running round on their front garden too. That's why they got to have a lawn, see. Can't grow vegetables or flowers or anything like that. The rabbits eat everything. Anytime you look out of the window you see rabbits running about."

"But that's OK. Because they can catch them to eat."

She'd laugh. "Yes, but they can't eat rabbits all the time. Even once a week they'd be fed up with them. Anyway you got to skin them an' they got an awful lot of little bones. I love rabbit stew though, I do. I wouldn't mind it once a week if someone made it for me."

She would chatter on about her holidays in Norfolk, the game shooting, the acres of forest, how once the Wash overflowed and nearly reached their door several miles inland as it came over the flat Norfolk countryside, the vast fields of potatoes they grew, the market town of Kings Lynn, the coast, Hunstanton, Cromer and the Broads. Although she had other sisters in Canada and Gelligaer, it was the Royal Norfolk one I was interested in and felt important myself being related to someone who not only had spoken to the King and Queen, but been invited to their palace for drinks.

"Have you ever seen the King and Queen Gladys?"

"Oh yes. One day I was there pottering around in the kitchen making Welsh cakes with Ray (her sister Rachel). She looked out of the window and there was the King going up the wooden steps to the loft across the yard. Bill's got a sort of office up in the loft, see. "Oh Gawd!" said Ray, "There's the King going up to the loft and I 'aven't dusted up there this week. The Queen stayed in the Land Rover, but I did see her in her wellies and headscarf."

After a year or two, one of Gladys's younger brothers, Tommy, came to live at the Lan to help Uncle John with the farm work. He looked very like her with his round, plump, pale face and surprised look. He was cheery as well, smiled at everything you said but didn't talk as much as his sister.

On winter evenings, Uncle John would finish work for the day much earlier and after tea would linger in the kitchen. As there was no electricity in the farm, an oil lamp was placed on the table and we ate in a warm, cosy gloom with the fire providing a little more light glowing in another corner. If anything needed fetching from the dairy, one's way was feebly illuminated by a candle. After tea, people talked around the table about farming, relatives, deaths and funerals, scandals, and very occasionally, politics, or something from the *Western Mail* that Tommy had fetched up from Gellifynaches. I mostly listened, my chin resting on my folded arms on the table, now and then peering into the further dark corners of the room. I could make out the mens' muddy, hobnailed, heavy, unlaced, bulgy boots under the brown painted bench along the wall by the door: the dark rocking chair with a heap of old newspapers on a little shelf underneath: the mantelpiece with its wooden, shellacked tea caddy made by my carpenter father with 'TEA' carved on the front and probably given as a Christmas present: letters and postcards with blue tuppenny stamps shoved behind one of a pair of ornamental brass candlesticks: the reliable, round-faced clock in its dark wood case reassuringly ticking loudly away in the semi-darkness. I could make out the dark shape of the door in the furthest corner leading to the house-encircling corridor with the stone-flagged floor, a few paces along which was the dairy. I felt smug that I was this side of it, not beyond in the dark, cavernous house where goodness knows what creepy crawlies or ghosts of past tenants roamed.

When it was time for Mam and me to leave, Uncle John would light a portable oil lamp and the three of us would trudge off like Scott, Evans and Titus Oates (except that we had eggs wrapped in newspaper and sometimes a piece of spare rib) to conquer the hazards of the night – in this case the steps and path down through Lan Wood. Mam, when not chatting to her brother would be issuing words of advice to me about the terrain although I was a lot steadier on my feet than she, or mumbling to herself about the difficulties of night marching.

"Mary! Be careful on those steps! They're slippery! Can you see your way? John, hold the lamp up here a bit!" Then, stopping, "Oh, damn! I walked into a branch then. Nearly lost my bloomin' 'at! Oh, so Walter the Cefn's been telling you he's building a bungalow for his son has he? Is the son getting married then? Mary! Don't go too far ahead mind! Oh, jawl, I've stepped in something soft now!"

And so it continued until we reached the meadow by Gellifynaches and Uncle John turned to go back up alone through the wood. Sometimes I walked backwards watching the light of the oil lamp going higher and dancing through the branches like a will o' the wisp as it swung in the hand. Soon we turned down to Pentwyn and the steep road down to Pontypridd with its assorted lights, the dominant blue neon sign of the County cinema and the bus back to the Vaughan's Arms.

# 12. Dreaded Exams

It's a truism that time goes quicker as you get older. Although from Form One to Five had seemed a lifetime, the two years in the Sixth Form, like a snapping of the fingers, were coming to an end and A level exams were fast approaching.

The majority of girls heading for universities were for those in Wales. There were a lot fewer to choose from in the UK generally in those days, but there were fewer applicants too, so once accepted, that was it. If you passed your three A levels with whatever grades, you were in. If you passed in only two subjects you might be rejected from your chosen course and have to search around for an alternative having a vacancy once the authorities had done their maths; so you might have applied to read Law and ended up with Art History. Those who managed one A level were usually destined for a third year in the Sixth. We had been recommended to apply to Teacher Training Colleges as a fall-back in the event of not making it into the highest echelons of learning, so I was bound, with luck, for Aberystwyth, or without for London and Goldsmith's College.

Returning to school after the Easter holidays, faces showed strain and as the summer term progressed, unusually, these faces didn't look attractively and healthily brown as they had in previous years. Strain was visible on staff faces too and the key phrase was a variation on "finishing the syllabus".

In French, under Miss Llewellyn's calm, well-organised tutelage we were easing into the final strait on schedule. Grammar exercise books were full of the clearly explained, thus easily understood eccentricities of the French language, vocabulary notebooks strained at their staples with words and meanings we'd been tested on, and the significant aspects of the set texts had been firmly implanted in our minds. As usual, in that era, when using the language in actual speech hadn't assumed the importance it has in today's exams, we were a little uneasy about the imminent Oral. Still, as for myself, I'd been to France twice on a school trip so learned an essay I'd written on the Paris monuments. Everything considered, we were not unnecessarily worried about French.

English had proceeded in much the same way with the charismatic Denise Ormond. Her energetic, single-minded, individualistic and largely discursive approach ensured we knew the texts inside out. We'd been to see the set plays, among others, performed in various places, Bristol, Cardiff and London. We'd performed the two Shakespeares ourselves as school productions' had been cajoled into appreciating the poetry and even the thirteenth century Geoffrey Chaucer, and had enjoyed the novels which she'd brought to life. Now we were spending the lessons reading through past questions, discussing what they meant, what answers the examiner was seeking and how best to provide him with them. The only difficulty was doing justice to five answers in three hours. Timing was of the essence.

"Keep the question constantly in mind," Miss Ormond would say. "Make the point and support it with reference to the text. Summon your armies and choose your regiments wisely to convince the opposition." Indeed we did feel we were going into battle with these A level exams!

In Geography, we were at panic stations! We hadn't completed the syllabus and it didn't look as though we were going to. This was not surprising as basically we had to know the Geography of the entire world. We had multitudinous bookfuls and folders of notes and maps on Physical and Economic Geography, basic Geology, Map Projections, Natural Vegetation, the Geography of North America, Wales, Practical Geography, but we hadn't done much European Geography or any Ethnography. In fact, a month before the exams we didn't know what Ethnography was! When Miss Orsman came in one day in May just a few weeks before the practical exam and started handing out pictures of naked men with spears and blow-guns, we thought she'd gone off her trolley. Then when she began to tell us how they bred head lice and ate clay voraciously, we cast worried looks and raised eyebrows at each other wondering when the men in white coats would arrive to take her away, and whether because of the stress of A level Geog we'd be going too. Apparently though, we were somewhat relieved to discover, this was Ethnography and the naked, scowling people were of the Witoto tribe in the Amazon basin.

Due to lack of lesson time we were required to stay after school to acquire some knowledge of parts of the course hitherto untouched, and to practise the touched bits. In what is probably an ostracised, politically incorrect study today, we learned about the African Nama Hottentot women who have much posterior fat, considered a sign of beauty, and the Masai who take blood from the neck veins of cattle and drink it warm. Despite Miss Orsman's conviction and grave manner in her approach to these lessons, a lingering suspicion remained throughout those final days that our normally unorthodox teacher was possibly, at last, crossing that fine line between derangement and sanity. This sentiment was encouraged by the non-Geographers.

"Finished the course in Geog yet?" friendly Historians enquired.

"Er...no...not yet," we'd answer.

"Cor, you're leaving it a bit late aren't you?" Jennifer said as though it was our fault.

"Well, you see Jennifer, the Geography syllabus includes the whole world, and it's a lot," explained Anne Morris.

"Yes, that's why we got to have all these extra lessons see Jen," added Caryl.

Turning to Florence and me, her normal companions on the walk down to Porth after school, Jennifer complained, "I s'pose I'll be walking home on my own again tonight then. Oh, I dunnow, s'not fair. You should tell her you need time to revise your other subjects!"

"What are you actually doing then, now, at this late stage?" enquired Gillian Morgan.

"Oh, about native people who drink fresh blood and make butter to grease their bodies with," I said.

Gillian stared in horror and disbelief. "You're joking!" she said.

"Yes, we are. Honest. It's part of the course. At least, that's what Ossie says. And she should know. These particular ones are the Baganda tribe," I informed her, pleased I'd remembered some of the last minute piles of information being stuffed into my head over the short timespan.

She chuckled. "Well, I'm glad I took Music. I don't fancy that sort of thing much myself."

Jennifer was sceptical. "Miss Orsman must have gone off her rocker, finally. That doesn't sound like part of the syllabus to me!"

"Yes it is, Jennifer. It's Ethnography. What would you know about it anyway?" Anne Morris insisted

"Well, John Davies who lives by me did Geography last year and he didn't have to know about natives and things. I know 'cos he showed me all his books," Jennifer was quite worryingly assertive.

"Don't be silly, Jennifer. Miss Orsman wouldn't teach us things we didn't need to know," reasoned Florence.

"Well, she's been very peculiar lately you know Flor," Jennifer went on. "She came into the form room yesterday and asked if anyone had seen Bernice Lewis because she wanted a word with her. And she left last year. She's in Edinburgh University now."

The Geographers cast glum looks around, thinking they'd never get to university in view of their partially finished course and absent knowledge.

"And she was walking down the corridor yesterday talking to herself, loudly too, something about people who have lockers should keep their doors closed. I heard her," chipped in little Pat Morris who was taking a passing interest and no doubt feeling smug in the safety of English, French and History.

"I wish I'd taken History now," I said gloomily.

"Huh, it's a bit late to wish that now!" riposted Jennifer, breezily, "Like two years!"

One of the worse things about staying for an hour after school to do Geography was hearing the plings and plops of racquets, and occasional voices of girls playing tennis on the terraced courts outside the Geog, room or those practising athletics on the field. It was difficult to concentrate anyway knowing it was really freedom time, but even worse when hearing girls enjoying themselves in the sunshine, like those chasing a tennis ball not twenty yards away. Minds easily diverted from the intricacies of Mollweide's Map Projections to thoughts of being at home relaxing with a cup of tea and a cream doughnut while perusing the sports pages of the *Western Mail* or even contemplating getting some books out for a spot of revision for the exams, approaching like a runaway express. "*O temps, suspends ton vol! Et vous, heures propices, suspendez votre cours!*" Indeed!

Indubitably, the worst thing about these after hours lessons was the lift Miss Orsman insisted on giving the girls who lived in a southerly direction and on her route home. It was kind of her to think of this, of course, but to her pupils, especially me, it was prolonged persecution and not for the first time did I wish I lived in the Upper Reaches. Caryl and Florence who lived in Porth and I, bound for Trehafod, would be packed into Minnie the Morris with Ianto and we'd set off having more verbal instruction on the way. It was all right while Florence was in the car as she was good at Geography and knew all the answers, but from Porth it was only me and the dog, and he was ever a hindrance, growling and making smells close by. What was worse, at my stop, she'd pull in off the road at the Vaughan's Arms and settle down for a further fifteen minute discussion, constantly interrupted by my stomach rumblings which she ignored and my stupid answers which clearly made her despair, to judge from her expressions. So glad was I to finally escape, I'd run, liberated and incautious across the road and several times missed death by vehicle by only a few feet. At such times the peaceful Trehafod air, only ever broken by the friendly afternoon colliery hooter was rent by the horns of irate drivers and loud, uncarefully chosen words of warning.

Heeding the proverb, "All work and no play makes Jill a dull girl", I took a break from revision to visit my cousin Wyndham and his wife Vera at Gellifynaches Farm. The Geog practical exams were a week away and the examiner was a Dr Melvyn Howe from Aberystwyth University.

"Well, fancy that! Melvyn Howe! Old drinking mate of mine you know. From Ponty, see. Yes, of course, he's at Aberystwyth. Know him well I do. I was at his wedding. Married a girl from up the Common he did."

"Is he young or old?" I enquired.

"Well, about the same as me," said middle-aged Wyndham. "Young."

"What's he like then? Is he nice?"

"Yeah, course he's nice. He's one o' the boys. You needn't be scared of him," Wyndham assured me.

"Oh, I don't know about that. I feel sick thinking about it!"

"Tell you what I'll do. I'll get on the blower and tell him to give you a good mark."

I was horrified. Apart from anonymity being preferable to notoriety, I imagined I might well be disqualified if Wyndham were to try and influence the examiner.

"Oh, no Wyndham! You mustn't do that. He'd more than likely fail me right away if there was any sort of persuasion."

"No, don't worry. It's all right. He's a mate. He won't mind. Anyway," he touched his nose, "he owes me one."

Came the fateful afternoon of the Geog Prac and a tense Miss Orsman ushered in a tall, dark-haired, bespectacled, smiling man she introduced as Dr Howe. After a few preliminary words of explanation, he looked around and cheerfully asked, "Which one of you is Mary Davies by the way?"

I tentatively and shame-facedly put up a hand.

"Ah! I know your cousin Wyndham Mann," then peering at me, "Oh yes, I can see a family likeness. Well, I've had instructions from him to make sure you pass, so I hope you know your stuff."

Miss Orsman's eyes opened wider than usual and her chins vibrated visibly while the other examinees looked at me in petrified disbelief. As far as I can remember the exam went pleasantly and smoothly without any noticeable problems.

It was a year later, when a student at Aberystwyth, that I regretted my cousin's association with Dr Howe. Arriving late for one of his nine o'clock lectures, he spotted me trying to sidle around the wall to a spare seat, and announced to my embarrassment and the hundred and fifty or so other first year students, "Aha! Good morning Miss Davies. Up too late last night with your boyfriend eh? I know! I saw you last evening in the castle grounds! I'll tell Wyndham!" and grinned widely at my blushing discomposure.

It totally destroyed my idea of university lecturers being dry, humourless academics who only thought single-mindedly of their subject. That apart, his statement was a figment of his unbridled imagination. I was late because someone had "borrowed" my bike to get to their lecture, as often happened at Aber.

Getting off the bus at Porth on my way to school on the day of the French Oral exam, I was asked by a lady where she could get the bus to Trealaw. I pointed out the stop she needed, then muttering some sort of French to myself by way of practice, went into Morton's on Porth square to buy a bar of Cadbury's marzipan chocolate to buoy up my spirits for the forthcoming ordeal. When I passed the bus-stop, the be-hatted lady was looking around anxiously, the only one waiting.

"Did you miss the bus?" I enquired.

"Yes," she said, "I saw it pull out as I was crossing the square."

"Oh dear!" I sympathised, "You'll have to wait half an hour now, for the next one."

She looked worried and tutted.

"Look, I'm going in that direction," I said, " but I'm walking. Trealaw's not much further on than my school. If you fancy a walk, you can come with me. It's not all that far really."

I regretted my offer immediately as I wanted to practise my prepared French answers by asking myself the appropriate questions, mentally of course.

"Well, if you don't mind, yes please," was her answer.

"Perhaps a Trealaw bus will pass us, then you can get on that," I said hopefully, "It's uphill most of the way and you can see the bus coming and there's lots of stops."

So we set off and chatted amicably. I told her I had my A level Oral that day and talked about the school and the teachers, particularly the dotty Miss Orsman and our problems with completing the vast Geography syllabus. We got on very well with me doing most of the talking telling her about my liking for sport, our shop, my plans for the future and how in the Oral exam I wasn't going to tell the truth exactly, just go for the less complicated French.

"For example," I went on, "if your father has a job in a factory labelling bottles or tightening up screws, it's much easier to say in French he's a postman. Miss Llewelyn our French teacher told us to go for the easier option. Makes sense really, and the examiner isn't to know what your father does after all."

She agreed. I offered her a square of marzipan chocolate which she accepted.

We passed the Boys' School which I'd pointed out and we'd reached the garage outside which is a bus-stop when she said, "Well, I think I'll wait here now. I want to get a newspaper. I wonder if I could get one in that garage. Anyway, thanks for letting me walk with you. It was very pleasant. P'raps we'll meet again sometime. Good luck with your exam! Goodbye."

I made my way the short distance to school, doing a bit of hasty self-help revision, asking myself in French the questions I hoped the examiner would ask, mainly, "Have you ever been to France?" – "Oh yes, I've been twice on two school trips to Paris and I saw the Eiffel Tower, Notre Dame cathedral, the Louvre museum, the Sacre-Coeur and Napoleon's tomb in the Invalides. In Notre Dame, which stands on an island in the river Seine we saw the famous Rose window. In the Louvre we saw the painting of *La Joconde* by Leonardo da Vinci, the statue of the Venus de Milo etc. etc." The idea in the oral exam is to lead the examiner to ask the questions to the answers you want to give, then carry on talking, only allowing him the occasional word in edgeways, but it seemed to me you had to be lucky with the first question. You could hardly go on about Paris and French food if the examiner asked you your thoughts on the setting up of the new commercial TV channel, or the economic situation in Africa. In French? God forbid! Also, if you had a fair whack prepared, he could have a little rest from thinking up more questions and undoubtedly be grateful for it.

The morning dragged. The examiner was in the Boys' School first and coming to us in the afternoon. None of the French class felt like eating lunch. Even the thought of what remained of my chocolate made me feel sick. We were to have our ordeal in alphabetical order and as usual, I, cursing the family name, was first as unfortunately Margaret Algate didn't take French. The call came from a briskly cheery Miss Llewelyn who led me to the little room opposite the staff-room. She knocked, popped her head around the door saying, "This is the first candidate, Mary Davies. All right then?" Smilingly, and with a little encouraging pat she stood aside for me, knees feeling like rubber tubes, to enter. Scarcely had I crossed the threshold than I stopped in surprise. My jaw dropped, my mouth fell open as I stared wide-eyed at the person before me, none other than my be-hatted lady companion of that morning, except that now she'd taken her hat off. My mind was in a turmoil – in English. What had I unwittingly said to her on the walk up from Porth? I could feel myself blushing as she said, "*Ah, bonjour Mary. Nous nous rencontrons encore une fois.*"

"*Oui, madame. Bonjour madame. Encore une fois.*"

Another secret of the oral exam is to repeat part of what the examiner has said, which, it is to be assumed, must be correct French. She smiled and went on, "*Alors, votre père est facteur, n'est-ce pas?*"

Her friendliness as she now dominated proceedings, unlike earlier when I had been doing most of the chatting, was relaxing, and I was able to smile as I said, "*Non madame, il est menuisier.*"

This clearly puzzled her, "*Ah! Menuisier ou magasinier?*" she enquired, obviously remembering what I'd said about the shop. I more or less tried to tie things up with what I could remember of the morning's spontaneously and foolishly donated revelations but clearly left her slightly baffled which is probably why my test went on for half an hour, twice as long as anyone else's. However I didn't have to resort to the poem we'd all been told to learn in the event of being totally unable to say anything and certainly didn't need to burst into French song like one famous A level candidate a few years previously, to the examiner's complete amazement on finding himself being serenaded. But I made sure I caught the packed school bus home.

The written exams didn't appear to pose many problems other than my forgetting to put my exam number on one English paper, convincing myself I'd fail because nobody would know whose it was, and spending anguished periods when I thought about it, which wasn't often. No-one managed to complete the Geography paper on N. America and Europe. This was due to lack of knowledge not the time factor, so the expected maximum mark there was only eighty per cent. We heard with envy the ping of tennis ball on gut string on the nearby courts as we wrestled with Alfred de Vigny's attitude to nature compared with Leconte de Lisle's, tried to recall appropriate quotations from *Hamlet* in support of a character sketch of Polonius, or desperately drew a blue line denoting a river on a map, hoping we weren't altering a landscape hitherto unchanged for thousands of years. All this while keeping a close eye on the time, rigidly allocating oneself the thirty six minutes per question. A level candidates were easily recognisable by their pasty, drawn faces in the welter of normal, healthy, tanned adolescents in late June. But after mid-July when it was all over bar the grief or happiness awaiting in August, we more than made up for lost time.

# 13. A Taste of Things to Come

After the first couple of weeks of freedom which we spent mainly in Bacchetta's cafe and Bronwydd Park in Porth playing tennis and lazing in the swimming pool, empty because it wasn't yet the long holidays, July 1955 saw us bored and impecunious. As I swam slowly up and down the pool thinking about the uncertain future and in a way, lamenting my lost, innocent childhood I thought about the time six years ago when I'd come here as an eleven year old.

When the summer term arrived, the First Year's double Games lesson for a month was devoted to swimming. Unfortunately the nearest pool – and that open air – was the one in Bronwydd Park, a few miles away. For some reason, everyone – aquaphobiacs, games haters and the plump were excited about this and no-one forgot to bring her swimming costume, bathing cap and towel on the appointed day. Dismay was first experienced on being told we had to walk to and from the Baths. The distance problem hadn't until then been given much thought as at eleven, worries about the future are not a major mental preoccupation. We had simply assumed we would be bussed there, or at least allowed to catch a service bus to Porth Square which would conveniently come along Cemetery Road when we were ready to go. The authorities had no such plans however and quick walking in twos, with Miss Jennett setting the pace was the order of the day. Her final instructions as we assembled at the school gate were, "And I don't want to see a long column stretching back up the road. No longer than this, mind. No stragglers please."

Getting to Porth was no problem as it was downhill, as far as Tynewydd Square anyway, it was early in the day so we were fresh and it being late April, the weather, though fine, was not hot. The haul up Caemawr Hill was a bit of a late disheartener, but if we arrived tired after our thirty minute march, no doubt we would be revived by a refreshing swim.

We changed hurriedly and went out into what now seemed near-freezing temperatures. Constant, involuntary screams erupted as one by one girls whose feet were hot after the walk, attempted to tiptoe through the icy foot bath. Some jumped back out and tried to climb over the barrier, others tried unsuccessfully to edge around the side.

"Oh, my God! If the pool's as cold as this I'll die of heart failure," objected Marjorie Woosnam. Shivering girls with blue lips stood around hugging themselves and rubbing their arms to stop them going numb.

"Swimmers and divers at the deep end, swimmers only in the middle and non-swimmers shallow end," Miss Jennett's instructions rang out in the clack-clack of chattering teeth.

"Stand still! Relax, girls! Stop shivering like frightened rabbits and get in the water!"

More howls and screams rent the peaceful park air as girls dived or jumped into the cold, clear pool. Those who had dived surfaced looking shocked and non-swimmers in two feet three inches of water stretched upwards to achieve greater height and preserve their upper bodies from frostbite as long as possible. This was short-lived though as Miss Jennett briskly gave orders, "Stand on the blue line, push off with your feet and glide to the side!" It was necessary to keep moving to encourage circulation of the blood. The Baths Superintendent, an altogether less demanding instructor, took charge of the more accomplished who were allowed to use the diving boards and the slide to the envy of the rest. Not that anyone could stand around watching or hypothermia would set in.

After approximately ten minutes in the pool, just as bodies were getting acclimatised to the glacial conditions, the whistle blew, the lesson was over and we were urged to change quickly as we had to be back at school in half an hour. Dripping, skinny bodies skidded and slipped back into the changing cubicles, grateful to huddle in the warmth of a towel. There was no time for huddling however as Miss Jennett kept up a continuous commentary urging us to get a move on. "Three minutes to change so don't dawdle! We're leaving in three minutes."

"Oh's" and "Ouches" issued from the small cubicles girls were sharing as they bumped into each other, rummaging for their clothes in the restricted space. Garments fell on the wet floor, vests were put on inside-out and knickers back to front as damp bodies struggled to dress. Socks were lost, ties abandoned and blouses left unbuttoned when, five minutes later, no-one having emerged, Miss Jennett's increasingly impatient voice rang out again, "One more minute and we're setting off. Girls who are not ready will spend their lunch hour doing twenty laps of the field."

"Oh gosh, my hair's all wet. I'll catch my death. My mother'll be off!"

"I can't find my beret," someone grumbled.

"Where's my watch? I gorra find that. It's my sister's. She'll kill me," a panic-stricken voice wailed.

"Oh, look! You've got my blouse on, stupid. That's mine that is!"

"Who cares?" was the disembodied reply, "We'll change back in school. There's no time now."

We were an unkempt, motley crew marching back through Porth. Despite bathing caps, everyone's hair was in a state of wetness ranging from dripping rats' tails on those who had barely bothered to apply towel to head, to damp fluffy on girls with short hair who had made an effort but had mislaid their comb.

Miss Jennett did see a long column on the return journey, so long in fact that its rear was out of sight and tended to give her apoplexy. When she, tripping along ahead, was nearing Porth Hospital, the tail-enders were only rounding the bend at Tynewydd Square. Some, it must be admitted, were deliberately lagging so as not to be seen eating the choc ices they had bought in Gambarini's.

Although it was uphill, the return journey only took five minutes more than the outward. No doubt the crocodile was spurred on by reminders from Miss Jennett about laps at lunch time relayed back down the hill from group to group.

Miraculously we were back in time for the lesson after recess. We were all dry too by the time we reached school, though some were damp again with perspiration and a strong smell of chlorine hung over the class for the rest of the day. Teachers entered the form room, sniffed the air then enquired, "Have you been to the Baths by any chance? Open the windows please!"

Miss Pennington joked in her sardonic, academic way, chuckling to herself. "It's a good job we're not in the Lab today. If these fumes came in contact with the Bunsen burners, you'd explode," she said cheerily, clearly relishing the thought.

In spite of the distance, the icy water, the rush and the threat of laps, everyone seemed to be looking forward to the following week's outing. The Welsh must be a sadistic race, not only for putting their naked children into cold water in the open air in April at 53° latitude of the Northern Hemisphere, but for those offspring to enjoy the occasion! Perhaps sadism is inherited or perhaps it was just an excuse to get out of school for an hour and a half.

I had a kindly aunt in lower Trehafod and around this time she turned up one evening with a pink and green, rather fetching, woollen swimming costume with cross-over straps at the back that she had knitted. There were no shops dedicated solely to sport in those early post-war days and the choice of swimsuit was limited to plain wool in sombre colours or brightly coloured, flamboyantly patterned, satin, bobbly affairs suitable for babies, and you had to go to Cardiff to get one of these or anything much in the sporting line. Consequently I was rather pleased with my unexpected present and decided to take it to the next swimming lesson instead of my navy bathers. I was quite fond of my towel too – a large white one with a red inscription across the middle that proclaimed "Furness – Bermuda Line" the meaning of which puzzled me for years.

Friends admired my costume and it fitted nicely – until I got into the water that is. I was aware of something amiss before surfacing after the first entry – a sort of weighty, dragging feeling with something hindering my knees as though I was trailing weeds. I swam to the side to investigate. Some girls who had not yet plucked up enough courage for total immersion, having only toe-tested the water and thought better of it, were grinning and pointing at me from the pool edge. Turning to look back I nearly shouted with fright to see a dark green shape lazily floating behind me just under the surface. At first glance it looked like spirogyra, but was of course my new swimming costume – one of the type clearly intended not to get wet! It had become most horribly stretched, at least three times its original length as it floated behind like a clutch of ducklings faithfully following their mother. A thought struck me. If most of the wretched garment was behind me, what was in front? In panic and horror I made a quick inspection, fearing, but accurately guessing what I would find. Nothing! By now the others were aware of my predicament, were having a good laugh and my embarrassment was total.

"Go on Mary! Swim over there, let's have a look at your tail!" my so-called friend Hope Higgs demanded. Others were more positive if relatively unhelpful.

"You might as well take it off for all the use it is," advised Barbara Jones, "Anyway, it might drag you to the bottom."

"Don't be soft! I can't take it off! What about the Superintendent? He's a man!"

Barbara was dismissive. "Huh, a man! He's old enough to be your grandfather!" She swam off irritated, delivering a less than comforting Parthian shot, "Don't expect me to save you from drowning then!"

"Oh, don' drown will you Mary," pleaded Mair James, "You've got my money in your bag, remember?"

"It might be best if you wrapped it round you and tied a knot in it," suggested Marjorie, ever practical.

By this time Miss Jennett had been attracted by the little gathering of chatting, non-swimming girls and wanted to know what all the fuss was about. The situation was explained to her and a rare smile crossed her face. She disappeared for a moment, reappeared with a towel and beckoned me out of the water and into it. Which I did with some difficulty, gathering up yards of dripping wool, attempting to wring it out while still wearing it and replace it on those parts normally hidden from public view. That was my shortest swim ever with the longest swimsuit ever. It would have adequately clothed a giraffe.

I felt very glum on the return journey. My pretty new bathing costume was four feet long and all out of shape. I'd walked all that way and had no swim. I'd been the object of all Form One ridicule – and now it was starting to drizzle.

Me, Hope Higgs, Marjorie Woosnam and Pamela Nicholls were lagging at the rear of the ragged procession. Miss Jennett was out of sight.

"I know, we'll all have a choc ice in Gambarini's," Hope decided, "And I'll pay for yours Mary and you won't have to pay me back. It's OK." No doubt she was feeling remorseful about her earlier lack of sympathy!

As we emerged from the cafe, marvel of marvels, the Trealaw bus was arriving at the stop on the Square.

"Come on girls!" whooped Marjorie, leading the way, "On the bus!" Buses don't hang around long enough for you to have a debate as to the wisdom or foolishness of to catch or not to catch, so we had to make a split second decision. Some of us were uncertain, but with Marjorie in her Boadicea mood marching forth, and the conductor being irascible with, "Look! You coming on 'ere or not? We 'aven' got all day! Make up yer minds quick!" we piled on and ran upstairs. Soon we were overtaking the tail-enders, waving gleefully to them through the windows as they trudged up the hill in the rain. Their response was to stop, gaze at us open-mouthed, grin, then point, laughing. As we passed those at the front with Miss Jennett striding purposefully ahead, we ducked out of sight on the floor to the surprise of the other passengers. At the Porth County stop we scampered off the bus and ran to hide in the lane until the rest of the damp, hot, tired, chlorinated band arrived. Then we emerged and merged to be counted with them. I was feeling a lot happier by now.

And my scarf-length swimsuit? It never regained any sort of

shape so Mam unravelled it and made bed socks – socks being all she could knit – for all the family and friends. But my aunt never knew.

Caryl and I decided to look out for a holiday job in some rather more exotic location than the Rhondda Valley. Many would say anywhere fitted the bill. Caryl soon espied, in the *Western Mail*, an advert for waitresses and chambermaids in Paignton, south Devon at the Hydro Hotel. She immediately applied for a job there and to our astonishment, in typical impulsive and independent fashion, planned to depart within days to start her new employment.

"I'll write and tell you what it's like. Then if it's OK you can come down too. They said they had plenty of jobs," were Caryl's parting words. True to her promise, she sent a sepia postcard of a timber framed hotel which looked Elizabethan, very elegant and rather attractive.

"It's great here," she wrote, "lovely weather, hotel's right on the sea-front and the work's OK. It's my day off today and I'm going to the beach for the afternoon. Getting a tan already. Jobs here if you want them, but don't take too long deciding. Ring me on Paignton 12345 after 7 pm. Love, Caryl." Well, what were we doing stuck aimlessly in tedious old Trehafod and Porth when glamorous Paignton was beckoning? Visions of the beach, sea and sun, easy work with lazy days off in a delightful location overwhelmed our imagination. And getting paid for all of this to boot! It was barely credible and quite irresistible, so Florence and I took the train south too.

The reality was something of a jolt to our eager optimism. True, the weather was good, the hotel close to the beach and we did have one day's freedom in seven plus a half day on Sunday. As well as our weekly chambermaid's wage of £5, for which we were expected to work from 7.30 to 5.30 with an hour for lunch, we were lodged in a house in Goodrington, a mile away, where Flor and I had to share a room and a double bed and fed in a tin shed at the back of the hotel on whatever food remained after the guests' meals. To get to the Hydro in time to start making and taking early-morning tea trays to the bedrooms, we had to be up at 6.30 for the mile-long trek to the hotel. Since dinner was never served to the staff before 8 pm, we could either hang around after work for a few hours charting the progress in decibels of our stomach rumblings, or go back to Goodrington then return later for the meal. This was largely fatal, as once back in a room with a bed and in a fairly exhausted state, mentally from the monoto-

1. English trip to London to see *As You Like It* at the Old Vic, 1953

2 & 3. Geography field trip to Ystradfellte

4. Aberystwyth First XI Women's Hockey team, 1956-57

5. The French Department, Aberystwyth, June 1959. Staff in the middle, begowned, from left: Dr Hoggan, Denis Fletcher, Dr Margaret Phillips, Prof Briggs, Dr Yvonne Niord

6. Aberystwyth from Constitution Hill, with the University beyond the pier, and Alex in the foreground

7. Mary on the Prom, Constitution Hill and Alex in the background

8. Alex girls sunbathing. Florence Wilton ('Flor') on the extreme right, with Merle Picton next to her

9. At the Rag Ball with Stephen O'Leary from Treorchy, 1959

10. With Margaret Algate, by the War Memorial at Aberystwyth

11. Weekend recreation with Flor and Yvonne Lanoe, at Amboise

12. Flor on her twenty-first birthday, Blois

13. Mary, Flor and Margaret Sanderson visit Dorothy (left), an *assistante* at the Ecole Normale in Tours

14. Mary at Blois

15. Mme Fouchaux at 23 rue de Sébastopol, Tours

16. Cycling round the châteaux, June 1958, near Beauregard

17. Blois town from the Château

18. Tours Cathedral

19. Streets in the old quarter of Tours

20. Mary holidaying in the south of France, 1958

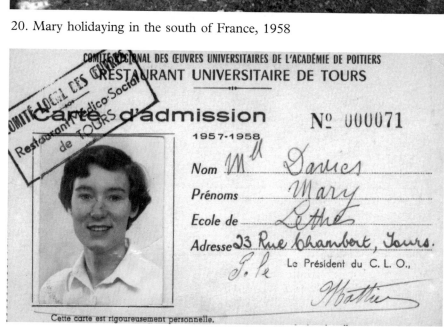

21. One of the many identity cards with which Mary was burdened

ny of cleaning bedrooms and physically from the effort of it, one tended to fall asleep for several hours and thus miss the vital re-fuelling process. Entire mornings of days off were spent in bed, refurbishing the energy store and rejoicing at not having had to arise, march and tea-make while normal people were still in dreamland.

While ourselves sending the occasional, reassuring postcard home, "Everything fine here. Weather fine, food fine, work fine. See you soon", we couldn't understand how Caryl had been so enamoured of hotel life after a few days when we were disillusioned after a few hours.

"Well," she confessed, "you don't like to admit you've made a mistake. And I was lonely on my own. Anyway, it's not so bad, and I didn't tell you any lies." Didn't tell us the truth either, so there we were, all three of us in the soup, or not in the soup, as it were, because there was never any left after the guests had finished.

In those far-off days, forty years ago, before the days of counselling, molly-coddling and taking into account people's feelings, pupils' results at O and A level were published in the *Western Mail* for all to see. If you failed, everyone knew and was interested; if you passed, no-one, except your parents, cared. No grades were given, simply a capital letter for a subject passed and a lower case letter for a fail. For an oral pass, the letter was starred, so I was hoping for E, F*, G, not e, f, g. We had ordered a *Western Mail* for results day in mid-August and as it was my day off, it was also my thankless task to get the paper and report back to the other two working at the hotel.

I don't know whether it was worse for them or me. They, at the hotel wouldn't be able to concentrate on their jobs – they'd be nervously putting incomplete tea trays at the wrong doors, knocking up late-risers too early, running for and spilling forgotten milk, looking at their watches, biting their nails, constantly going to the toilet, wondering what to do with themselves. By 9 o'clock, I was worrying more about their results than mine, praying I wouldn't have to report a fail to either of them, wondering how I would perform such an unpleasant task. Would I blurt out, "I'm sorry – but you failed Geography!" or would I just shove the paper at them with, "Page 7, right hand column, half way down"?

In fact it was all right once my shaking hands had found the page and my panicking eyes the correct place. We all had capitals but Caryl had one lower case, so she'd probably still be acceptable for her course at Southampton University. Florence and I were bound for Aberystwyth to read French. Telegrams arrived later from parents, the sun shone brighter, the sea twinkled and the Hydro Hotel wasn't so bad after all. Nevertheless, all attractions now lay in the Rhondda Valley where our friends were. We could hardly wait to get back. Paignton had palled and we were impatient to give in our resignations and work our notice. Pale, tired, probably underweight, and after we'd bought our train tickets, financially on a par with six weeks earlier, but elated, we returned to the family circle two weeks after the results to think about leaving home more or less for good.

# 14. Autumn Migration West

As the start of October 1955 drew closer, I began to understand how an upper class seven or eight year old must feel when he or she is packed off to boarding school for the first time – increasingly panic-stricken and lacking in confidence. The thrill of passing the exams had worn off and been replaced by apprehension of what lay ahead. I'd never even been to Aberystwyth as at that time there were no university Open Days where you could look around to see if you liked the place where you planned to spend three years of your young life, no interviews with tutors telling you about courses, no counselling helping you with problems about student life, money, health and accommodation, no anything. I simply sent the authorities a form with my A level subjects, signed by Miss Hudd and they replied, more or less saying, "OK, we'll have you if you pass". I don't remember even advising them of the course I wanted to pursue. The idea was, I think, they'd tell me when I got there. Information was sent that I was to share a room called Bal 14 with Florence Wilton in Alexandra Hall on Victoria Terrace, Aberystwyth. Was this "Bal" place something to do with dancing I wondered. Perhaps they didn't have enough rooms to go round and had to put people up in the ballroom.

My mother bought me a blue woollen dressing gown with a zip from chin to toes and other clothes, jumpers, blouses, a pair of warm, plaid trousers fashionable at that time, skirts, pyjamas, underwear, a black blazer with a slit at the back, a matching china cup, saucer and plate and a trunk to put them all in.

One day I watched as a green British Road Services lorry, with a minimum of fuss, collected this trunk and smartly departed down the hill, swaying like a pine tree in a gale, taking most of my material possessions with it. I trusted I might meet up with them again in this Bal 14 on Victoria Terrace, but I felt far from confident.

We were to attend a Freshers' Conference the weekend before the term began on the Monday. On the Thursday morning I met Florence at the Porth bus depot at 10 o'clock to catch the coach to Bridgend, the first of several en route to our university town in mid-Wales. At Bridgend bus station there was no sign saying, 'Aberystwyth' so after enquiry, we discovered we had first to get to Neath. Other individuals of our age stood uncertainly looking around, on their own and in small groups.

"I wonder if they're going to Aberystwyth too?" I mused.

"Well I expect so Mary, if they get on the Aberystwyth bus at Neath," Florence answered. "We'll have to wait and see," being far too shy at that stage to ask.

Lunch-time saw us at Neath bus station, enlarged by a Port Talbot contingent. Again no Aberystwyth sign on any stop or coach. More enquiries. This time we found we had to get the coach to Ammanford but had an hour to wait

"D'you think we'll get there before dark?" asked Florence.

"D'you think we'll get there today?" I replied feeling increasingly dubious.

As the journey slowly progressed, more and more young people joined the procession in a general north westerly direction to the college by the sea, and the Bridgend bus station people were still with us. More got on at Pontardawe, including a thin young man with sandy hair and a shorter, dark-haired fellow with a mischievous face. At last, at Ammanford there was a stop with an Aberystwyth sign, and a man, standing on the mudguard of a coach, cranking with a handle through place names until Aberystwyth appeared in the space, to a collective cheer.

"I don't know whether this bus is actually going as far as Aberystwyth, no. You might have to change in Lampeter you see," he announced in what was definitely not a south Wales accent as he wound on to Lampeter, now to a collective groan. It seemed there would be too many for the vehicle to accommodate, but after a *mêlée* reminiscent of the school bus, we all squeezed on and set off bumping and swaying along winding, hilly, country roads. People were refused access at Llandeilo.

"I'm full now, sorry," announced the conductor. "There's a special been put on today. Be along in fifteen minutes. You'll have to wait for that, yes indeed", and off we went with a jerk, clanking of gears and clouds of oil fumes to Lampeter where the driver and conductor had a little break for a cup of tea and a cigarette while the students, bored rigid, sat on the bus watching them in the cafe on the opposite side of the road. We didn't need to change coaches again at Lampeter but were quite prepared for it. We'd got on and off so often we were doing it mechanically. In fact, on that occasion, I believe we did lose a few students at Lampeter who automatically got off the Aberystwyth coach, looking for the Aberystwyth coach which still had Lampeter on the front.

The afternoon was well advanced when we reached the coast at Aberaeron, and all heads turned westward to look at the sea and catch a glimpse of the coastline of Cardigan Bay. We passed through hamlets with lovely Welsh names which roll majestically off the tongue – Aberarth, Llansantffraed, Llanrhystud, Blaenplwyf, then despite hunger and fatigue, excitement mounted as we entered Aberystwyth, having a good view of the place from the elevated, southerly suburb of Penparcau and finally pulled up outside the railway station in Alexandra Road. We'd made it! It was 5.30 and still light! It had only taken eight hours to travel 110 or so miles.

'Bal' turned out to be not remotely connected with dancing, but an extension building to Alexandra Hall, the main women's residential hostel at the university, perched at the end of the Prom at the base of Constitution Hill. It was soon obvious that nothing was given its full title at Aber Uni. 'Bal' was short for 'Balmoral' while the Hall was universally referred to as 'Alex'. The other women's hostels were Carp and Cere (Carpenter and Ceredigion Halls) and the mens' Plyn and Panty (Plynlymon and Pantycelyn). The regal nomenclature gave an idea as to when these places were built when architecture was in its no-nonsense phase circa 1896. Alex is rectangular and solid, made of grey Llandovery Grits sandstone. A five storied construction facing, and built to repel the sea, and all its dastardly tricks, not thirty yards away, it has a sturdy porch with weighty, nigh-impenetrable door built to frustrate man and all *his* dastardly tricks *vis-à-vis* women. Iron railings further protected front ground floor rooms from invasion by undesirables.

One only saw glimpses of daylight through the ground and first floor windows during the winter, as they were boarded against the sea in angry mood. One ate meals in a dining room lit electrically during daylight hours and listened as the sea crashed against the Prom, shaking the building and throwing pebbles which hammered at regular intervals against the protective panels. Students having front rooms on the third and upward floors found themselves popular at such times as crowds gathered in them to watch the sea's antics. Gasps accompanied each new mini tidal wave which threatened to hurl itself over the roof and engulf the building. During such storms, students had to use the back entrances. Beach pebbles landed on Queen's Road behind Alex so you had to keep an eye out for groundward bombardment. For most of the year though, Alex and the sea lived happily together. In calmer seasons, wavelets flopped prettily and largely ignored

133

on to the beach, but at night the backwash over the pebbles troubled the sleep of those not used to such sounds.

Another sound, apart from the scrunched pebbles, which disturbed people who lived further down Victoria Terrace was the Life-Boat. Its station was in Queen's Road and the launching stage on North Beach. After a sea flare or some other maritime emergency, the life-boat would be trundled cumbersomely on its trailer along Bath Street into Terrace Road causing rumblings and a fracas enough to make you wonder whether the Russian army with its tanks and assorted machinery had come to town. Particularly worrying was when you were in the Celtic or Coliseum cinemas watching a quiet film. The thunderous racket of the passing life-boat made you think an earthquake was in the process of activating. If it was a western, thriller or disaster movie with lots of shooting and bangings, or a noisy war adventure you were watching, the rumpus outside added credibility to the story. The first floor Coliseum cinema shook with the vibrations as well, so you really had value for money.

As a Geography student though, on hearing the initial rumblings, my mind automatically flashed to the world map of the earthquake and volcanic belts we'd drawn with Miss Orsman in school – purple bands for earthquakes and red dots for volcanoes – before thinking, "No, it's only the life-boat. No earthquake belt around Cardigan Bay!" However, small measurements on the Richter scale had been noted in north Wales. Hmmm!

For those in the Pier cinema the life-boat din made not one iota of difference, bashed and battered as it was by the sea in most seasons. The screen was constantly on the move with a particularly noticeable sideways shift every seventh wave. The Pier, however was a specially good place to watch pirate films and queues were long and anticipatory of virtual reality for such films as *The Flying Dutchman, Moby Dick, Horatio Hornblower, A High Wind in Jamaica* and the like.

A curious ritual was enacted just outside Alex where the Prom ends in a steep wall overlooking a rocky cove. Everyone walking along the prom would touch one of the end railings atop the wall with a foot. Some would give it a tap, turn, and retrace their steps. Others would stop, touch the rail with their foot and gaze at the cove, Alex or the hill behind before resuming their walk. Whatever and whoever, no-one reached the end without touching the rail, so much so, that the black paint had worn off and the metal shone through as though polished. What was this strange ceremony performed by everybody and his uncle?

"Oh, that's kicking the Bar," one of the Third year Ellis twins from Swansea informed us. "People kick the Bar to make sure it's solid. This part of the Prom was washed away once, you see, and students were evacuated – in the Thirties I think – so people give it a kick to make certain it's firm. There's another Bar at the other end of the Prom, down by the harbour and people kick that too. Nice walk it is. Only a mile there and back."

Balmoral, adjoining Alex, was another big house on the Prom acquired by the university to house ever increasing numbers of female students and it was in room 14 that Florence and I were to live. It was on the top floor at the back overlooking Queen's Road and what looked like an abandoned quarry and a grown-over tip. There were two single iron beds with thin mattresses, a wardrobe, chest of drawers, a large table-cum-desk with two chairs and an armchair. What heat there was going to be, was to be provided via a radiator evidently from the Mesozoic era. The walls were painted yellow. We had not brought any posters which might relieve them of their sickly hue, so a few days later we collected some pretty pebbles and shells from the beach which we sellotaped to the walls. The only trouble was they kept falling off and landing painfully on our heads if we happened to be sitting, lounging or sleeping on one of the beds underneath. Initially the only cheering sight was my dark blue trunk in the middle of the room. I felt immediately homesick on seeing it.

"Why had I come to this unwelcoming place with the depressing view so far from Trehafod when I could have gone to Cardiff University, lived at home and travelled up and down daily on the train?"

"What about washing and things?" Florence wondered.

We set off in search of the ablutions and discovered the nearest were two floors down, serving three floors, each with four rooms.

"We'll buy a bowl," I decided.

"What for? Flor enquired.

"Well to wash in, silly!"

"What if we need the toilet in the night?" Florence was worried.

"Well then, you've got three options Flor. (a) don't drink after 7pm, (b) run down a few floors in the dead of night or (c) use the bowl we're going to get."

Florence looked at me horrified. "Mary, we can't, you know, use the bowl then wash in it. Anyway we said we'd get water last thing to wash the next morning and avoid the queue."

"Perhaps we'd better buy a torch as well then."

These were our first purchases at university.

"I still don't fancy wandering around this place at night. It's spooky enough in the day. And cold!" Flor grumbled.

Our neighbours in no. 15 were two quiet, unassuming north Walians, Mair Eluned Jones and Mair Penry Jones from Brynrefail in Merioneth. They were clearly at university to work and seemed bothered about the sybaritic aspect of college life

"Are you going to this dance for Freshers tomorrow night?" they enquired of us. "It's not compulsory is it? We don't have to go do we?"

"In any case I can't dance," added Mair Eluned, "I'd look very foolish on a dance floor you know."

They were delightful, friendly girls but I never saw them pleasure-bent, although I suppose they enjoyed themselves in their own way.

The interior polished, wooden, rickety staircase and floors were not conducive to calm and concentration. You could hear if someone *breathed* gently on the stairs and landings without talking of movement, and as most people ran or stomped, thumping and creaking noises formed a background to living in Bal. When the meals bell rang, we stomped along too.

# 15. Small Fish, Big Sea

The Freshers' Weekend was organised to help people settle in to university life. True, you did get to know other new students and the lay-out of the college buildings and town with its twenty-two pubs for a 10,000 population. But there were so many rules! A register was taken in lectures so you mustn't miss them; you had to be prompt or you were refused entry; academic dress – gowns – had to be worn or you would be turfed out, and these useless garments had first to be tracked down and purchased. Hall fees, all £40 of them for the term, had to be paid within the week and one worried the grant cheque wouldn't arrive on time. "What happened if you couldn't pay? Would you be sent home?" I wondered hopefully.

One talk from Brian Heath, President of the Students' Representative Council, as this newly graduated Ll.B student was grandly entitled, pompously informed us, "Hitherto, at school, you have been big fish in a small sea. Now you are small fish in a very big sea," which didn't exactly nurture anyone's self-esteem. I heard one awed Fresher, still wearing her white school blouse address him as 'Sir'.

Green and red horizontally striped woollen scarves and the University of Wales blazer badge, as well as the gown were to be bought at Daniel Thomas's, which must have been Aberystwyth's most profitable shop. At least, a college scarf around your neck and a badge on your blazer, albeit luminous in its newness, made you feel part of the establishment.

Several girls from Porth County had chosen Aber as their place of tertiary study. Margaret Algate and Evelyn Jones were ensconced in Carp, further down the Prom, smaller and apparently more comfortable than Alex. Nearer the university and lectures too! Margaret Evans from Treorchy who was going to study Philosophy was in Ceredigion and Gillian Morgan who was doing French was sharing a room in Alex with Samantha Pritchard from Wrexham. As far as we knew the only Rhondda boys were Graham Cummings, a lawyer-to-be and Terence Hole studying science and always reliable at Saturday night 'hops' or college balls to ask you to dance and avoid possible wallflowerdom.

Aberystwyth looked a pretty bleak place to me, considering it doubled as a seaside resort, with its pebbly beach, black groynes, tall, grey, sombre houses matching the grey sea, long promenade with a rickety pier at the far end near the dark, Edwardian mess of the main college buildings which looked like the London Courts of Appeal but with a statue of the formidable-looking Edward VII gazing mournfully out to sea. The whole dominated by the slagheap of Constitution Hill with its toy railway! The weather was cold and overcast, I hadn't slept well in the strange twanging bed, I'd been running around since yesterday to advisory lectures, talks and tours of buildings. To boot, it was Saturday, normally a relaxing day. I felt thoroughly miserable.

Although I hadn't seen Aberystwyth south, I heard about it from a boy I met at the Freshers' hop, Peter Williams from Newbridge, a musical French student who later spent a year in Toulouse where he played the trumpet with *Les Crazy Stompers* at the university there. He had been a rugby-playing trumpeter at school but abandoned sport for music, an altogether safer bet for preserving limbs and features intact.

The previous August after the A level results, he and Howard Young, also a rugby-playing French student from Newbridge, had decided to have a look at Aberystwyth, so came up for the day on the train. Leaving the station and having no street plan, they decided to ask for directions to the harbour. They didn't know much about the town, but as most seaside resorts have harbours which are picturesque, interesting places and usually fairly central, they wandered in that direction. After looking round the harbour they settled on South Beach for the few hours before their train back.

"Hmm. Not much to this place is there?" said Peter, "I'd expected it to be more thriving. Have I done the right thing I ask myself, choosing to come to this dreary hole?"

"Well it's a bit bleak, I agree," answered Howard, "but we passed quite a few pubs and one or two chip shops on our way here. The town looks all right. Where's the university I wonder?"

On their way back to the station, they decided to take a look at the castle ruins which can be seen from South Beach on a rise before the road turns the corner to become the New Promenade. Imagine their surprise on turning the corner to see the pier, university and wide sweep of Marine Terrace with its Victorian buildings, the King's Hall, boarding houses, hotels and student hostels in front of them.

"Good God! There it is! There's Aberystwyth!" exclaimed Peter. "We missed it!"

"Ah, this place is not so bad after all," said a relieved Howard. "Thank God for that!"

Unfortunately, as their train was leaving in half an hour or so, they didn't have time to discover what they'd come to see, but up until then, both boys had been thinking they'd made a mega mistake in their choice of university.

We were very well fed in Alex, though many would disagree. To someone to whom food was not particularly important other than as a nourishing process, and who had been raised on plain fare, I found it more than satisfactory.

We ate in the big Alex dining hall, at tables seating ten and thus comprised a 'family' group. There were the three of us from Porth, Nan Smith and Tessa Jones from the Rhymney Valley, Samantha and two of her friends from Wrexham, Betty and Frances Jones and our Bethesda neighbours in Bal, Mair Eluned Jones and Mair Penry Jones. The five Joneses were not related. We assembled quite naturally and stayed that way for our first two years when the three of us from Porth departed for France and went our separate ways.

Breakfasts were individually collected from the 'hatch' running half the length of the room. Bacon rashers lay pink and tender on the hot plates if you were early, scrambled, fried, boiled eggs, sausages, fried bread, and, to my initial surprise, sautéed potatoes were there for the taking. Several kinds of cereal were on offer and you helped yourself to tea from huge teapots at your table. I suppose you could have had 'seconds' if you so desired, but not many appetites are that keen at 8 am.

Lunch at 1 was an altogether more formal affair. Miss Powys-Roberts, the Warden invited a group of four students each weekday to lunch with her and the Deputy Warden, Alice Evans, a dark-haired lady who worked at the Plant Breeding Station and played for their hockey team. On Sunday, extra-mural guests were invited. One received a written invitation in one's pigeon-hole to be at the Warden's room on the first floor at 1 pm and the natural reaction was, "Oh God! It's come. I've got to lunch with the Warden next week." Sympathy and advice flowed from all quarters, "Oh, poor thing, make sure you get there on time."

"Never mind, you get lovely food on her table."

"Yes, but you're so concerned with talking to her and doing the right thing, you don't get round to eating it!"

"Make sure you're wearing a skirt, not trousers. Enfys wore trousers and they got a very long disapproving stare."

"A word of warning" – among many! – "Don't start eating before her or she'll glare at you."

"You get napkins on her table. Don't tuck it under your chin!"

Other horror stories of spilled water, errant peas and splashed gravy were forthcoming.

If you had a 12 o'clock lecture which finished at 12.50, you had ten minutes to gather up your stuff, hare along the Prom, get to your room to dump your books and present yourself *chez* the Warden, usually with a red face, damp and out of breath. She was a gracious, gentrified, cool and unhurried type of lady, the sort with whom you felt you had to watch your p's and q's and particularly your ing's and h's. When, on such an occasion, she asked me what I'd done in the summer, I replied, "I went to the Island of Wight Miss Powys-Roberts," and some-one else who lived in Essex, told her they came from 'Hongar'. But even if one over-reached, she was good for standards.

In her comfortable, spacious lounge above the main door you were offered coffee in fragile china cups with a bowl of multi-coloured, flat crystalled sugar. I had never come across this before, was momentarily wrong-footed by it, but saw others putting it in their coffee so did likewise. Once the lunch bell rang you proceeded to the dining room then entered in silence and single file, following the Warden to her table under the main window, watched by 200 other students, some of whom would wink, grimace in sympathy or make silly faces as you passed.

Plates of meat, tureens of vegetables and a gravy boat were brought to her table whereas other tables had to organise fetching them from the hatch. Twenty neat slices of pork, beef, lamb or ham in summer for salad would have been arranged on a meat-platter for each table and there was always potato in some form plus roasted ones on Sunday, and another vegetable. Gravy and the accessories of mint and apple sauce, stuffing and Yorkshire pudding arrived as appropriate. Beverage was in the form of water. Lunch desserts were always of the filling kind, 'stodge' as most girls called them – pastry fruit tarts, spotted dicks, treacle and jam puddings, roly-polies served with jugs of hot custard. Lunch was clearly the most important meal of the day. After all, students needed their large calorie intake for the demands of the afternoon's work. No-one, certainly, could complain of Dickensian treatment. In reality, after lunch, it was as much as you could do to stagger weightily up to your room for a lie-down before taking on the rest of the day. Some in fact slept until woken by a tinkle at 4.30 when tea was served in the form of cake, biscuits and cups of tea.

There was another full meal at 7 pm. This time the cooking was more exotic in the form of fish and chips, ham and chips, sausages and chips and corned beef pie and chips. Occasionally there was cheese, potato and onion pie on the menu when many girls, Florence and I included, would disdainfully decline the offered dinner and go and order egg and chips in town or at Ashley's restaurant further along the Prom.

After the evening revelries, whether they be work or entertainment, students would surely be hungry so at 9.30, boxes of cream crackers, urns of milk and huge lumps of Cheddar cheese were placed on the gleaming steel hatch counters for whoever required sustenance. By 11 pm, little of it would be left, the cheese having been hacked into surreal, crenellated shapes reminiscent of Cézanne and cubism, and the crackers reduced to a pile of crumbs.

The only unsatisfactory meal as far as I was concerned was Sunday tea. There was no evening meal that day. All sorts of individual cakes, from the highly desirable, fancy cream and chocolate gâteaux down to dry buns of the Chelsea and Bath persuasion were set out, together with fruit, slices of bread, milk and the usual hefty lump of cheese. However, you had to be smart to get your hands on a delectable morsel. Florence and I were rarely in time for anything more than a scuffed bun which had lost its glaze, sometimes its top, no doubt jostled aside in the stampede for the delicacies, plus dry, scattered bread slices, a rejected, misshapen apple and cheese. There was always plenty of mutilated cheese. We ate apple and cheese sandwiches for three years at tea-time on Sundays at Aber and yearned for them when we left, like most women a stone or two heavier than when we arrived.

The cooks held beetroot in high esteem. It usually accompanied the mashed potato, was inseparable from Spam and always sat abundantly in diced or sliced form somewhere on the salad plate. It was said that Hall food came from the college farms, wherever they were. Whether they were experimenting with beetroot production in the Plant Breeding Station and had wildly succeeded but had neglected the marketing angle I don't know, but one term beetroot was on the menu every day. Personally I was quite happy with this, but rumblings of revolt escalated. A common-room meeting was called by the Head of Hall, Shirley and her deputy, Avril to discuss the beetroot polemic.

"What do they think we are, giving us beetroot every day? Pigs?" were the cries.

"I've eaten so much beetroot my teeth are permanently stained purple," objected another. Shirley said that after the earlier rumblings of dissent, she had mentioned this to the Warden who in turn was seeing the Cook. Cook had not, even had it been possible, heeded the grievances.

"We must go on strike!" some rebel enthused.

"Yes, strike against beetroot!" went up the cry.

Finally a motion was passed that next time beetroot was on the menu, (the next day) the meal would be boycotted. Much to my shame, thinking of all that waste, and chagrin at missing chips, Spam and beetroot, with ice-cream and peaches to follow, I with 200 or so, mainly indignant, others that evening filled the coffers of the town's cheap restaurants, cafes and chip shops. I just hoped some pig was really appreciating my meal when he got it. Beetroot, sadly, never again that year graced Alex's tables.

The highlights of the Freshers' Weekend, if you disregard the Principal's address and the Freshers' Service in St Michael's and All Angels on the Sunday morning was the Freshers' Hop held in the Parish Hall. More and more students were appearing in the town over the weekend and the Parish Hall was packed. On the stage was Ralph Davies and his band, so the logo on the music stands said. On the floor young men in suits or jackets and ties, crowding the walls as though for a royal event of national importance, gazed around at young women with shining hair and fancy frocks who stood chatting in groups and anxiously looking at the young men, hoping a dance partner would soon materialize. Dancers jostled the lookers and gazers, gradually encroaching on to the floor area until finally there was no space between – the hall heaved with a core of bobbing bodies and a periphery of packed onlookers.

"You've come up early," said one young man to another, "Keen to start work eh?"

"Not at all,"" answered number two, "Come up to get a look at the new talent and put my claim in if anything takes my fancy."

Announcement of the last waltz generated a general rush of man to woman then the un-partnered started to make for the exit. I was last-waltzing with Wyn Phillips of the Pontypridd Legal family, also about to train for a law career. I'd met him in Paignton with Graham Cummings in the summer where he was on holiday. At the end of the dance he chivalrously offered to walk me back to Alex. Outside the entrance, after getting my coat, to my surprise I had difficulty finding him among the hundreds of escorts milling around waiting for their girls. Another surprise was in store on reaching Alex. Couples in close conversation and holding hands lined the front railings while others, arms around each other were disappearing around the side. I was puzzled.

Where were they off to? We had to be inside via the front door at 11 – a matter of minutes.

"Oh, don't you know? The back of Alex is famous. Or notorious rather," said Wyn.

"Notorious? For what?" I enquired.

"Well, you know, for...er...necking...and things."

In my three years I was occasionally offered a stroll around the back and sometimes accepted. It was one more step in my education, if not entirely academic.

Sick Bay was housed in the ground floor rooms on the side of Alex facing Constitution Hill. You couldn't actually see the hill only a high, dark wall supporting a path from the end of the Prom up to Cliff Terrace. There was nothing to distract you from your sick-bed – you could just concentrate on getting better. In fact, with nothing to look at, few visitors because they were all at lectures, writing essays or taking baths, boredom quickly set in and illness didn't last long.

The guardian of Sick Bay was Sister, an elderly, white-haired lady who always wore a light blue dress, with a dark blue cardigan in winter, and white, flowing nursing headgear. She had three remedies up her sleeve (or in her cupboard) – aspirin for what she couldn't see, plasters for what she could, backed up by a hot water bottle if the former failed. One of the Hoole twins went to seek her out, feeling sick and with stomach pains. When an aspirin didn't work, Sister gave her a hot water bottle which did at least hasten the appendicitis she was suffering from and it was removed just before it burst.

I was in Sick Bay once with 'flu. Given the obligatory aspirin, I was put to bed and ministered to in the form of Sister bringing dainty meals on a tray, plumping up my pillows and uttering words of encouragement. The days dragged but the evenings were another matter as from 9.30 on, with the light off, you could watch to see which couples were making their way round to the back for a bit of slap and tickle. Most of my visitors came to sympathise at that time and we had an entertaining time sitting in the dark by the window discovering who were the latest pairings. One of my sick visitors saw a young man she thought was her boyfriend escorting a girl round the back so that particular visit quickly put paid to any protracted liaison as far as she was concerned.

Balls, such as Rag, Freshers' and Leavers' further enlightened me about life. On the advice of my cousin Wyndham via Dr Howe, I had brought an evening gown with me. "Tell your mother to get you a dance dress. Melvyn Howe says all students do is drink and go to dances."

My dress was royal blue, strapless and silky. It had, of necessity, a boned top which was covered in sequins and there was a long, matching stole which proved to be something of an encumbrance. It was all right if you stood still but kept slipping to the floor if you moved, an essential factor in a dance. I, sometimes my dancing partner, normally ended up wearing it as a scarf wound around the neck, occasionally the corporate neck. The gown had been bought at James Howells in Cardiff. My mother was very proud of it, constantly enquiring about its welfare in her letters.

Big balls, held in the King's Hall, were eagerly awaited long in advance. The bands of famous bandleaders such as Joe Loss, Syd Lawrence and Ted 'When the Saints come marching in' Heath came to play. For some of the men, dancing was the last thing on their minds. They bought a ticket, expensive at 10/6d each, and simply went to watch and listen. At some point the band's drummer would give a virtuoso, solo display. Everyone would stop dancing to listen appreciatively, then applaud thunderously when he finished, dripping sweat, exhausted and pleased with himself.

Florence hadn't brought a ball gown, so when her grant arrived and fees had been paid, and she was still solvent – in fact she became known as Moneybags Wilton – we went to Lewis's in Great Darkgate Street to buy the sophisticated, calf-length, black gown with diamantes on the bodice they had on display in their window. It fitted her to perfection and with her fair hair and some earrings she was persuaded to wear, she had never looked so chic. In fact she was unrecognisable. Hitherto I'd had difficulty in persuading her to relinquish her white ankle socks – a relic of school and best left there – for stockings. But she had come a long way in the woman-of-the-world stakes since she had confessed to me at the beginning of the term that her favourite pop-song or piece of light music was 'Just a song at twilight'. At eighteen! "You might as well have chosen a hymn Flor," I told her.

Shirl the Girl, Shirley Jenkins from Aberdare, a beautiful, tall, slim, red-head and her friend Bernice Jones from Gowerton, a pair who certainly weren't behind in growing up, gave Flor (and me) a few tips about make-up and how to use sellotape instead of a bra when you had a low cut dress. The life-education of Florence, a shy, demure girl from Porth was progressing in leaps and bounds. We enjoyed the Balls, Freshers' in this case, very much, but were rather surprised at how Florence attracted the coloured gentlemen students. They queued up to dance with her! Most were the sons of great men in their countries, Ministers of State and the like. One or two were princes. We ascribed her appeal to her fair hair and blue eyes – a complete contrast to her admirers, also to her sweet, innocent nature. Whatever it was, it never failed her during her years at Aber. If there was a black student present, he gravitated to Florence.

We were granted an extension from the usual 11 pm to 11.30 pm, sometimes 12 for a Ball, after which time if you hadn't crossed your name off the signing-out book and had to ring the bell to gain admittance, you were 'gated' for the following evening. The post-Ball rush brought we cosmopolites back to reality as we scampered back to Hall along the Prom, carefully combed-and-set hair streaming in the wind, all semblance of curl being completely blown out, stocking seams askew, mascara smudged with perspiration and ball gown gathered up to facilitate the gallop. If you had an escort, he often offered to carry the handbag or the bag with the spare shoes which some girls took for the stroll thither and sprint hither. Elegantly dressed women students, partnered by men in tuxedos, had the sparkling, fragile appearance of Hollywood film starlets until you got down to their feet, encased in furry boots, wellingtons if it was wet, or sturdy shoes.

Whatever, you had to be back in Hall before a certain time. Whenever you went out after the evening meal it was necessary to write your name in the book and cross it off when you returned. That way the authorities knew who was where. If you weren't back before the ceremony of the closing of the front door and had to ring the bell for Clarence the porter, you were gated. Girls had thought of various ways of late, illegal entry such as getting friends to open the fire-escape doors or those at the back on the ground floor. Unfortunately these were alarmed and to set them off in the early hours was a 'sending down' offence. The latter were locked anyway. Apart from Sick Bay whose windows were only accessible over high, spiked railings, no-one slept on the ground floor. Administration had foreseen all student tactics and taken appropriate action to thwart them.

Clarence the porter was a dear old fellow who'd pop his head outside at 11 pm to make arm-beckoning motions to lovers lingering at the Bar or on the front railings and would keep the door open if he saw you sprinting the last hundred yards up the Prom. He took his duties seriously and at midnight, Lights Out, he did a conscientious tour of the building. Spotting a chink under a door, he'd knock so you'd have to temporarily extinguish. "Thank

145

you. Goodnight." he'd call. When you could no longer hear his footsteps on the corridor floor, you could re-light and be up all night if you wanted, as was often the case before exams.

After a big Ball, sleep being out of the question for a few hours and another chance to wear a posh gown a long way off, we'd get milk from the hatch and make Cocoa or something similar, then with our night-caps, gather in one room, after Clarence's rounds, and discuss the evening. This was often Gillian and Samantha's room. Sam liked dancing but Gillian didn't. When we once tried to persuade her to come along, she emphatically asseverated, "Huh! If you think I'm going to that clod-hopping cow-barn you've got another think coming!", so we let sleeping dogs lie. However, she patiently tolerated our animated chat, mainly about the boys met and the clothes worn.

"Ah!" sighed Betty Jones, "I danced with that boy, Anthony something. Tall, fair hair, square chin. Very good-looking. He's a rower."

"Green. Anthony Green," Frances supplied the information, "Keen on a girl in Carp from north Wales, Wrexham I think."

"Oh, thanks for letting me know so promptly Frances. Who's she anyway? And where was she tonight then?"

"Don't ask me. P'raps she wasn't there," answered her friend.

"He sits next to her in Geography. Anne Morgan," said Jean Rogers, "But if you ask me, she's after him more than the other way round."

"Oh I hope so," sighed Betty, "I think he's gorgeous."

"So do most girls," added Flor.

"Did you see John Rowley?" asked Sam, "He hardly had a leg to stand on when he came in and wasn't exactly on the wagon during the dance. He was sick on the steps as I was leaving. It splashed all over Joan Thomas's dance shoes. White satin they were with gold bits. She wasn't best pleased I can tell you!"

Gillian put her oar in. "And you paid ten bob for the pleasure. Huh! Got better things to do with my money I have. Why do blokes need to consume so much beer anyway?"

"To get drunk of course," replied Frances

"But what for?" Gill was incredulous.

"Well..." Frances shrugged. "Fun I s'pose!"

"You'd have enjoyed the dance though Gill. Really you would have," said Florence, "Terrific band they were. You must come next time."

"No I won't," was Gillian's response, "I can quite easily listen to dance music on the radio without someone being sick on my feet, thank you very much." There was laughter at her unyielding stance.

"Cor, did you see Jungle Juice's dress?" asked Frances. Jungle Juice was a glamorous first year student from a small hostel down the Prom, who always wore lots of make-up, very high heels so she tottered everywhere, and had black waist-length hair. Contrary to her overpowering appearance she was one of the nicest girls at Aber.

"Yes. Pretty colours. I love shot silk especially that purple-red. But my goodness, no wonder she had queues of blokes wanting to dance!" Jean giggled. Gill's curiosity was aroused.

"Why? What happened?"

"Ah, see, you should've gone Gill," a few chorused

"Oh well, don't tell me then if you don't want to. I don't mind!"

"Well, she had a strapless, low-cut dress you see Gill," I explained, "And it was too big. When she moved about inside, her dress sort of stayed still and her partners had a good view of everything down her front. They danced transfixed."

Gillian tutted, "Oh, that's disgusting that is! Flippin' boys! They're all sex maniacs!"

It was very convivial. The clock ticked on to tomorrow. The cups were long empty. People began yawning and hauling themselves off beds and chairs to go to their rooms. Gradually silence crept over Alex and all was peace and quiet for a few hours.

# 16. Academe

The main college building on the sea-front opposite the pier was where most lectures took place, though I spent time in work and play in other buildings scattered around Aberystwyth. The Geography and Geology departments were in uninspiring, grey buildings in Alexandra Road while some French lectures were in a house in Laura Place adjacent to the main college and facing St Michael's church. The Union building was here too with its Snack Bar, packed at the 11 am break between lectures and where you could indulge your appetite with most things except sinful alcohol. There was a Self-Help area where you could get second-hand text books and first-hand cheap stationery. 'Support Self-Help' a poster proclaimed, 'We are virtually giving books away'. They were giving them away for half the original new price, then two thirds of the second-hand cost, and so on we discovered – a bargain in any student's fiscal manoeuvres.

The other option for text books was Galloway's bookshop in Pier Street. Crammed with books in every conceivable nook and cranny, ancient shelves bending under their weight, there was scarcely room to turn in the narrow aisles between. The books were right up against your nose so you went cross-eyed trying to read them in the dim, bare-bulb glimmer of the darkest recesses. Sudden movements often resulted in a cracked head or funny bone on some protrusion. A steep, rickety staircase led up to a narrow gallery with a creaking, unsteady floor and more books piled higgledy-piggledy to the ceiling. There seemed nothing Galloway's couldn't get for you if it wasn't in stock and the chief advantage was you could arrange to have things 'on tick' allowing later payment when the grant cheque had arrived.

French oral classes were conducted in a top, fifth floor room of a ramshackle house with red-painted woodwork on Marine Terrace opposite the pier. Concentration on French conversation was difficult here as one had such a marvellous, distracting view of the sweep of the bay right round to Alex. You could see who were the latest items in the couple's lists as they sauntered arms entwined along the Prom, who was rushing along with gown and books under arm late for their lecture and generally observe what was going on. Once I saw a woman student ride off on my bike that I'd left outside leaning against the wall. She obviously found the Prom too long a haul that day, or perhaps she was lunching with her Warden. I saw her dismount outside Ceredigion and park the bike against the kerb. I just hoped it would still be there when I passed later.

The sea was always fascinating, but rarely gave French conversational inspiration, blue and twinkling in summer with swimmers, yachts with bright sails and boats taking visitors on trips, or grey and menacing as it surged over the beach with swollen waves after a storm.

There was a women's entrance to the main college building via an innocuous door in Kings Street. This discreetly led to toilets and a cloakroom from where one had direct access to the Quad, the focal point of day-time student life. Between lectures one either milled around in the Quad and looked up at those leaning over the Balcony who looked down on those milling. Even people who didn't have lectures, research students who were working in the Library, took breaks on the hour to join in the general crowd-scanning. At 10.50, coffee addicts rushed up to the Union to spend their break queuing then normally managed to get their boiling hot drink when the bell was ringing for the next lecture.

The thinner part of the main college building, stretching in the direction of the ruined castle, crazy golf and harbour was the science block. A tower at its extreme end had mosaic pictures of men doing clever things with geometric and scientific equipment. Arts students rarely penetrated these quarters unless it were to be shown around by a boy or girl-friend. It smelled differently, acidly pungent, while the Arts precinct smelled of dust and old wood.

Large classes in the Arts were generally accommodated in the West classroom – a 50 feet long, narrow, raked room, chilly in summer, glacial in winter with tiny, draughty windows overlooking the Prom and pier. The route there from the Quad and balconies was a tortuous one – up stone steps, through narrow, arched doorways, round corners with columns and more steps until you were in a kind of dark alcove with a door. The West classroom was on the far side. If you got lost and were late, as you entered the room you looked up at the faces of the entire class who then stamped with both feet on the wooden floor in philanthropic welcome. No chance there of reaching a seat unnoticed, and that seat would be a window one, unbesought by all else because of the gale blowing through it. The silken-voiced novelist, short-story writer and scholar of Icelandic Literature Professor Gwyn Jones always lectured to us in that room on Anglo-Saxon – Alfred's Wars with the Danes – a study which caused considerable problems to considerable numbers; Mr Earnshaw gave Yorkshire-mock-grumpy type lectures on the novel and Dr Price intellectual, kindly ones on Shakespeare to classes shivering in unison.

French classes were held in smaller rooms off the Quad. Over the three years of the degree course we came into learning contact with Dr Margaret Phillips (Maggie Pip), Mlle Yvonne Niord, Mr Denis Fletcher, Mr John Killa Williams, the handsome Scotsman Dr Hoggan and Professor E. Briggs. Maggie Pip, pale blue-eyed and wispy grey-haired had lectured on Classical Drama to the parents of some of the students and was rather like a benign grandmother herself. She would tell stories about the war in Aber – we were never sure which one – of seeing spiked mines floating around the headland off Alex and submarines surfacing in the bay. Sometimes these tales would be in French, sometimes English, sometimes a mixture. The two languages were interchangeable as far as she was concerned. Our notes were a *mélange* of both. She'd arrive with a *"Bonjour messieurs, mesdemoiselles"* then speed off in French.

"Aha, it's French today to start then," Margaret Donovan from Merthyr would whisper to her friend Wendy Collis, "French thinking caps on!" Dr Phillips would carry on for fifteen minutes then suddenly flap her hand up and down and gasp, "Oh, it's so hot! Would someone please open a window? Ah, thank you Mr Williams. That's much better." Speaking English would impel her to continue in that language for the following quarter of an hour until, asking a rhetorical question, she'd say, "If you like, *n'est-ce pas?*" then she'd be off in French once more until an English interruption. Someone might mistake the door, knock, put their head around and mutter, "Oh, sorry, wrong room!" Her French train of thought would be broken and English would fall in torrents from her lips until another, "If you like, *n'est-ce pas?*" when we'd be back to French. And so it went on. In and out of the tongues like a yo-yo. Notes frequently changed language half-way through a sentence. We were all fond of this gentle, rather scatter-brained lady whom you felt you could approach with any worries or problems you might have about work.

Then there was Mlle Niord. 'Niord', as every-one called her or 'Ee-aw' if she gave you a poor grade accompanied by a load of sarcasm which was quite often, didn't suffer fools gladly. Clearly a highly intelligent lady herself, in her mid-thirties, she struck me as a cool, female version of Victor Mature. Tall and willowy with black hair, an aquiline nose and slightly droopy eyes, she displayed a lot of pink upper gum when she smiled. She took us once weekly for Prose Translation (Thème) and this was the least liked class of all. Students spent longer on their prose than on anything else, fearing her humiliating comments for grammatical errors ("You people appear to me to have the IQ of a piece of toast"), sometimes doing the translation five or six times with a final, desperate polish before handing it in. Getting to the end of her prose lectures you felt a sense of relief and release, as on a Friday afternoon before a relaxing weekend, especially if you had managed to avoid being singled out for a tongue-lashing, in English, so that everyone clearly understood.

In our final year after our year abroad and the class had been slimmed down, Mlle Niord would bring a box of chocolates each week which she'd pass around in the interval between the double lecture when she was teaching the Humanists and Pleiade poets, Ronsard and Du Bellay. We saw her in a different light then. She was much more 'sympa' and sympathetic, especially towards the men and Howard Young in particular, but she may have changed because she was in love as we later discovered.

On returning to Aber after our year spent as 'assistant(e)s' in France, to our delight we found the French Department had appointed a new lecturer, Dr Hoggan. He was young, tall, Scottish, had fair, wavy hair and was very handsome. Women forgot to take notes in his classes but simply sat, gazed and smiled at him, whereupon he would blush, as the men scribbled busily, unaware of the waves of silent ardour pulsating in the room. Before the end of that year Mlle Niord was wearing Dr Hoggan's engagement ring and they were married, I believe, the following summer. No doubt he got A+ and chocolates every time for his Prose translation! We wondered whether Dr Niord would become Dr Hoggan too, or two,so that the Department confusingly boasted more than one Doctor of the same name.

We had heard about Mr John Killa Williams MA, TD, (generally known as 'Killa') from Miss Llewellyn before we'd reached Aberystwyth. This amiable, urbane, dryly humorous man taught us Semantics. He was also an A level oral examiner. Just prior to her exam one highly-strung candidate heard her teacher say the examiner was usually known as 'Killa' and envisaged the spelling differently. Reading an affiliated intention into the mis-spelling, and being on the point of a nervous breakdown with anxiety anyway, she promptly fainted into her surprised teacher's arms.

Killa told us he looked forward to his month-long, paid, June and July holiday examining in schools along the north Wales coast uncluttered by the seasonal hordes, enjoying the good weather, staying in hotels and being pampered in the institutions. After the exertions of marking college exams, this was one of the most agreeable times of the year.

Everyone was in awe of Professor Briggs with whom we came into contact mainly in our final year when he gave lectures on French philosophers through the ages – Descartes, Diderot, Pascal, Saint Simon, Henri Bergson. "Je suis Henri Bergson, Juif!" the famous philosopher proudly announced to the invading Germans in World War 2. A man of such world-wide renown they couldn't possibly dispatch to a death camp in a cattle wagon.

Prof Briggs was a short, balding man with eyes that twinkled behind glasses in a round face. He looked as though he existed solely for the intellectual life. He was unhurried, calm and cerebral in everything he did and one couldn't imagine him in a setting other than the groves of academe. He was though, an aficionado with a tennis racket. Playing one evening on the college courts in Llanbadarn with Merle Picton, Miggs Morris and Florence, I was distracted by a familiar figure running athletically around a few courts away.

"Gosh! There's a bloke over there who looks exactly like Prof Briggs. Uncanny resemblance!" The others looked.

"Oh yes. So he does," said Merle, "But it can't be!"

"It is Prof Briggs!" Florence was quite definite.

"Go on Flor! It's not. Don't be silly! Prof Briggs couldn't play tennis like that!" The controversial person jumped for the ball and made a winning smash as we watched.

"It is you know," she insisted.

She'd just acquired a new pair of glasses and saw things larger than life. Having a penchant for Cadbury's Turkish Delight chocolate then only made in 2oz bars, she'd gone into a shop asking for the new 1/4 lb bar they had displayed in the window.

"No love, we've only got small bars. They don't make them any bigger."

"Yes, they must do. I've seen one in your window."

It was only on production of the aforementioned chocolate that she believed the shopkeeper, realised her mistake and attributed it to her new super-vision specs.

I knocked the ball away a few courts to have an excuse, retrieving it, for a closer look at the mystery player. He noticed me in the break between points, smiled and nodded saying, "Evening Miss Davies." It was Professor Briggs! My astonishment and admiration were unqualified.

In tutorials he invited us, sitting around the far end of the table from him, to approach and sit nearer him. Everyone shuffled up, but on the next and succeeding occasions we were all back at the other end like rabbits scurrying back into their holes. His immaculate French was sprinkled with latinate words – primo, secundo, tertio – and if we ever saw him outside the lecture ambiance (apart from on the tennis court), such as when we went for a stroll along South Marine Terrace where he lived, it was always a formal, "Good afternoon Miss Wilton, Miss Davies" with a shy smile and a touch of his hat. In his nineties now, he lives outside Paris.

One couldn't imagine Prof Briggs rounding up students in the town streets in an open topped car like Dr Denison of the German Department once did. He was, so it was said, not the promptest of lecturers to meet his class. One day his group decided to wait the obligatory five minutes then be off to the Penguin, Home or Seagull cafes or do a bit of shopping and wandering around town. To their surprise they heard themselves being hailed by name from a passing car driving slowly by. It was nothing to do with electioneering, only their lecturer mobilizing them from his vehicle.

The same German lecturer had David Nehemiah, rugby-playing student from Swansea in his class. When Dr Denison first asked their names he discovered one particular name was shared by a few people. Nia Jones from nearby Bow Street who commuted daily gave her name,

"Nia Jones, sir."

"Thank you." He wrote her name in a book. "And you?" nodding at the next girl.

"I'm Nia Morgan."

"Ah, lots of Nia's in this group I see. Right." He jotted down the name. "And the young man there, next to Nia Morgan."

"Er... Nehemiah sir."

Dr Denison paused in his writing. "This I do not believe. You are having me on aren't you?"

I understand his tested credulity. In the first class I taught, there was a Roger Gabriel and a Gabrielle Rogers. I just hoped the two didn't eventually marry each other.

One morning a guest lecturer, a Dr Richard Cobb from the History Department we were informed, was to lecture us on the French Revolution. A tall, gangly, rather unkempt man with a thin, goose-like face and large glasses and mouth entered the room. As we were first year students, most of our teachers, as a gentle introduction to Academia, spoke English to us for part of the hour, then a carefully-paced, clear French, nonetheless demanding for eighteen year olds who had been raised on the grammatical, written language rather than the informal, oral one. We fully expected Dr Cobb, as a historian to speak in a dry, English narrative. To our shock and confusion, he launched forth in a 100 mph French of which we could catch one word in twenty as he manipulated his flaccid mouth gear around the language while we watched in fascinated horror. And we were supposed to be taking notes! People looked at each other with puzzled frowns and raised eyebrows of incomprehension. After five minutes of this I felt a nudge. Margaret Hatton was sitting next to me. "Er... what's he on about?" she whispered.

"The French Revolution, I think," was my hushed reply.

"Can you understand much of this?" she enquired, head bent for concealment.

I had to admit, "On a scale of very little to none."

"Thank God for that! Nor can I," was her reply as she started to doodle on her blank page. Fortunately we were able to read up what we assumed Dr Cobb to be lecturing on. Later in Union Debates, I had difficulty understanding what he had to say in English, though what I did catch seemed very clever and dialectically persuasive. In the late eighties, as chairman of the Booker Prize Panel he made a speech before announcing the winner. As I watched him on television I experienced the *déjà-vu* feeling of being hypnotised by the liberated dance of his mandibles and the strain to catch every word. By this time he had been awarded the *Légion d'honneur*, the red ribbon of which, it is alleged, he wore on his pyjamas.

Edward Nevin was a lecturer in Economics whom most students knew – the women especially because he was young and handsome as well as charming – happily married, however, with several children. When it was advertised that he would be speaking in a Union Debate, it was necessary to get to the Examination Hall where they were held, early, foregoing your pie/ sausages/ ham/ fish and chips, if you hoped for a seat. Students crowded in, several deep around the walls to hear what was always a convincing case from him, given smilingly in a nonchalant, humorous, often teasing manner. He later became Professor of Economics at Swansea University.

Another genius who would fill a debating hall was Gwyn Alf Williams, lecturer in Welsh History. Dauntlessly speaking with a stammer, his style was in complete contrast to Dr Nevin's. Often invoking his extreme political views, he was blustery, arm-waving, glaring, hilariously funny in a self-deprecating, mock-indignant way when his voice would rise to a breathless squeak. He attracted students like worker bees to the Queen. A *mêlée* of youngsters with college scarves would be seen tramping up the Prom. What was this one wondered? An open-air, mobile conference? A protest against Saturday morning lectures? An attack on Constitution Hill by the Harriers club in full dress? Students marching for the abolition of fees? It was none of these. It was the Gwyn Alf Travelling Prom Show or Moving Scrum. Being so short himself, he couldn't be seen. Occasionally one might see a central waving arm or a shock of tough, greying hair through a gap in the throng, because he was always the pivot of the group which moved around him like American presidential bodyguards. It reminded me of little boys playing football. They don't bother with positions and the ball itself is rarely glimpsed. When it does spurt out from the fray, the little boys chase it to another part of the field, tightly surrounding it for another five minutes. Gwyn Alf and Richard Cobb were apparently drinking mates and their bacchanals were legendary.

Another well-known, but nameless, Prom character was a lanky, straggly-bearded lecturer of Maths. He would amble along pensively, seemingly oblivious to his surroundings. It was said this was his method of solving his mathematical conundrums by thinking them through. As he thought, his pace would quicken until it became a trot, then a rather ungainly run, then a dash, sidestepping other strollers as his beard streamed in the breeze. No doubt, reaching the solution to his problem, he was racing home, anxious to get it all written down before he forgot it.

A handsome, neat man with wavy, grey hair and heavy bags under his eyes was often to be seen walking along the front. Students acknowledged him and he always smiled back or raised the hat he usually wore.

"That's the Principal, Goronwy Rees," said Margaret Algate on one of our rare encounters for she now lived in Carp and had made a new set of friends. At school she was a mine of unprompted information and already at Aberystwyth only a few weeks, she knew everything and everybody. "He went to Cardiff High School. They don't like him much here, they say, 'cos he's not Welshy enough. He's got five kids, an' he's written some books. Always wears white socks. You have a look!"

"Gosh!" was my tongue-tied riposte to this welter of data, probably the five kids and the white socks most impressing my imagination. I warmed to him instantly, erroneously inferring him to be from my part of the world, the urban south-east and English-Welsh. I too had experienced feelings of rejection by the north Welsh and remembered how indignant I'd felt when a child. Though my mother's first language was Welsh – she had not spoken English until she was ten – I had been brought up in English. On holiday in Pwllheli one summer in the late forties, we'd gone into a shop where Mam naturally, spoke Welsh to the shop-owner who then said something to me in Welsh.

"I can't speak Welsh," I said.

"What, can't speak Welsh!" this woman barked in English, "And you call yourself a Welsh girl! Huh, you're not Welsh! You're an English girl if you can't speak Welsh!"

My ten year old blood boiled. "No, I'm not! I am Welsh! I'm as Welsh as you! More Welsh in fact because I'm from *South* Wales which is much more important than up here!"

"Mary!" My mother blushed in mortification.

The woman looked at me in narrow-eyed hostility. "You cheeky little girl! Children up here don't speak to their elders like that anyway! No indeed!"

I pulled at my mother's arm to leave the shop, which she did, without her purchase. I got a considerable ear-bashing afterwards though and she remembered and recalled the incident, in support of other grievances that cropped up, for years.

In Aber too, members of the student Welsh club, the *Geltaidd*, all paraded along the Prom, noisily and high-spiritedly, presumably after meetings. Their group jollity exuded an air of exclusivity and rejection to non-Welsh speakers. Individually I never met an unpleasant student whose first language was Welsh although I did find the English accents of the north Welsh droll. No doubt they were as amused by mine.

Goronwy Rees, I learned thirty years later on reading his autobiography, *A Chapter of Accidents*, was neither from the south-east nor English-Welsh. He was born in Aberystwyth to a Calvinistic Methodist minister and his farmer's daughter wife, also from Cardiganshire, was brought up Welsh-speaking, although he did attend Cardiff High from where he won an Oxford scholarship. After Oxford he had become decidedly English in outlook and subsequently only lived in Wales during his principalship from 1953-57.

Nevertheless the students, especially the women, adored him. He mingled with the student body, went to Hall and College Balls and danced with the girl students; he supported Aber teams at inter-varsity games; he invited representatives of student groups, clubs and teams to tea at his large house in Penglais which stood in a field at the end of a long drive; he took walks with his wife and children on the Prom. He appeared informal for a great man, far more congenial than some of the lecturers.

At Easter 1956, *The People* newspaper published a series of sensational articles about the Russian spies and defectors, Guy Burgess and Donald Maclean, written by a Mr X, shortly afterwards identified as the Principal of UCW Aberystwyth. Everybody was shocked, none more so than the College Authorities. Soon, rumours abounded that Goronwy Rees would be shown the door. In the summer the students, at a General Meeting passed a resolution of support for him. It was about this time that Clement Attlee came to address the Union. He was applauded as he entered the Examinations Hall, applause which became thunderous on the appearance of the Principal behind him. It was a show of approval, the like of which I've never seen accorded to anyone and he was clearly moved by it. I was amazed to later discover he was a manic-depressive and considered, even by his friends, to have been woefully mis-cast as Principal of a mid-Wales, small-town university.

Whatever, when I returned to Aber in October 1959, there was a new incumbent in the Principal's residence under the wood in Penglais, Dr Thomas Parry, who seemed very nice but not half as exciting. He wore black socks.

# 17. Socs and Other Diversions.

During Freshers' Weekend there was a club-joining session. The various societies displayed their attractions on tables with pamphlets, timetables, folders and adverts and behind tables in the form of enthusiastic students, athletic-looking ones in the case of the Games clubs – Football, Golf, Rugby, Hockey, Harriers, Rowing, Netball, Badminton, Table-tennis, Swimming – earnest ones for the political clubs and dreamier types for the Arts, Music and Literary socs. Others on a scale from the extra to the ordinary tried to persuade you to part with a few pence for the Film Club, Drama Soc, Gram Soc, Overseas Students Soc, Urdu Soc etc.

The most popular of these bodies, apart from the Sports Clubs were the Film and Gram Socs, and the *Geltaidd*, to judge from the numbers who paraded the Prom. Due to the socs secs. persuasiveness or fanciability, many freshers joined more clubs than there were evenings for meetings, and, spoiled for choice, ended up going to none.

The Gram Soc met on a Sunday evening downstairs in the Union Building in Laura Place. It was packed out every week and you had to get there early to claim a place – a seat on the stairs or on the floor. There were no chairs, considered far too staid, and space-wasting to boot. If you wanted a seat where you could also sit with your back against the wall, you had practically to camp there for the afternoon. Classical records were played and the majority of students flocked there, not so much for the music but because there was nothing else to do in Aber on a Sunday night, and because, during the music, the lights were put out. Many first dates, after the previous Saturday night's Hop were to the Gram Soc and it was a weekly topic of interest to see who turned up with whom. Who was Romeo Jones's love of his life for this week? In the darkness, while looking appealingly soulful listening to Beethoven's *Pastoral*, you could hold hands with the new love, possibly have the odd nuzzle during the romantic *Romeo and Juliet*. Then afterwards, the ever-open Penguin and Home cafes on opposite sides of Pier Street being closed on Sunday evenings, you could have an intimate chat over a cup of coffee in the National Milk Bar in Terrace Road followed by a stroll back to Alex along the Prom, watching the sea shimmer in the moonlight with little waves breaking breathlessly on the shingle. Ah, Youth!

Having played hockey in the school team for several years and still feeling reasonably fit, becoming part of the hockey set-up was my first Club priority, so I went along to the trials. Previously I'd played at Right Back. Now, however, I noticed Backs abounded. Anne Ellis, the captain asked where I wanted to play. "Anywhere where there's a vacant position, really. I don't mind. I'll try and adapt," I said, adding hastily, "Except in goal."

"Well, we're short of Half Backs. On the left especially."

"OK, I'll play Left Half then."

"Are you sure? Don't you want a trial in your proper position?"

"Well, you play Right Back don't you?" The captain nodded. I wasn't going to displace her was I?

"So I'll play Left Half," I said.

I'd never played on the left side of the field before, but somehow found the angles easier, the position more comfortable and spacious. With your back parallel to the sideline, you have the entire field of play before you whereas on the right you can be forced into touch and have fewer options. The arm swing from the left seemed more natural. Though right-handed, I decided there must be something sinister in my make-up because I also high-jumped from the left.

The first match, the following Wednesday afternoon was a Second XI game against the Plant Breeding Station and I was down at Left Half. The following Saturday I read my name, again in that position to play for the Second XI against Aberaeron Grammar School, away, in the morning, and for the First XI against Newtown, at home in the afternoon. Surely this was a mistake? Even if it weren't, would I be able to get back from Aberaeron with enough time to have lunch and get to the ground at Llanbadarn? This was a bit more than I'd bargained for. I didn't really need, or indeed want, that much exercise, but as Anne explained, "Well, you see, we've got a shortage of Left Halves. None in fact. Only you." My attempts at explaining I wasn't really a Left Half were waved aside, "So we've put the First XI's bully-off to 3 o'clock so you'll be able to make it. You don't mind do you?" Oh no, I'd only ache for a week!

At least I felt wanted! I played in two matches in one day on four occasions, once mid-week and three on Saturdays. Mid-week wasn't too bad as you could slump in a seat in the cinema for the evening although it needed a few strong friends to pull you to a standing position at the film's end as one's joints inclined to fuse after a few hours in a certain posture. On a Saturday though, I had to miss the social event of the week – the Hop – hop being the least function my sore limbs could perform. It was no consolation either, lingering in a hot bath thinking of everyone else enjoying themselves, dressed up and meeting new friends. And the next day, when stiffness set in, was perhaps worse, as you tended to forget your pain and sudden movement would cause further yelping anguish.

Finally after having to leap (painfully) one Saturday evening from a luxuriant bath for a fire-alarm (false) and stand steaming out in the road (dripping wet), clad only in slippers and my blue, long-zipped (fortunately) dressing-gown while the fictitious conflagration was tracked down, I begged to be released from this torture of a bi-match day.

In the hockey circle I met up again with former school opponents such as Angela Dove and the brilliant Centre Half and future international, Rose Watkins, both from Whitchurch, and Barbara Thomas from Mountain Ash. Strange, they now seemed ordinary, friendly, fallible girls, quite unlike the dour, super-Amazonian women of a year or so back.

By dint of sharing coaches for away matches, we became acquainted with the men's hockey club, and besides a joint hockey dinner at the Talbot Hotel, we played practice matches against an assortment of their Second and Third teams which I hated. These lesser players seemed to me to have little skill, only strength and would belt the ball far too hard to be controllable. They also paid scant regard to feminine fragility, only wishing to display their power and virility. Many of the First team players were Cardiffians who had played hockey at school, such as the captain Tony Harris, John Vodden, Brian Shears, Mike Jeffcott (Penarth) and the handsome chemist Graham Thomas. It was an advantage having a hockey-playing boy-friend as Cardiff being so accessible, you could easily meet up in the vacations.

Female hockey players were handicapped by having to run the gauntlet of the rugby team supporters. The changing rooms were at one end of the University's Llanbadarn playing fields and the hockey pitch at the other. To reach one from the other we had to pass, in our red shirts and socks and navy shorts, in front of the rugby stand where the male spectators would stamp on the wooden steps and chant the Laurel and Hardy theme, "La la la-la-la, La la la-la-la" and clap each time one of us went by. The clamour initially brought blushes to maidenly cheeks, but by the end of the season we were inured, chanting with them, waving hock-ey sticks and bowing, especially when we'd won.

The other exercise, albeit semi-serious, was swimming. Before we'd left Porth County, Denise Ormond said, "You must go and see Mr Blaze at the swimming pool up on the hill behind the National Library. He's in charge of it. You'll get a hearty wel-come. He's an old friend of mine. Remember me to him and to his wife. Mrs Blaze is blind. Oh, and make sure you don't take him by surprise. If there's no-one there, he swims in the buff."

Not many weeks had elapsed before Florence and I, having a free afternoon and after a long toil up Penglais Hill, found the building tucked away behind Nat Lib from which it is totally, annoyingly, inaccessible across a few cultivated fields. That first time we had to retrace our steps, climb a bit more hill, turn south at the Agriculture building, pass the new men's Hall of Residence, Pantycelyn, on our right and follow the only road to the pool.

Mr Blaze, an elderly, short, wide and balding man with pene-trating blue eyes and a few wild wisps of hair, gingery on his head and white on his pink chest, was indeed pleased to see us.

"You're the first students I've had up here all day. I was think-ing I might as well lock up and go home for my tea. Nice to have someone to talk to."

In truth, apart from Pantycelyn and the Agri building where students, presumably mostly from Pantycelyn were too busy studying to swim, the pool was a long way and an arduous walk from the nucleus of collegiate activity. Aber is now the college on the hill, but then it was decidedly the college by the sea. Of Denise Ormond, Mr Blaze said, "The best actress we've ever had in the Dram Soc. She was the best Puck I've ever seen in *The Dream* and that includes the professional theatre."

To the south the pool had a fine view of Aber and to the north a good view of the back of Nat Lib, positively less impressive than its front. It was very peaceful up there, no noise of traffic or peo-ple, only the twittering of birds or the occasional drone of a plane or distant tractor. Apart from Swimming Club evenings and galas against the other Welsh universities and colleges, the pool was under-used, though the pupils of Ardwyn Grammar School had morning swimming classes there.

I never saw more than half a dozen swimmers at one time in the pool, so it was possible to glide around without having peo-ple's elbows poke you in the eye and feet kicking you in the ribs. Florence hadn't swum as much as I, so to build up her stamina and speed we'd have end to end races. I'd give her a start or swim

161

slowly alongside then just quicken up at the end to win. Mr Blaze remarked, "I bet you two bob she'll beat you one of these days."

"OK then. You're on," I replied.

One afternoon, I was ahead and swimming casually when suddenly she shot past at great speed, raising a bow wave – at the end of a rope pulled by a gleeful Mr Blaze. He in turn was using up so much energy and stomach muscle hauling a not insubstantial Florence, his trousers, normally held up by his corpulent middle, were around his lower hips, crucially balanced so as not to reveal quite all. The scene was so comical, Flo half out of the water creating a tidal wave, hanging on to the rope for dear life and Mr Blaze heaving away and losing his pants, I started to laugh which is the last thing you should do when out of your depth in chlorinated water, or any water I suppose. I swallowed pints of it and touched the bottom. It wasn't quite a case of drowning, but definitely one of a race lost, if not exactly under ASA rules.

If it was the end of the afternoon, Mr Blaze would give us a lift in his blue Austin A40 car and drop us off in North Parade in the centre of town but in our final year we took bikes with us back to Aber. Though it was necessary to push them up Penglais Hill, we rode them back, hair drying in the breeze as we careered back down the hill to Alex and our evening meal.

On hot summer days when the glazed doors forming the side of the pool overlooking the town were slid back, you could take your towel and sunbathe either on the grass outside or on the wide, tiled pool verge and read or doze. Usually reading became dozing in the warmth and silence, only disturbed by sleep-inducing lapping or gently splashing of water and the noise of crickets in the nearby fields.

Despite swimming every week, Florence wasn't deemed to be getting enough exercise so Frances Jones suggested she should row. Rowers needed to be reasonably well-built and strong. Fragile little creatures were no use she argued, so Florence, being no weakling, would be ideal. I took up the cudgels on rowing's behalf.

"You never know Flor, this could be your sport. You might take to it like a duck to water and be so good you'll be chosen to row for Britain in the next Olympics. Good grief, you could be the next Gold Medallist in the women's single sculls. I can just see you up there on the rostrum, in your blazer, with the Union Jack flying, them playing the National Anthem and tears pouring down your cheeks!"

"Oh, go on! I don't know anything about rowing."

"Well, everyone's got to start somewhere – and they'll teach you anyway. I think you'd be good at it. I mean you don't have to be able to run fast or anything like that. You just sit and use your arms. And you only have one oar to think about."

Florence was clearly thinking along Olympic lines, the Gold Medal podium and her own boat.

"No, you have two in single sculls surely?"

"Well yes, of course in single sculls you do, or you'd be going round in circles wouldn't you?"

"Oh aye." She was persuaded. "OK then, I'll give it a go."

The trouble with rowing at Aber was that it was on the sea, not the river and you had to 'catch the tide'. This always seemed to mean getting up at some ludicrously early hour as apparently Aber's tides only operated at 6 o'clock in the morning. The first try-out in an 8's boat was at 7.30 am one day in the harbour. Having recklessly encouraged Florence along this path of dawn endeavour, I could hardly refuse when she asked me to accompany her to the venue for moral support.

The coach, Anthony Green, admired of Betty Jones, was there, dynamic and enthusiastic in shorts and blazer with what looked like a towel around his neck tucked in the V of his coat. The women just looked cold and sleepy and yawned a lot.

"We'll just row up and down in the harbour at first to get you used to the feel of the boat." he explained.

They went down a little ladder set in the harbour wall on to a miniscule margin of shingle and with much waving about of arms and unsteady balancing acts, eventually all got into the skiff which looked about as sturdy as an enlarged pea-shell. A helpful hand pushed them off and they were afloat. Neither Florence nor I, watching, had expected moving seats. I couldn't hear what Anthony Green was telling them but shortly each placed her feet deliberately in a certain position, hung on unwaveringly to her oar and started to pull, more or less in unison. There was a lot of splashing and frightening of indignant seagulls and they were off. Unluckily no-one seemed able to control her sliding seat, so as some were shooting forward, others were reversing and getting knee-jabs in the back. What with the seagulls, the breeze and the sea, I couldn't hear much, but expressions said it all.

"Stop!" I heard a male voice roar, and they came to a halt. For a while they just sat in the boat sliding forward and back on their seats. Then they took up their oars again. But to no avail. Moving bottoms forward for the dipped oar then back for the pull with

163

legs at full stretch seemed an impossible feat of co-ordination for the majority, with the result that backs went on being thumped, faces displayed stoic pain, Anthony Green looked fed-up though doggedly continued to instruct, and the flimsy craft wobbled about in the water, barely moving. From the quay it all seemed very comical and it couldn't have helped that the sole spectator was overwhelmed with gales of laughter. Their awful torture went on for 45 minutes before it was abandoned. Visions of Flor on an Olympics rostrum were fading.

"OK girls. Not too bad for beginners I s'pose. See you on Friday. Same time, same place," Anthony Green bade them farewell.

"Huh, he'll be lucky!" groaned Florence, "I think my back's broken. If I recover, I think I'll just stick to gentle strolls."

Poor old Flor, she was so stiff the next day she couldn't even stroll and spent the day lying on her bed with a hot water bottle. No-one mentioned rowing again.

# 18. Perambulations

If you were feeling an excess of energy and the weather was nasty you could take an indoor ramble in Alex – it was so vast with its long main corridors and lateral ones as well as various little recesses, alcoves and niches about the place. You discovered all sorts of unknown places – small individual bathrooms with ancient baths on curly feet, and washrooms besides the modern, multi-ablution complexes built on each floor. There were student kitchens with kettles, pans, irons and ironing boards, sinks, usually with the draining board loaded with unwashed or unwiped utensils. Doors led to more isolated corridors and some opened on to fire-escapes. On one ramble I discovered a large and forgotten basement room with a sprung floor. In a box room were old badminton rackets and semi-feathered shuttles. I rounded up a few friends and we spent some enjoyable hours further de-feathering shuttles playing badminton with no posts or net – no court marked out either. Evidently an earlier venue for dances and parties, in my final year this room was made into a lounge with a carpet and arm-chairs where Alex young ladies could entertain their men friends. But it was too big. Voices echoed for everyone to hear so conversations were whispered and one needed to be on the move to keep warm.

Exploration of Hall was useful for telephone duty. Each student was required to stay indoors, approximately one evening per term to answer the phone located in a booth in the entrance hall, and run and fetch the desired girl. You had to be fit for this job as sometimes it was necessary to get up to the fifth floor then breathlessly shout, "Rhiannon Bell, Heather Halhead, Gloria Tatchell (whoever). Telephone!" Often a person would be out or untraceable, whereupon you had to belt back down to the phone, and, if the caller's money hadn't by then run out, inform them of this.

Before chasing after the caller, you had to consult the room list on the notice-board by the front door. This was easy enough, it being alphabetical, until you came to the Margaret Joneses of whom there were at least ten. They were known as Margaret (Gowerton) Jones, Margaret (Newcastle Emlyn) Jones, Margaret (Pwllheli) Jones, Margaret (Crumlin) Jones and so on. Margaret Jones calls were detested.

"Where's she from?" you'd ask

"What?" or, "I beg your pardon?" people would respond in surprise, not expecting a chat with the unknown at the end of the phone. To the repeated question some wanted to know, "Why?"

"Well, we've got dozens of Margaret Joneses here and they're in different rooms see, so is it Margaret Llangollen Jones you want or Margaret Cardigan Jones or who?"

Sometimes, caught hanging around within earshot of the phone, you were asked to fetch girls for their boy-friends who'd come to call unexpectedly. Sometimes the girls didn't want to see them.

"Oh, tell him I'm out will you please?"

"She's out," I'd tell him on my descent, feeling like saying, "She said to say she's out," but restraining through a sense of feminine solidarity.

"No she's not, because she hasn't signed out. I've looked in the book."

"Oh well, she's not in her room. Her friends don't know where she is."

Once, the suitor, a lanky, spotty lad with black curly hair, given this information looked as though he was about to cry.

"She just doesn't want to see me. I know. She won't answer my phone calls either. I think she's finished with me. Do you know if she's going out with anybody else?"

He was very crestfallen. On that occasion I didn't know the girl but offered him a seat in the corridor and a glass of water to recover. This was a mistake on my part, as the phone, being unprecedentedly idle for fifteen minutes, I had a woeful mini account of his life history ending with, "Will you go out with me?" I hurriedly invented hordes of young men I was promised to every evening for at least the next six months.

If there were sometimes downcast young men in the foyer, the noises emanating from the Common Room were always joyful, particularly after a meal, apart that is from Miss Stocks and Shares who now and then moaned on her daily consultation of the appropriate page of *The Daily Telegraph*. The table-tennis table was located there and the gentle exercise involved in the game was deemed ideal for one's digestion. Rarely was singles played, so great was the demand, but one frequently saw three players at each end. People who'd never previously played became experts and even turned up later with their own bat. When Hall meals began to take their toll in *avoirdupois*, and calories were discovered as evil elements, our 'family' group played an energetic game which included six a side, hitting the ball then running to the other end of the table to hit the following shot. Needless to say there were many collisions and tumbles with bodies piled up on the floor, prostrate with laughter, distracting for those trying to concentrate on the serious news in the paper. No doubt unbecoming behaviour for twenty year olds, but eminently possible in those days of single sex residences. Essays, study, charts, maps, translations, reading, dissertations would pull students reluctantly away after dinner in the evening.

Sundays were work, walks and occasionally, worship days. Work was *de rigueur*, not so much through conscientiousness, but because then, students weren't so aware of their rights. If they were, they certainly didn't enforce them – and would never have been so audacious as to defend themselves or answer back a reprimand from a teacher – and some of them could be vituperative – for a late, or lacking piece of work.

Walks took place on fine Sunday afternoons, otherwise it was more work or table-tennis. Hundreds of students swarmed over Constitution Hill – it was infra dig and a needless expense to ride up on the cliff railway – getting to the top gently via the zig-zag path, or arduously straight up over the shale getting shoefuls of grit.

In summer, mainly on fine afternoons and all day Sunday, the railway ground up and down, which was a considerable irritation to students having rooms on the Consti side, especially as exams approached and with them, serious revision. Animated summer visitors doubled Aber's perambulatory population and signs, "Silence, students working", or "A bit of peace please! Exams next week", were to be espied in student hostel windows.

Unaccompanied men wandered over Constitution Hill and could be seen sitting and gazing, often with binoculars, over the town. Only, as I discovered in my final year, they weren't so interested in the views of the Prom, pier, bay and beach, as what was going on in the women's rooms in Alex.

One day I'd been reading, propped up on the pillow on my bed in the corner opposite the door, and looked up to see a man lying on the hill reflected in the mirror on the wardrobe facing the window. He was looking straight at me. I got up and looked out of the window, but now he was casually looking sea-wards. I went to tell Florence next door.

"Hey, Flor, there's a bloke sitting on Consti opposite my room and looking in." She didn't believe me.

"Go on! How could he see in the room? Where is he?" We peered out of her window but the man had gone. "No. I expect he was just someone having a rest on his way up."

167

A few days later the scenario was repeated only this time he had binoculars. It was sinister. I wondered what to do. Suddenly I jumped up, pulled the curtains and ran to Florence's room before the peeper realised what was happening. Typically, she wasn't there. And I stubbed my toe on the bed leg, rushing in the darkened room. I needed confirmation that these weren't the demented imaginings of a mind unbalanced by frenzied revision.

The answer to the problem seemed to be a bit of furniture re-arrangement, particularly the wardrobe through whose mirror the pimp could see into the room. As far as I was aware, it never happened again, but I couldn't help regarding with aggrieved suspicion any single men I saw walking on Consti. It probably also explains my fondness for net curtains.

At the summit of Constitution Hill you had a fine view of the bay, the pier stretching out over the tranquil sea with a constant white border, people like black flies moving on the Prom and the normally unseen roof of Alex immediately below. Behind were the irregular tops of the town and college buildings and away to the south, the dolls' houses on Penparcau Hill and the sporadic dazzle of light as the sun caught a windscreen or window. Pen Dinas Hill with its TV mast rose level with our vantage point, and the eye went beyond to the mistier coastline, dark green right down to the water's edge at valley openings or ending abruptly in sombre, indeterminate cliffs above a sea gradually lightening to the horizon.

Sometimes we were a group going for a walk, with the north Walian Joneses, Betty, Frances, Eluned and Mair Penry, Gill Morgan, Sam Pritchard et al, but once a term was enough for most, whereas Flor and I were stalwart walkers. We usually pursued a northwards route along the narrow path for half a mile, now and then venturing near the edge to peer down, daring the grassy bank not to give way and thinking you shouldn't be challenging nature.

"Cor, good place this to, you know...er...jump...if things got too much," said Frances.

"Oh, I think I'd just walk out of Alex in my pyjamas, down the beach and on into the sea without looking back," decided Betty.

"Why in your pyjamas?" Gill wanted to know.

"I don't know. Seems appropriate. Wouldn't want to ruin my best clothes I s'pose," mused Betty, "I just imagine that sort of thing in night-clothes somehow."

"Proper clothes would be better," Samantha advised, "They'd

weigh you down and get it over and done with quicker. Anyway you wouldn't be coming back to your best clothes."

"You might change your mind half-way," piped in Florence.

"Haha, you wouldn't half look daft coming back into Alex in dripping wet pyjamas," added Frances.

But instead of committing suicide over the cliff as tragically a few depressed students have done, we carried on to Clarach and had ice-creams and pop.

The path turned gradually around the cliff and the new panorama was of Clarach Bay, pebble beach with snack shack above, and beyond, the green valley floor with holiday caravans neatly lined up on the south facing side. Our road back ran under the north slope of the valley then rose steeply as it turned back through Cwm woods to join the A4487 back into Aber. On winter Sunday afternoons when the hikers weren't nearly as numerous, people would kindly stop, unasked, in cars and vans and enquire whether we wanted a lift. But we strode on past farms, isolated houses and the experimental crops in the Plant Breeding Station fields to the main road at the top of Penglais Hill. From there it was downhill all the way back to our bald buns and cheese and apple sandwiches.

Another pleasant summer walk was alongside the northernmost of Aber's rivers, the Rheidol. It was preferable for the weather to have been dry for some weeks, otherwise wellies or hiking boots were needed as the path lay across cow-fields and places where these animals had laid claim to river access where there was more fertilizer than grass. The Rheidol banks were littered with flat, skimming stones, ideal for ten minutes of ducks and drakes competition. Not being serious hikers and therefore not having maps in plastic bags hanging upside down round our necks, or rucksacks, brown corduroy trousers and oiled wool socks tucked into our boots – come to that only sandals really – we usually got lost. But Florence had a survival technique. She'd march up to a tree, walk round it examining the trunk then suddenly proclaim, "That's north! Come on, we must go that way!" and then tramp determinedly off while I meekly followed. At first I thought she was undergoing some mystic process, communing with the tree sprites as it were, until I discovered it was all about moss. The southerly aspect dries up the tree so moss only grows on the north facing side so she maintained. When I investigated a tree it looked equally green all the way round to me, so I left this particular art entirely to my friend. I felt happier with points of the compass via the sun, but half the time there wasn't any.

Sometimes we found a route, sometimes we just reasoned the river was parallel with us and going to Aberystwyth, so aligned our way back more or less with that. On occasion we came to the road and hitch-hiked back to Aber, there being no Sunday buses in that part of the world – locked up like the town's twenty-two or so pubs. Once, we arrived back standing in a farm trailer pulled by a tractor, among the bits of hay, manure, sheep wool and cattle-cake it had held. But as Mam would say, "A second class ride is better than a first class walk!"

Another time we found ourselves in Llanbadarn Fawr, and coming across the pretty little church there, decided we'd go to the service the following week. That Sunday we were hardly in a fit state after our trek, to present ourselves to the Lord, let alone the good church-goers of Llanbadarn. We noted the time of evensong – 6.30 pm and resolved, if it was fine, to cycle over next week. It wasn't, but the succeeding Sunday was, so, faithful to our design, we turned up at the appointed time.

We were greeted at the door by a smiling, ruddy-faced gentleman, with brownish teeth and vocal chords obviously constricted by a stiff, white collar and wearing a tight, navy suit. He smelled of mothballs.

"Oh, hello. Good evening. How are you?" He handed us a prayer-book. It was in Welsh. Not being a true offspring of my maternal grandfather who never attended an English service in his life, I was discomfited.

"Ah, this is in Welsh. Have you got a prayer-book in English please?" I enquired.

"Oh, dear me! Well, yes we have, but the service is in Welsh tonight you see, so we're using the Welsh hymnals. It's the last Sunday of the month you see," he added by way of an explanation.

"Ah!" I replied, sounding enlightened in my complete bafflement. We smiled at each other and he nodded.

"Well, we can't speak Welsh, so there's no point in our coming in really," I explained, "Do you have services in English at all?"

"Oh yes, indeed. It'll be in English next Sunday. It's in Welsh on the last Sunday of the month you see. Or on special occasions. It does say so on our notice board actually." And sure enough it did, in small wording as a translation we hadn't noticed underneath the Welsh.

"Well, look now then. If you can come next week, the service will be in English for you."

"All right then. We'll do that. Ta ta."

It was a pleasant evening. We rode back to Aberystwyth to spend our time in some other unexciting pursuit, it being the day of rest, seriously observed in mid-Wales. The following Sunday was even finer and at 6.15 we were back in Llanbadarn. The same fellow was at the porch. His face fell on seeing us.

"Oh, there you are. Hello. Oh dear, I'm so sorry but it's a Welsh service again tonight. You see..."

"Oh, no!" Florence exclaimed, disappointed to say the least after our efforts to dress up, get the bikes out and cycle a couple of miles, "But you said last week it would be English this week."

"Yes, I know. I'm very sorry, but this is the last Sunday in the month again."

"But it was the last Sunday of the month last week, you said." objected Florence.

"Yes, I know that, but this month has got two last Sundays you see." We didn't see, just looked at each other in baffled incomprehension.

"Well, how can you have a month with two last Sundays in it?" I asked.

The old chap was looking very apologetic and wringing his hands.

"Oh, now then, it's because, do you see, this month has got five Sundays and the service is in Welsh always on the fourth Sunday, and on the last Sunday of the month?"

"And this is the last Sunday of the month," Flor and I chorused.

"Yes, yes indeed. You're right. I didn't realise last week there was going to be another Sunday this month. I thought it would be the first Sunday of next month but that's next week. Oh, dear dear, I'm sorry the service is not in English for you."

So were we. There was nothing for it. We bade our good-byes, retreating to a promise we scarcely believed, of, "It'll definitely be in English next week. Definitely. I can assure you now. Perhaps you can come back next week," – a promise getting fainter as we rode away. If we'd gone, no doubt next week would have been a 'special occasion'. Sadly we never did get to see the inside of Llanbadarn church.

# 19. Good Intentions Thwarted

Not only did you have to be a good Geographer, but a good walker too, to study the subject at Aberystwyth. The Geography department, housed opposite the station, was a good five minutes walk further away from Alex than the main college. There was a lot of competition for places on the course, as at that time, Aber was the only Welsh university offering an Honours degree in this key discipline. Hordes turned up for lectures at the Alexandra Road buildings, especially in Part 1 and every year the degree results list was the longest of any department, even Law, also unique to Aber.

The professor was E.G. Bowen whose text book, *Wales* we had studied at A level. He was typically Welsh – small, dark haired, sallow-skinned, reserved, neat. Coincidentally he had a sister who lived in Trehafod, so I discovered in my first year, two streets behind me in Rheolau Terrace. This was Mrs Williams, known locally as old Mrs Knifey, who used to speak Welsh to my mother in the shop. Apart from being tall, and gaunt as a blade, she could well have been a twin to her brother. Professor Bowen taught us Physical and Welsh Geography and Geomorphology, fast and concisely in the vast, terraced lecture theatre where in fact all Part 1 lectures, apart from Practicals took place, to accommodate the huge numbers. He was barely recognisable outside the lecture room, hiding himself under a trilby and scuttling around Aber like a fifth columnist.

Dr Melvyn Howe, who taught us Economic Geography with reams of statistics to remember, was liked and respected by the students. He had a quick wit and while highly endowed intellectually, was able to operate on the same wave-length as the undergraduates. There was a certain amount of banter in his lectures, 99% of it coming from him, but his lectures were well ordered.

Mr Fogg's classes on the other hand, were riotous. He was an Anthropologist. A solidly built man with a round face, gingery hair and a moustache, there was something vaguely effeminate in his bearing. Though he must have had a huge sense of humour, I never saw him smile. His prevailing expression, purposely cultivated, was of uneasiness, and indeed the students responded to his bizarre individuality. He appeared to invite frolicsome behaviour. Shuffling into the room, he was invariably greeted with whistles, stamping on the wooden floor and mild cheering. This would ·be acknowledged by a casual wave of the arm. He was sometimes late, but no student budged from his seat. They wouldn't miss his classes for a dozen free boxes of Carson's chocolate cream cups, popular at the time. He used slides a lot and as we also needed to take notes, the lights would be flashing on and off like in an electrical storm. The equipment never worked smoothly for Walter Fogg. Whether it had been slightly sabotaged for even more hilarity, was debatable, but he seemed to expect the apparatus to malfunction. He never got angry, would simply 'tut', fold his hands over his tummy, frown at the appliance and sometimes poke it, more in hope than understanding. One of the technically knowledgeable students, or the technician, if he was around, would step forth, to more cheers and stamping, to correct the capricious machinery, then we'd carry on. His classes were probably the most popular in the university. Students who had nothing remotely to do with Geography came to his lectures to witness his eccentricity. There was often standing room only.

One day, at the beginning of a lecture he showed a slide of a scowling native with a substantial bosom and a corpulent belly, entirely naked but for some necklaces and a piece of bone through her nose. "Er... this is a woman," he said to wild laughter, stamping and cheering.

On another occasion in Part 1, he was talking about the physical characteristics of the men of a certain tribe and began to hold forth about their unusually large penises. Two young ladies in the audience from private schools who, no doubt, had hitherto led sheltered lives, rose and pink-cheeked with indignation, walked to the door. They had clearly had enough. Just as they were about to leave, Mr Fogg, in his rather husky voice and dead-pan manner said, "Mmm. I'm afraid you've missed the last train ladies!" The room erupted. His lectures were enormously enjoyable but I don't suppose they ever sent prospective teachers from the training department to learn teaching skills from them. Or on second thoughts, perhaps they did!

One afternoon per week from 2 to 5 pm, we had Practical Meteorology. These classes were taken by an English Northerner, Jim Taylor who explained warm and cold fronts, pressure zones and occlusions. We were given lots of photocopied maps in rapid succession, a series of data, and flamboyantly drew jellyfish rings, bulging this way and that, all over Europe.

Very early on, Mr Taylor explained that he had a research student whose MSc was based on meteorological records – rainfall and temperature – at three points on Pen Dinas, a hill 415 feet high, with a monument and an Iron Age fort on its top. This student was largely dependent, poor fellow, on the help of the First Years for the success of his research, in that the sets of statistics had to be taken daily at a certain time and place and entered in a log-book kept in the loft of Pen Dinas farm. He obviously couldn't go himself every day and this is how Part 1 were to be of, as it turned out, dubious, assistance. Naturally we needed to be shown where these strategic points were, so instead of Pracs, half the class set off on an early October afternoon, on foot, via Trefechan Bridge over the Rheidol river for Pen Dinas, south of Aberystwyth and west of Penparcau Road. The rest were going the following week.

"Wear strong shoes and don't over-exert yourself beforehand," warned Mr Taylor. "It's a fair way and you don't want to be tired before you start."

From past experience, Florence, Margaret Algate, Evelyn Jones and I knew that "a fair way", from the mouth of a Geographer, meant a very long walk, but we looked forward to the ramble as a welcome change from classes.

It took an hour to reach the little, white-washed farm at the foot of Pen Dinas where we were shown the log-book – a curly-paged, much-thumbed, swollen and rather disappointingly ordinary exercise book with a pencil attached with a bit of string – and the columns for the statistics to be obtained from the east, south and west meteorological stations on the hill.

"Now, it's necessary to get around in an hour," Jim Taylor was emphatic. "These statistics are recorded between 2.30 and 3.30 every afternoon, so you must set off from here at 2.30 and be at the last base before half three. I can't emphasise enough the importance of that. All right?"

We nodded and looked earnest.

"The science of meteorology is a precise one and timing is of the essence. Now, we have to walk at a fair pace to get round all three stations and take the readings. No dawdling from here on!"

Margaret raised her eyes to heaven, "Oh Gawd, there he goes again! 'Fair pace' means 'run' I expect. My feet are not half aching in these tough shoes my mother insisted I bring. But I suppose we must try to keep up!"

At that stage she fancied John (Westgarth) Dodd ("His middle name is Westgarth, you know. Isn't that swanky?" and "John Dodd says this, John Dodd says that"), a keen student always at the front and she didn't so much want to seem eager, as to keep him in sight.

We followed a steadily climbing, sheep path and in twenty minutes the front of the column, mostly men, including Terry Hole from Porth County who had legs three yards long, halted, while the rest of the panting line reached the spot, a wooden perforated box and a calibrated jam jar under a bit of chicken wire. We gathered around the lecturer who looked anxiously at his watch. "Right then. Not bad. We should do it. The first base is not difficult to find. Just near the path here. The thermometer's in there." He noted down the temperature on paper then picked up the jar, entered the rain level, threw the water away, replaced everything and was off. We trotted behind in single file, restored after the brief pause and encouraged by the shallower gradient. Approximately twenty minutes later we were at Base 2, looking south. This was harder to locate, some yards above the path. But how would we know where to stop?

"There are a few indications," Jim Taylor pointed out, "That large, rectangular stone there, and if you look south you should just be in line with the Isolation Hospital down there. See, that big, white building on the northern face of that slope. Other side of the Ystwyth."

We could just make out a white blob among the greenery as we balanced precariously on the steep hillside among the ferns and tufts of grass.

"It's nice up here," Evelyn Jones admired the landscape, "There's a lovely view of the coast and the valley down there. It's so peaceful. Mind you, I wouldn't like to be up here on my own in the dark, would you?"

"Oh yes I would! Why not?" said Margaret mockingly, "Especially when it's raining as well, and foggy. You'd have a nice drop of water to record in the jam jar then." Evelyn looked at her, frowning slightly, unsure of whether she was serious.

But, having performed the same operation with the box and jam jar, Jim Taylor was off at a cracking pace, taking advantage of the now downhill path.

"Cor, you could easily sprain your ankle or miss your footing here and go rolling down the hill," said Flor.

"Yes, it's a dangerous sort of place to send students to," I agreed.

Well before the hour, we arrived at the last, westerly station which again was a bit tricky to find, near a jutting piece of rock of which there were several.

"You see," said Jim Taylor, "it's not impossible to get around in the hour. We've done it today in a big crowd with eight minutes to spare. OK then. I'll put a sheet with dates on the main notice-board for you to sign when you're able to do the circuit. In pairs please. I don't want you going on your own – for obvious reasons. Now, I'm just going to record today's data in the log-book and you're free to go. Thanks everyone. Well done!"

Florence and I signed up for an afternoon in early November.

"I hope it'll be fine," said Florence. A passing male student overheard and paused. "Ah! Signing up for the Pen Dinas ramble, are you?"

"Ramble!" I echoed, "Race, more like!"

"Na!" he scoffed, "You don't have to run round that mountain, specially not if it's raining. Most people just go up to the farm, have a fag in the loft or a kip in the hay, invent some statistics and leave it at that," Flor and I were shocked.

"But what about the student's research?" I asked.

"Well," he said, "Temperatures don't vary all that much from one day to the next in mid-autumn. Just take note if it rains in the night and morning before you go, then all you have to do is jot down something like the other figures."

Then, seeing our still concerned expressions, "Well, you can go round if you want to of course. If you like punishing yourselves. But personally..." He shook his head. "Still, you do what you want. Good luck!" He grinned and went on his way.

Our afternoon arrived, grey, cold but dry. We set off after lunch, resolved to do the thing properly and found the route to the farm with only a modicum of error. Since we had time, we checked the log-book in the loft. It was up to date.

"Right then?" I asked Flor. "Ready for the race?"

Red-faced, puffing and feeling decidedly damp at the hair-line and arm-pits, we reached and found the first base with no trouble, took down the information, threw away the rain-water, replaced the material. Twenty five minutes later, Flor, checking her watch said, "I think we must have passed the second place Mary."

"Well, I've been looking out for that big piece of rock but I haven't seen it."

"What about that other point of reference? A line between the monument and the white building it was, then up from the path."

We both looked down at the Ystwyth valley. You couldn't make out the river in the misty air, let alone the Isolation Hospital.

"Oh, great! What are we supposed to do now?" I felt defeated.

"Just carry on looking I suppose."

"But we haven't got time. We're late as it is. We're not going to get to number 3 in the hour even if we run all the way and we'll have to make up figures for this one like that bloke said."

The path was muddy and slippery. Florence grumbled, "Huh, I'm not risking my neck running, for anybody. If that research chap wanted statistics from a daft place like this, he should come and collect them himself!"

"But he couldn't come up here every day himself Flor. Fair does! Once in a life-time is too much for me!"

"Oh well, he shouldn't have chosen such a mad scheme then."

We were fifteen minutes late getting to where number 3 should have been but wasn't. Jutting lumps of rock were everywhere but none near a wooden box with meteorological impedimenta inside.

"Oh, this is hopeless!" I confirmed. "We might as well pack it in!" Which we did.

So the cynical student's advice prevailed. We might just as well have had a chat or a chocolate in the loft for all the use we'd been. Not one of the other first year Geographers we spoke to had had total success on Pen Dinas. Some had completely forgotten to go while others had gone on the wrong day. I imagined the anonymous student working out his erroneous statistics to the third decimal point and applying the standard deviation principle and felt awfully guilty. I hope he got his MSc. His research though must have been the most unsound ever produced in the history of the university!

Because it wasn't my main concern, I found Geography enjoyable. It was the third of my subjects and all I had to do was pass the exam at the end of Part 1. I didn't even need to pass well, as in French for example, in which I wanted to specialize.

In the autumn term we were to go on field trips. The first of these was to Devil's Bridge. It was a crisp, sunny Wednesday afternoon and we set off with our notebooks and 1 inch OS map of Aberystwyth which cost 4/- new or 2/6 second-hand give-away from Self Help. Several coaches to transport the masses of first year students, hired from Howells, a little firm in Ponterwyd – it had to be little as Ponterwyd was only a small village itself – stood waiting for us outside the station. We piled on and were soon on the A4120 climbing up the beautiful Rheidol valley on its south side, with panoramic views across Aberystwyth.

"Aren't they kind in the Geography department to take us on these trips," mused Evelyn Jones, "And we don't have to pay. Not like school. You had to pay for Geog trips in school."

"Well, it's not exactly for sight-seeing you know Evelyn," Flor remarked.

"You're telling me!" chipped in Margaret Algate, "We're supposed to take piles of notes. Anne Richards from school, you know, couple of years ahead of us, she told me. She's in Carp. Said there'll be an exam question on these trips."

"When?" Florence wanted to know. "Which exams?"

"Well the Christmas ones I suppose," answered Margaret.

However, unpleasant thoughts of exams were cast aside as we gazed at the magnificent scenery. The Stag, a curious scar left by lead mine workings was pointed out to us on the opposite side of the valley by Mr Harold Carter, a handsome lecturer who didn't teach Part 1 but who was on our coach. He indicated the Rheidol Falls, then further on more evidence of old lead mines on the steep valley slope. The road turned and suddenly we were faced with the wild scenery of Devil's Bridge where the Mynach river joins up with the Rheidol after falling some 600 feet. Once off the coach we attempted to take notes from Dr Howe's explanations of how the seething river water had scooped out great chasms or pot-holes in the rock then plunged down another 100 feet. Some were more successful than others at note-taking. This depended on your proximity to the speaker. Three feet away and his words were drowned by the racket the water was making in its delirious quest for sea level. I gave it up as a bad job, though I did catch something about Aberystwyth Grits, but wasn't sure whether he was referring to we students or some species of rock. I couldn't read my writing anyway what with trying to look at what was being pointed out, trying to balance the notebook in my hand and being jostled in the throng. Then I dropped my pencil which rolled off under a few hundred student feet and probably ended up in the gorge. Anyway it meant the end of note-taking, so I simply enjoyed the impressive scenery as we walked down the precipitous Jacob's Ladder steps to the Devil's Bridge, the lowest and probably the oldest of the three bridges constructed over the cataracts and the great ravine, black with age.

We returned to Aber via the road from Rhayader. From Devil's Bridge to Ponterwyd, the Rheidol has carved the longest and deepest gorge in Wales. More waterfalls, chasms, pot-holes, old lead mines and Swiss-type vistas with glorious 'New England in the Fall' leaf colours. Geographically speaking, Harold Carter kept mentioning 'glacial diversion' but by this time we had relaxed and were enjoying the ride back via the road north of the Rheidol. It was a memorable field excursion even if I was vaguely bothered by my lack of written information. I resolved to borrow someone's notes and copy up.

A fortnight later on a very blustery afternoon, we were off to Borth on the coaches, this time to see how the sea currents had created and built up a four-mile-long sand bar extending well beyond the estuary of the Dovey river whose mouth is considerably narrowed, and sheltering an extensive marsh. At low tide one may see the remains of a submerged forest and appreciate the evidence of the encroachment of the sea.

We got off the coaches and walked wearily for miles, this time in rather a tedious landscape, sand stinging our faces and any exposed bit of flesh. Again, note-taking suffered because of the gale, blown sand, difficulty of hearing and the fatigue of trying to maintain an upright stance in the tempest.

Finally we had a field trip, following the Ystwyth river this time, to Tregaron with its peat bog, the largest in Wales, and on the return trip a detour to Strata Florida which, apart from the ubiquitous lead mine, seemed to me more historical with the remains of its ancient abbey, than geographical. Still I was at university to be educated, so showed interest.

I had now, like most of the others in the scrum, abandoned notes, although this last field-trip was the most propitious for that art – no noisy water, no wailing hurricane blowing sand into head orifices. It was a balmy, Indian-summer day, the bog wasn't making any noise, the abbey was deathly tranquil, the lecturer booming, and there was more space. Whether we were fewer I don't know but the participating legions had plenty of room.

The Christmas exams arrived. There was no mention of field trips in the Geography revision list and all went well in that quarter. I did have some trouble with English though, having a low mark in Anglo-Saxon, probably after Professor Gwyn Jones was unimpressed by my attempt to conjugate the definite article as a verb. For some reason too, Mr Earnshaw had failed me on his paper, the twentieth century novel. This puzzled me as I thought I'd done enough to pass there. All was explained when I sought him out in January.

"Well!" he pointed out indignantly in his direct, no-nonsense, Yorkshire manner, "You wrote six sides on *Nostromo*! I don't read more than three at Christmas. Bound to be a load of tergiversation!" I blinked.

"Oh dear, I'm sorry," I said, "If I'd known, I'd only have written a few sides."

He smiled, or rather bared his teeth mischievously.

"If you can't answer the question adequately in three sides of foolscap paper, you don't deserve to pass anyway." However, my failure there didn't seem to matter.

But as far as Geography went, all was satisfactory. The field trips became a pleasant memory as a congenial few hours away from lectures getting acquainted with Cardiganshire.... Until the summer exams. Sitting one fine, sunny afternoon in the Exam Hall, yachts with bright-hued sails darting about on the glinting sea not a hundred yards away, I stared horrified at a question inviting me to 'Compare the geomorphological characteristics of the upper and lower reaches of the Rheidol valley with particular reference to those you have seen in the field. Illustrate your answer with sketch maps', and 'Explain the development of the Dovey estuary and how the sea has affected the topography of the area', again with the aforementioned sketch maps. I did my best, cobbling together some pathetic answers from pure, incomplete, rudimentary recall. My best wasn't good enough. I was 'referred' in Geography. That meant that, together with a dozen others, including my hockey-playing friend Brian Shears from Whitchurch, Myra Evans from Pontypridd, Betty Jones of my Alex 'family', from Wrexham, glamorous Bernice Jones from Gowerton, Anne Morgan, beloved of Anthony Green and Jean Rogers, another Alex acquaintance, my summer vacation would be spent, not only re-revising Part 1 Geography and field trips in particular, but would be abbreviated by my having to present myself for re-examination at Aber the following September. As I was quite keen on spending another two years at Aberystwyth, I directed my efforts into acquiring the most comprehensive field trip notes and maps which I learned totally, so they were etched on my brain for years. I managed to pass the September hurdle. Ironically, no question was asked on field trips!

# 20. The Ravages of Rag Week

Rag Week was the hedonistic highlight of the year. Lectures were suspended for the latter part of the week and it was an excuse for students to do all sorts of silly things in the name of charity. The townspeople probably dreaded the second week of February, continually pestered as they were to put their hands from pockets to collecting boxes jingled at them by students in various outfits, clowns', Walt Disney-type animals or other outrageous clothes and painted faces to match. Sometimes, students, especially girls, were conspicuous by what they were not wearing. A favourite undress for males was two halves of a coconut shell over the upper half and a grass skirt over the lower (usually covering florid, skimpy underpants), the whole topped by a face made-up to a bright copper colour with equally embellished turquoise eyes, false Miss Piggy eyelashes and iridescent lips. The rugby team, or young men composed almost entirely of neck, favoured these costumes for a dance-type routine in the Rag Show whereby they pretended to be ballerinas, clumping heavily on the trembling stage in football boots.

Since Rag Week came round in mid-February, the weather was not always sympathetic to these various states of disrobement, but students were prepared to risk pneumonia for the cause. Fun and horseplay also played a major persuasive role, and the more audacious the costume, the more money was collected. People approached by lively, noisy, exuberant creatures, to all evidence from another planet, were the centre of attention and could hardly, being so in the public eye, refuse a donation or purchase of the rag magazine. This was a compendium of foolish or filthy jokes and silly cartoons which nobody wanted but everyone bought – price at least 2/- the cover proclaimed.

Teams of students in fancy or normal dress, but always sporting the red and green scarf, were dispatched on selling trips in cars and a freely loaned coach from Howells, Ponterwyd, to towns around mid-Wales to persuade their residents to part with their cash. To judge from the amounts collected, people in soporific places where life was repetitious and humdrum, welcomed these annual raids because they contributed generously.

Money was raised in all kinds of ways. Pedestrians were encouraged to place coins in a line along the edge of the pavement, 'The Mile of Pennies'. One year a circle of coins was successfully completed going from Galloways' bookshop, down Great Darkgate Street, along Terrace Road and back along Marine Terrace. Another year, a continuous line of coins was attempted from North Bar (the kicking variety) to South Bar. Unfortunately there was a spring tide and a lively wind. It was reasonably remunerative as far as the Crazy Golf. Beyond the college buildings it petered out for want of passers-by; the middle section was strong and silver by dint of the affluent Aberystwyth middle-aged and retired, braving the February weather to walk their dogs, but the part on Victoria Terrace kept being washed into the road by the sea and run over by passing cars.

Some students were required as appealers to good will on behalf of the selected charity. "I wonder if I might appeal to your good will to support the West Wales Hospital Trust for Contagious Diseases / The Society for the Preservation of the Red Kite in Mid Wales / The League for the Protection of Abandoned Babies, by putting a coin or two, three or four down in our line? Although it's called a mile of pennies, it doesn't have to be copper...Notes, even, could be weighted down with coins" – the latter tacked on as a hopeful addendum. Others were needed to guard the line from little boys, rarely spotted in Aberystwyth, who appeared from nowhere by magic when they surely should have been in school, and who kept telling you how much they'd counted and asking what it was for.

Small boy: Cor, you've got a lotta money 'ere, 'aven' you?

Student: Mmmm.

Small boy: I counted about £10.4.6 from that shelter down b'there.

Student: Oh yeah.

Small boy: Are you goin' to be 'ere all day then?

Student: Mmmm. P'raps. (Then, seeing the kid taking too great an interest in a half crown coin and moving in vigilantly) Shouldn't you be in school today? It's not the holidays.

Small boy: I'm bad.

Student: (unsympathetically) You look all right to me.

Small boy: I got a cold.

Student: You ought to be indoors then. In the warm.

Small boy: Who are you collecting all this money for?

Student: Charity. Not for little boys anyway. Look, isn't it time for you to go home for your dinner?

Small boy: Na, my mum's in work. I got money for chips. I can stay an' help you if you like. I'm eleven. (The kind offer made despite child-strangulation looks from the be-scarved young woman)

Student: No, it's all right thanks. You go an' have your chips.

There were auctions of goods donated by the town traders, street shows with lively music and drama, the Rag Procession with Miss Fresher and her retinue prominent on one float, and the various college departments providing other decorated floats vying for the first prize of a green and red rosette and another excuse for a celebratory drink. One year there was a soap-box sprint at 10.30 am with a Funeral Procession at 11 for the victims of the previous event. Students turned up in large numbers to watch, fascinated, the Yard of Ale Drinking Contest, and give vociferous support to a drinker from their department. Hywel Ceri Jones valiantly represented the French department one year, probably getting in some practice for his obligatory year in France. Many looked groggy or stupefied or both after this particular exercise and their clothes gave off beery fumes for the rest of their university days.

The Bun Eating Contest was another favourite. Miss Fresher, no doubt feeling public-spirited in her high profile role, was a contestant one year. She starved herself for a week, and won, slowly masticating her way through fifteen or so fresh, buttered, currant spiced, to great acclaim. Sadly though it turned Miss Fresher into Miss Fatter. 'Miggs' Morris's stomach was stretched, she always felt hungry and consequently put on many surplus pounds. It didn't help to live in Alex where plenty of food was readily available. It took several terms and much exercise to get rid of the extra poundage. Happily in the interim she still had her pretty face if rather more of it in the cheek and chin.

Kidnapping was a choice, if unofficial, money-raiser. All sorts of things were purloined from people to portfolios and the pantaloons of the Union President. One lecturer lost the roof-rack off his car in Laura Place, spotted, parked, by an opportunist group of students. When he emerged from the Economics department, he drove off without noticing it had gone. It was retrieved for a pound after a phone call. Another young lecturer in the English department stopped to talk to one of his students in the main quad. He put his brief case down to indicate something on a piece of paper – an imprudent move at such a time of year. It was smoothly swooped on and swept up as though by a professional cutpurse. At the end of the conversation, the man went to pick up his case. There ensued a series of puzzled looks, sudden head movements, twists and turns, short, rapid walkabouts and a scanning of the quad and balconies as though the case might have developed legs and scarpered of its own accord, before the realisation that Rag Week had reared its bagging, begging head once again and a donation would be necessary for its return.

Possibly the most daring kidnap I heard of was one, a few years later involving a national institution. So outraged was the Establishment that a *Times* editorial was dedicated to the castigation of "irresponsible students". It was a few weeks before the Boat Race. Some bold students had decided it would be a major coup to abduct the rudders of the two boats. One originated from Cambridge where the offensive started, so knew exactly where to go. Amazingly the boat-house containing the precious skiff was unlocked and unguarded. It was a matter of minutes to detach the rudder and be off to Oxford. Here, the lie of the land was not familiar to anyone, but casually strolling along the bank of the Thames, one of the intrepid band enquired of an old fellow weeding the river path where the boat-houses were.

"Oh, that one on your left has got the Isis boat and the Oxford boat is in the one further on. Come to have a look at it have you? It's going to be the winner this year, no doubt about it." he obligingly told them. Again it was not a difficult task to part boat from rudder. They nonchalantly exchanged a few more pleasantries with the weeder on the return walk, then got back to their car and headed for Aberystwyth. However, the Authorities were not amused. They unsportingly refused to pay the £50 ransom, demanding the return of their rudders forthwith. On that occasion the Deaf Ladies Bowling League and The Association for the Promulgation of OAP Sports (APOAPS) did not benefit.

At times Aber were the victims of kidnapping by others, notably our nearest rivals, Lampeter. In the fifties Lampeter still retained an aura of the Theological College and one did not suspect them capable of the dirty tricks that all the other colleges played. Apart from that there weren't many of them. There were no women there then and the Lampeter men often turned up at our Saturday night Hops in a state ranging from merry to paralytic drunk, so I suppose it was evident they were not all saints and seraphs.

Once they lured, then stole, Miss Fresher the day before the Rag Parade at which her presence was vital. A ransom was demanded by Lampeter for her reinstatement in time for the Parade. A gang, including her boy-friend, who had had wind of her whereabouts went to Lampeter to rescue her. Not knowing which room she occupied at the Black Lion, they threw gravel, in the early hours, at a few windows chosen at random, with no successful response, until chased away by irate guests threatening to call the police. Aber on that occasion paid up and Miss Fresher adorned the glamour float in the usual way.

Another time the Lampeter priests-to-be devised quite an elaborate (for those years) scam. They got hold of a small removal van, dressed up in workman's overalls, and with official-looking paperwork, presented themselves at the Union saying they had come to collect the grand piano for its annual service. There were music students present who must have known that pianos do not need to be removed to be tuned, but that a blind man arrives to perform the operation on the spot. Struggling to manoeuvre the piano up the steps from the lower floor, a Lampeter lad asked, "Could you give us a hand here? This 'un weighs a ton and the last thing we want to do is drop it!" (Indeed, or they'd be the ones paying for repairs!)

"Yeah, OK. Come on lads, let's give these boys a hand here!" several young men unstintingly gave of their strength. Instructions, "Up a bit on the left, now back a bit to get through this doorway. Whoa! Gently! It's stuck on this side. Right! OK now" followed and the piano was successfully moved by Aber and disguised Lampeter men out of the Union on to the van and driven away. Another one up to Lampeter, but at least the piano wasn't imminently needed on a Procession float so the ransom wasn't speedily forthcoming.

Dances abounded during Rag Week, the grandest being the mid-week University Ball in the King's Hall with some famous band to play. The week ended with a Fancy Dress Ball. Not that the majority of students had worn anything other for most of the week anyway, fancy dress had become a symbol of mid-February extrovert youth, strange behaviour and the rattle of collecting tins shaken on their cord handles. Some didn't bother to change out of what they had been wearing all week, but now it was an excuse for young men and women to get close to each other and in view of some of the scanty costumes, closer than normal for a dance situation. Themes were announced for these romps such as, 'A Dance called Fred', 'Hubert and Henrietta meet Porky Pig', 'Bits and Pieces'. Nobody could make much sense of them even if they were intended to. Most students could lay their hands on a sheet though and turned up in it, tied at significant points, to represent phantoms, Greek / Arabic / Indian potentates, glamorous models, Druids, bards and Kings. Bath towels, again readily to hand, were much used, and again strategically pinned and with appropriate

185

make-up transformed their wearers into Romans in togas, Vikings, beach lovelies and Scots people (if you had a tartan towel). Cowboys and pirates abounded simply by donning a pair of wellingtons, a mother's wedding hat, an eye patch, a check shirt, neckerchief and waistcoat. It must be said though that most didn't know who or what they were. By the end of the evening, a lot didn't know where they were.

It was a different matter for the Pyjama Dance, an afternoon event in the Pier Ballroom, in 1957 anyway, as bed-wear was essential to gain entry. This resulted in many young men appearing in boxer shorts displaying messages and pictures of varying impudence; one or two spirited young sprigs turned up in briefs. ("Well, I don't normally wear anything in bed, but I thought it'd be too cold to come starkers"). Girls' attire ranged from cute Baby Doll sets to solid-looking flannel nighties covering every ounce of flesh and which surely must have clothed the wearer's ancestors or been borrowed for the occasion from the Welsh Folk Museum.

The more serious side of Rag Week was the Eisteddfod when the four constituent colleges were in competition and held in Aber, Bangor, Cardiff and Swansea in consecutive years. Aberystwyth had a fine reputation for music and habitually won the Blue Riband event of the eisteddfod, the choral competition, even if overall success wasn't always ours. At that time the composer William Mathias was doing post-graduate research under Professor Ian Parrott.

For months beforehand, students having been urged to join the Choral Union, weekly practised the set piece for an hour, a practice which became nightly during the week preceding the event. Under the direction of the enthusiastic Rowland Jones, aided by his successor Roy Bohana, I made myself hoarse singing 'For Unto Us a Child is Born', only to discover a few days before the competition that I'd be playing hockey in the inter-collegiate match when the choral competition was taking place.

It seemed the entire student population of Aber removed itself for the day to the town of the college hosting the eisteddfod. There were not only eisteddfod competitors but sports teams as well crowding on to the Ponterwyd coaches. At least, in my first year we rode to Bangor in Mr Howells's vehicles, but because several of the coaches had difficulty making it back to Aber after the intervention of Bangor students introducing sugar into the petrol tanks and no doubt hoping for a big bang, we afterwards went by rail. Rampaging students have difficulty in access for train sabotage, kept as they are in stations and reached only via ticket offices, collectors and guards. The decision-makers must have thought train mischief was beyond the wit of the average student. So we all got on one very long train for our trip to Cardiff the next year and were able to return without mishap other than a few lost students. One-upmanship wasn't all on the Bangor side however, as not only were street-name signs missing in the neighbouring area of the Bangor campus as they were all in Aberystwyth, but there were no plaques or room numbers on the doors in the university either as someone had packed his screwdriver along with his football boots. He made a lot of money for the Aged Persons Marathon Running Club too, selling the prizes off in the coach when it managed to get going back to Aber.

The trouble with the Rag extravaganza was that after the exhilaration of the comparative emancipation from responsibility it engendered, it took several more weeks to get back into the work ethic. One needed a holiday to wind down. After Rag Week one year, not being patient enough to wait for the Easter vacation, I decided to make up an excuse to go home for the weekend and surprise my parents. I didn't have any special commitments and had recently been scared to sleeplessness by the film *The Kraken Wakes*, itself exacerbated by the shuddering pier on a rough night. The college authorities naturally didn't like people disappearing off to various bits of the UK during term-time, so one had to have a convincing excuse. Mine was that my aged grandmother (who had quit this life when I was three) was very poorly, not a complete lie if one thinks of it in the cosmic context. Non-existent relatives seemed to be the basis for absentee excuses. At least I wasn't trapped into giving the reason a lad in the French class did, desirous of being home for his girl-friend's birthday three weeks away and anxious to get permission settled. Not having properly thought out his plan of modest deceit, when asked, "Why do you need to go home in three weeks?", he unguardedly, rashly replied, "My uncle's very ill and I...er...I have to be home for the funeral."

As it took nearly all day to get from Aberystwyth to the Rhondda, and as, from Bridgend, I unwisely caught the bus that tours south Wales before getting to Pontypridd, slowly, grindingly, visiting village after outlying country village, I arrived home well into the evening, to be greeted by my immediately worried mother and mildly surprised father.

"Oh! Oh! Mary! There's Mary!" exclaimed wide-eyed Mam looking up from her darning over the tops of her glasses. "Well, there's a surprise! Is everything all right? What you doing home? We weren't expecting you for another three weeks. Have you had anything to eat? Oh dear, your bed's not aired."

After I'd explained I merely wanted to come home for a couple of days' break and they had mentally ascertained that I hadn't been expelled, wasn't in disgrace, debt or pregnant, and after Mam had insisted on rustling up some hot food, we settled down to a typical late fifties evening, having a chat round the fire, drinking several cups of tea and listening to the nine o'clock news.

Having been brought up on a farm, Mam was an enthusiastic advocate of good, plain food. She made all the cake eaten in the house, mainly rhubarb, apple, plum and gooseberry tarts and fruit cake. "Oh, we can't abide that ol' shop cake. Jack won't eat it you see!" she'd proudly say. Foreign food, lasagne, risotto, paella, moussaka, chow mein, curry, like foreign holidays wasn't then widespread. We ate bacon for breakfast, beef, lamb or pork, hot on Sundays, cold on Mondays, chops on Wednesdays, smoked haddock on Fridays and hake and chips on Saturdays. The other days were filled in with mutton cawl, beef stew, steak and kidney, boiled ham, pea soup, sausages, salad (tinned salmon, tomatoes, cucumber, jibbons and lettuce) and chicken for Christmas. At that time too, Mam, (though my father who'd eat anything put in front of him was always the reason given), had taken a dislike to factory bread and went through the performance of making her own. "That ol' bought bread goes stale after only one day and it's all crumbs!". She had an earthenware bowl in which she'd vigorously attack the bouncy dough, pounding and beating it, really enjoying herself giving it what for, then put it in the hottest place in the house, to rise – sometimes in the airing cupboard, sometimes in the side oven if the fire was low.

Eleven o'clock arrived and after the chores of the day and the excitement of my unexpected arrival, Mam was ready for bed. Earlier she'd put two glazed stone, hot, sand bottles in my bed to air it. Feeling I too needed welcome oblivion sooner than later, I went upstairs. My pyjamas, normally left on my pillow had obviously been removed for washing so I went to fetch them from the airing cupboard. Drowsily I opened the cupboard door. I wasn't drowsy for long though as a huge, whitish mass of some unknown, hot, soft, spongy substance sprang at me from inside, spilling over my legs before I could perform a backwards standing long jump. Images of *The Kraken Wakes* scurried through my mind as with an involuntary scream I beat a hasty retreat away from this multiplying, mutant frogspawn attacking me. Mam appeared, bare-foot on the landing in nightie, curlers and no teeth. "Oh dear dear, what's the matter? Why are you shouting?"

"Oh Mam, there's something horrible in there, coming out of the airing cupboard!"

"What?" She looked at me in wonder, then suddenly, clearly realising something was amiss, raised her arms and ran into the bathroom crying, "Oh no! My dough! Hell's Bells, the dough for my bread!" then seeing it gleefully spread on the floor, "Oh look, it's all spoilt. It's no good now! Oh damn! Dammit!"

The dough, forgotten because of me, had happily trebled in size in the heat, but now, on escape, lay deflated and punctured at our feet. Needless to say, Dad and I were very happy to eat crusty baker's bread that weekend but my mother was full of sorrow for her lost dough and refused to eat any bread. "Aw, I can't make you nice sandwiches to go back to Aberystwyth now. You'll have to have that ol' stale bread. Oh, there's disappointed I am! Next time you come home, you tell us first, so we can get organised mind!"

# 21. Reluctant Exile

In what should have been the third and final year of the degree course, language students were packed off abroad, so I didn't make too many unexpected trips home that year. None in fact, only returning once from France at Christmas from the September to July.

In school I'd had a pen-pal for a few years, Marie-Thérèse who lived in Angers in the lower Loire area, and though we'd never met, I'd received pamphlets and photographs from her of the beautiful region with its amazing river, fascinating castles, troglodyte houses and towns and villages sprinkled with vineyards. I decided that was where I'd like to spend my time in France. Marie-Thérèse and I had not written, apart from the desultory postcard, for a decade or so, and not wanting to land myself on her doorstep, I applied for an assistante's post at Tours, some seventy-five miles higher up the valley. The plan was to initiate a new, more adult correspondence, to re-kindle the friendship so that at least I'd know someone, have an ally in the foreign country. We'd been advised not to apply for Paris as eighty per cent of candidates put Paris as their number one choice. French spoken in this area of France, the favourite region of French kings from the sixteenth century, was also supposed to be the purest in the world. So Tours it was. Florence rather fancied the Loire valley as well so applied vaguely for this part of France.

In our second year we also shared a room but had moved from Bal to Alex – still at the back though, with the stimulating view of the road and disused quarry. I'd recently received my appointment in France – '*Vous êtes nommée assistante au Collège Technique à Tours, Indre et Loire*' – so France was very much on my mind. One night about a month into the summer term I had a vivid dream about Florence in a school in a Loire valley town called Blois, a town which I'd seen on the map but knew very little about other than it being in the direction of Paris from Tours. There she was supervising a noisy press of girls, trying to establish calm and order as they collected their lunch. "*Un peu d'ordre et de calme s'il vous plaît*" she was saying.

I woke up and, hearing Flor stirring in her bed across the room, said, "Flor, guess what? I've just dreamt you're going to Blois next year."

190

"Oh yeah," she replied sleepily and totally uninterested, "That's nice," turned over and started snoring. I went back to sleep and had another dream about Florence in Blois, this time something involving a swimming pool. In the morning I told her, "That school you're going to in Blois has got a swimming pool."

"Wha? What school? What you talking about?"

"You know," I said, "I told you in the night. I dreamed you were going to a school in Blois."

"Oh!" She blinked. "Oh yeah, I vaguely remember you saying something in the night. That was it was it? Blois eh! Where's that exactly?"

At breakfast Frances Jones collected the mail for the table. She handed Florence an official-looking letter. Gillian, who'd also received her placement to a school in Fontainebleau, took an interest in Flor's letter.

"That looks like the letter from the DES telling you where you're going, Flor. Mine was in an envelope like that."

Florence read it then looked at me frowning, "Gosh! I don't believe this!"

"What's it say then?" I asked.

"Is it about your school in France?" Gill wanted to know.

"Yes," slowly answered Florence, "It says '*Vous êtes nommée assistante au Collège Moderne à Blois, Loir et Cher*'."

"Well that's good. You applied for the Loire Valley didn't you?" asked Gill, "Aren't you pleased?"

"Yes, yes. But it's creepy. Mary dreamed last night I'd be going to Blois. Twice! And here it is!"

"Oh that's weird that is," said Betty Jones, making a face and finding the incident disagreeable. The whole table was taking an interest now and looking at me in an odd way.

"We've got a clairvoyant among us!" exclaimed Tessa

"Oh Mary, d'you know what's going to win the Derby? I could just do with a safe bet. I'm broke and there's at least six weeks of the term to go," Nan joked.

There was a certain amount of teasing but some were disturbed by the psychic element, attributing a spookiness to the whole business. I felt it was just coincidence but a few times in unsettled circumstances I've experienced similar strange affinities. and wondered whether the paranormal is to be scoffed at. Unfortunately I've never foreseen anything useful like the football pools score draws or the winners of the Irish Sweepstake.

It was a wrench to have to leave Aberystwyth for a year, a sentiment I hadn't expected to feel when I'd first arrived there and indeed was to prove small *pommes de terre* compared with the heartache when leaving for the very last time. However, the prospect of a year abroad was beguiling even if unknown territory. The only problem was, the closer it came the less I wanted to go!

Towards the end of the summer which Florence and I had mostly spent travelling daily to Cardiff from the Rhondda to check exam marks at the WJEC in Cathedral Road for £5 per week (riches indeed!), we collected year-long visas from the French consulate in Cardiff Docks, had numerous photographs, including profiles taken to satisfy the requirements of the French police and Immigration, and set off towards the end of September for a four day course in the Sorbonne in Paris on how to be an *assistant(e)*. We were told helpful things such as not to have a Scots accent when giving dictations to French kids because the words 'world', 'girl' and 'man' for example would be written as, 'wurruld', 'gurrul' and 'monn' and French children had no idea what these were. Useful sentences to help children phonetically were, 'Around the rugged rocks the ragged rascals ran' and 'This is the thing to wear to the theatre on Thursdays' to hone pronunciations foreign to them. Never mind that we had difficulty saying these phrases ourselves, French children would cope. I mentally checked I still knew, 'Peter Piper picked a peck of pickled pepper.' which would no doubt encourage their plosives and as an extra tongue-between-the-teeth-and-blow practice, 'The Leith police dismisseth us'. Then armed with a page of songs and a set of tourist pamphlets on *La Région des Lacs, Les Midlands, Londres, Le Pays de Galles* etc, I set forth for Tours.

The Aber French class of '55 was liberally scattered all over the country, Margaret Donovan in Gap in the Alps, her friend Wendy Collis with the champagne in Epinal, Merle Picton in Béziers, Hywel Ceri in Lorient, Peter Williams Toulouse, Howard Young Albi, Margaret Hatton in Rennes, Anne Tucker in Argelès Gazost from where she never permanently returned, David Arthur Phillips somewhere in Brittany and the others in equally far flung locations. It was as though someone had scattered split peas over a map of France. Where each had come to rest represented a British French undergraduate of 1957. Some split peas clearly landed on the same spot as I found that I had a companion *assistante*, Margaret Sanderson from Darlington and Sheffield University at the *Collège Technique* with me. Later we discovered a Robert Miller from Bournemouth via London University at the *Lycée des Garçons*.

As usual, similar to most of the embryonic relationships in my life, that with the *Collège Technique* was inauspicious. However, with this type of beginning, things can only get better, When I'd initially received my placement, I pondered, reasonably I thought, following the instruction to contact the school, "Ah, a *Collège Technique* will surely have a headmaster, so wrote to 'Monsieur le Directeur'" Unbeknown to me, as it didn't mention this on my official letter, I had been appointed to the *Collège Technique de Jeunes Filles* which, naturally, had a headmistress. There was a separate Technical School for both sexes in Tours. Eventually I received an agreeable but vague, worrying sort of letter from M. Charpentier, *Directeur,* to the effect that he hadn't been informed I was coming to his school, but it was a pleasant surprise even so, and welcome.

A week before the off, I had a frigid, formal letter from a Madame Helle (appropriate name I thought considering the tone of the missive!), *Directrice* of the *CT de Jeunes Filles* demanding, once I'd deciphered the handwriting, to know what was happening?, was I coming, as appointed to her school?, why hadn't I written as instructed?, and it wasn't her place to get in touch with me but vice versa. Letters, apologetic ones on my part, flew daily between France and Trehafod. Bidding farewell to an anxious, tearful mother, convinced she'd never see me again, I set off with one invitation to visit the Charpentier family in rue Albert Thomas and another to take tea on my immediate arrival at her flat on the school premises in the rue des Ursulines with Mme. Helle, who would then drive me to my lodgings with a Mme. Carré. Mme Helle's bark turned out to be far more ferocious than her bite. She was pleasant though formal, dignified, exuded an air of efficiency and was usually be-suited, reminding me of the rare female executive in the City.

At the Gare d'Austerlitz in Paris, Florence, Margaret Sanderson who'd winkled me out on the Paris course, and I, caught the Orléans-Bordeaux-St Jean de Luz train travelling through the Loire Valley. We said good-luck goodbyes to Florence at Blois, then gazed fascinated at the Loire scenery – the river, lazily pushing its tortuous way west through dozens of mature islands and sand-banks, the fairy-tale, cream stone castle of Chaumont perched on a bluff which you suddenly see among its protection of trees, the imposing, crenellated, squat tower of the castle at Amboise with its small-scale *chapelle St Hubert* and the doors and chimneys of the troglodyte houses in the chalk scarps on both sides of the river. Moored flat-bottomed boats moved gently in the flow and occasionally a punt in mid-stream contained an old man fishing, who casually raised his head to watch the passing train. Sand-coloured, manorial houses stood peaceful, and apparently uninhabited and rambling farms showed little signs of life apart from the odd strutting hen or dog basking in the sun. Now and then we'd see a bicycle on the road toiling along ridden by a workman dressed in blue overalls and black beret, or an old lady dressed entirely in black with a *pain* or *baguette* tied to the cycle rack. And all the time the braided river winding among its sand-banks and islands ran alongside, gleaming in the sun and the greenery on the banks was still dark and richly verdant in this early autumn.

Madame Carré turned out to be a queer old girl who lived in rue Chambert on the eastern side of the town, five minutes from the school. She looked on me more as a gentlewoman's companion than a lodger. After I'd initially accompanied her on a few outings, to the *vernissage* (preview) of a local painter's work at a gallery in Tours and to a local *foire aux fleurs*, she got quite cross when I declined further offers of outings. She would lie in wait for me in the evenings when I returned after dinner in a local restaurant and a coffee at the Hôtel de Ville or Univers Brasserie on the Place Jean-Jaurès in the centre of town, demanding to know what I'd been doing.

Mme Carré had been a Resistance worker in the war, had been captured and tortured by the SS. This torture had been in the form of cigarette burns to the face and as she sat in the dark in the evening listening to heavy classical music with the curtains open, the light from the street-lamps picked out these small circular marks on her face. I found it all very eerie. She was a bitter woman living all alone, her husband having left to work in Africa and her only son to be a soldier.

I hated hearing the sound of music around 9.30 pm as I put my key in the lock knowing I'd be pressed into joining her in the salon and it seemed churlish to refuse continually. However quietly I tried to creep past, she always caught me. When the music was over, she'd rail against the world and tell me stories about the horrors and deprivations of the war and how badly she'd been treated by life. Good for my French I suppose, but bad for my state of mind particularly just before bed-time.

She was a miserly woman, grumbling if the light was on after 11 and especially if the bedroom light was on when I was in the little adjoining wash-room. I suppose she spied on me from the back garden, otherwise she couldn't have known. My habit of using hot water once a week to wash my hair nearly drove her apoplectic. She only washed her thin, stiff, sandy locks once a month and thought my British practice excessive. She understandably hated anything to do with Germans or Germany, but didn't seem to like the British much, or anything for that matter.

Gradually I came to realise she was poking around in my room during the times when I was at school – clothes would be folded differently in drawers, letters replaced wrongly and un-Mary-like in envelopes, perfumes and toiletries arranged in new positions. I began to lay traps such as putting a strand of hair across the doorjamb when I went out and pieces of cotton across drawers. This was proof incontrovertible as they were nearly always displaced. When November came, and with it the central heating, she doubled my rent to 12,000 francs per month and I reckoned it was time to leave. I'd long had enough and I couldn't afford her. In Tours (salary amounts depended on the size of the town) assistants were paid 20,000 francs a month and food had to come out of this as well.

Margaret Sanderson had a room with a delightful couple, M and Mme Rutard in the rue de Sébastopol on the other side of town, and they knew a lady with a spare room to let. However, Mme Carré wasn't prepared to relinquish her monthly revenue without a fight. She demanded a month's notice. "*Si le gouvernement français est faible,*" she said, "*je ne le suis pas!*" With the help of Margaret, who, although slight of build was quite belligerent and confidence-boosting, I packed my belongings and decamped to 23, rue de Sébastopol, *chez* 85 year old Madame Amélie Fouchaux, a dear, dignified, white-haired, black-clothed lady whom I visited for some years afterwards.

I knew it was not the end of the story as far as Mme Carré was concerned. A few days later I was summoned to her office by Mme Helle who'd received a letter from my former landlady, complaining about these ungrateful, wasteful, contract-breaking foreigners and demanding an interview. Timorously, almost tearfully I put my side of the story expecting Mme Helle to stand firm with her kind. When she sympathised with me, a few tears of relief did flow. "We'll give her an interview with Madame Gatineau," she said and gave a brief, mischievous smile.

Mme Gatineau was the *surveillant général*, a sort of Deputy Head. There were two, one, Madame Fournier in charge of general administration in a more passive educational role and Mme Gatineau, responsible for discipline and the smooth running of the school. Hers was a very active role. She was continuously on the warpath. Tall, handsome, erect, aloof, fast on her feet with a loud, sarcastic tongue, she petrified staff and pupils alike. Woe betide a dawdling girl still outside class after the bell, Mme Gatineau would, radar-like locate the offender, "*Viens me voir tout de suite après la classe!*" If the child didn't have a one hundred per cent proof excuse it would be "*Retenue jeudi!*" and *retenue* meant not half a hour's detention, but at least two. One morning after *récréation* one teacher unwisely stopped to have a word with a colleague only to be vociferously encouraged on her way in front of the entire school by the *surveillant général* with, "There's no time to chat now. Please get a move on Mme____. Your class is waiting to be educated." Mme Gatineau was the nearest thing to a female hell-hound I'd ever known. I informed Margaret, "Mme Gatineau, not Mme Helle is going to see Mme Carré about her complaints about me." Margaret pulled a face, "Oh Gawd! Poor thing!" was her reply. "She'll eat her alive! Rather her than me!"

Margaret was taking a class when she saw Mme Carré come for her interview, very chic in a suit and hat, strutting confidently across the gravel forecourt. Ten minutes later she was reportedly scurrying off, looking very crestfallen as though she couldn't get away from the school fast enough. And that was the last I heard of her.

My new accommodation was an attic room with a sloping ceiling and a window with a flower balcony overlooking the street and from which I had a good view of the roofs of the western quarter of Tours. There were two other lodgers in the house, both students of pharmacy, Françoise, tall and quiet from Vendôme and Annick, short, dark-skinned and bubbly from Nice. Tours had no university then, only the faculty of Pharmacy, a branch of Poitiers University, and the *Institut de Touraine*, an Arts faculty for foreigners.

Mme Fouchaux was motherly and cuddly, the complete antithesis of Mme Carré. A devout Catholic, she had lost her only daughter to the nunhood in Madagascar, had not seen her for twenty five years and had little hope of setting eyes on her again. Despite this, she, unlike Mme Carré, bore no grudges and it was a happy household. Though much taller than she I was '*la petite mademoiselle Marie*'. I enjoyed keeping Mme Fouchaux company. She had never been out of France and to judge from her insatiable interest in what I told her about Britain and particularly Wales, I was the first non-French person she'd met. She would invite me into her *salon* for a cup of chocolate and a chat on those days I returned from school in the late afternoon, and when it was warm, we'd stroll in her garden. I often found on my bedside table a plate of strawberries, a *pâtisserie* of some kind, a vase of flowers or a bowl of some dessert she had made. Her unobtrusive kindness reminded me of my own mother far away and brought tears to my eyes. Great was the relief I felt at having escaped from the sharp talons of Mme Carré into the gentle hands of Mme Fouchaux, and grateful too.

# 22. Friends International

The French love bureaucracy. Since leaving Trehafod, I'd collected an increasingly voluminous pile of documents. There was the visa obtained in Cardiff; the *carte de séjour de résident* temporaire (temporary resident's card) from the *Préfecture* of Indre et Loire costing 430 (old) francs; a social security card plus a more impressive provisional one; identity card; cultural identity card; an international student identity card; a work permit; an *Institut de Touraine* enrolment card; two cards to gain entry to the student restaurant, one for lunch, one for dinner; a card for the town library and another for the Tours American library. I'd also picked up two cards in Paris for the *Cité Universitaire* and the *Institut Britannique* at the Sorbonne, and finally I'd joined the YHA (in France FAJ – *Fédération Unie des Auberges de Jeunesse*) so that meant another card, with three pages no less. My purse bulged and spilled cards. Now I knew why so many photographs had been necessary. To be allowed to breathe French air, it seemed you had to have a card with the correct photo on it. Some required full face, some profile. To obtain these cards, a passport, falling to bits by the end of the year, had to be presented. Though not a great fan of the EU, I trust that European integration means today's assistants are not so weighted down with certification.

Apart from the temporary resident's card, I'd had no difficulty obtaining my documents. In fact, they'd been showered on me simply by my waving my passport at the relevant authority. As for the resident's card, this had to be acquired from the chief commissariat for the district you inhabited. Initially, it took me three days searching around east Tours to find the place, being sent from one *poste de police* to another by grunting, moustachioed *gendarmes* I couldn't understand. Nobody seemed to know which was the pertinent police station or where it was. Now my *changement d'adresse* from 23 rue Chambert to 23 rue de Sébastopol necessitated a new card. Although the *changement* was decidedly worth the trouble, I wasn't looking forward to the hassle of the hunt, but with a new vigour I set forth and went to the nearest police station behind the main post office.

"I've come about a change of address," I said to the youngish officer manning the desk, placing my passport, visa, temporary resident's card, identity card, work permit and social security card on the counter, "I'm British."

"*Oui mademoiselle,*" he said, saluting and ignoring the ex mini-forest on the table, "What is your name and new address?"

Astonished I wasn't being mumbled at disinterestedly and sent packing with vague instructions to somewhere else, I told him, together with the old address. He wrote things on a slip of paper, stamped it and gave it to me with a smile. "*Voilà mademoiselle!*"

"*C'est ça?*" I enquired questioningly. "*C'est tout?*"

"*Mais oui,*" he replied, slightly puzzled and with a Gallic shrug,. "*Bien sûr c'est tout.*"

"Oh merci monsieur. Au revoir."

He saluted again and smiled. It was done in a matter of minutes and I'd anticipated at least a day's wasted search. I wondered at the unpredictibility of the French. Or was I just getting lucky?

The next time I saw that particular policemen, he wasn't smiling. I had a few 8 am classes and as rue de Sébastopol was twenty minutes walk from school, I'd normally leave at 7.45 and run most of the way. Zebra crossings in France were not to be trusted I'd discovered. Using one as I always did in Pontypridd (there weren't any in Trehafod), I almost came to the end of my study of French or anything else for that matter. I marched forth confidently, to be accosted by screeching brakes, cars only two feet away from my person, arms flailing and fists shaking out of vehicle windows and decidedly discomposed faces yelling at me. Thereafter I'd not crossed until a crowd had assembled with me. We'd look at each other, and anxiously, finding some assurance in numbers, edge uncertainly out on to the man-eating road, looking left and right, or rather right and left several times in rapid succession before scampering to the relative safety of the opposite pavement.

I had no time for this nonsense in the early morning and besides there were no crowds about wanting to get to the other side, so I'd cross at the lights on the rue Nationale. As is the case with traffic lights, they were usually the wrong colour, so if they were green, and there was a gap in the traffic, I'd hurry across. One morning a whistle blast startled me and the more patient, law-abiding pedestrians. My change-of-address policeman was at the blowing end of the whistle, beckoning. When the lights changed to red, I crossed penitently back to him. He saluted then started telling me off, wagging a finger at me, "If you ignore the lights again mademoiselle...mademoiselle..." He'd recognised me and wavered in his reprimand.

"Davies," I supplied.

"Ah yes, Mademoiselle Daveess, I will have to report you even if you are from England."

"Wales," I said, but he waved a hand dismissively and said, "Aahh!" before saluting to end the encounter.

During the year he caught me twice more crossing on green and the whistle blast was accompanied by yells of, "Mademoiselle Daveess, Mademoiselle Daveess!" causing everyone to take a great interest in the drama. The usual salute, the usual, "*Oh, je m'excuse. Je suis en retard. Pardonnez-moi s'il vous plaît,*" from me, followed by the wagging finger from him and, "Don't you want to see England again?"

"*Pays de Galles,*" I'd say and he'd reply with a wave of the hand, "*Aahh! Qu'importe! C'est la même chose!*" and a threat to report me next time, before saluting to end the interview.

If I saw him at other times, I'd say, "*Bonjour monsieur*" to keep in his good books, and he'd answer, "*Bonjour Mademoiselle Daveess*". Sometimes he was with another *agent*, and they'd say "*Bonjour Mademoiselle Daveess*" too. By the end of the year I was on greeting terms with most of the policemen in Tours!

Life for an *assistant* in a French school in the fifties was very different from that of *assistants* I have known in Britain. Here they work closely with the Head of the Languages Department at the school who becomes almost *in loco parentis* to them, finding them accommodation, often lodging them initially in their homes, then charting and easing their progress through the school year, always ensuring they are readily available to help with whatever problem might arise. *Assistants* are given much teaching advice and small groups of up to six pupils for conversation, groups which are carefully monitored so there is not more than one malcontent in it, who is speedily removed at the first manifestation of mal. They are often in a one to one situation with A level students and have all the school's facilities of paper, books, photocopiers, computers, overhead projectors, radios and TV sets at their disposal. Usually the British staff and the *assistants* become great friends and correspond for years, sometimes for ever afterwards. Not so in France. Although the statutory maximum number of working hours was only twelve per week, in other respects I was treated like another member of staff in this school of 1,500 girls in their blue or pink pinafore-type overalls. That is, just left to get on with it.

Complicated time-tables were left for Margaret and me in our shared pigeon-hole, with strange form-names such as 2eC2, 6eL8 and 1eP together with room numbers. There was no-one to oversee or guide us. If we had any problems we were supposed to go to Mme Helle, so we dealt with them ourselves. I only needed to see her twice during my *séjour* – once when she sent for me *re.* the Mme Carré affair and secondly when Margaret and I went to ask for a few extra days at a week-end to go to Brittany. So we were thrown in at the deep end.

Quaking with apprehension I managed to find my first class of third formers 4eB3. Trying to remember instructions from the Paris course, I drew myself up to my full height of five feet four and a half inches, took a deep breath, refrained from knocking at the door – they wouldn't have heard through the din coming from inside anyway – and went in, to be confronted by about thirty eight kids. There was an explosion of silence. They stopped running around, arguing, chatting, pulling and pushing and stood by their desks, looking at me with ready, smiling, impish faces. I hadn't expected so many for conversation. ( "They will probably give you groups of about a dozen or less for oral." they'd said in Paris).

"*Ah, Bonjour,*" I said, my mind wildly wondering what on earth I could do in the conversation line with this army. In fact it took me three lessons to get all their names.

"*Bonjour, Madame,*" they chorused.

"*Non, Mademoiselle,*" I informed them.

"*Bonjour, Mademoiselle,*" they re-chorused.

French children are no different from any others – easily bored and prone to noise-making unless you have something absolutely fascinating to occupy their attention. I tried conversation, which was what I was there for after all, asking them about their families and interests, the usual 'oral' in fact. It was hopeless! Individually they were delighted to use English to tell me about their brothers and sisters, the only trouble was that the other thirty seven knew all about their class-mates already, and rather than listen and correct mistakes of grammar and pronunciation, preferred to talk to each other, in French, about the latest songs, films, boy friends and clothes. I couldn't hear what the particular girl speaking was saying anyway in the racket. A stentorian, initial, "*Silence!*" only worked temporarily, the second, not at all. Lip-reading, I thought, would have been useful instruction on the Paris course.

Gazing at the animated scene, getting rowdier by the second, before me, I thought that if francs were needed and the way to acquire them was by taking this job or begging under the bridges of Paris, most of us would at least want to think the option over.

All of the classes, apart from 1eP, (6th form) numbered more than thirty, so plans of action had to be revised. I put the tall, thin pamphlets we had been given on the English regions, away in a drawer, clutched the songs, devised games on the lines of 'I Spy', 'Hangman', 'Famous People with clues', quizzes, bingo and winkled out a story book. No more, "What is your father's job?" or, "How old is your cat?". We would sing, play and write dictations. Which is what we did for the rest of the year. 'One Man went to Mow' is a bit hard on the adult nerves in an 8 am class but the children didn't seem to mind. Although their voices sounded cracked and hoarse in the early morning, they sang with more verve, if less tune, than in the afternoon when all they wanted was a story, preferably in French, or to sleep. After a singing class, when moving around the school I would often hear girls and staff humming, 'Row, row, row your Boat', 'Clementine', 'On Top of old Smokey' or 'Ten Green Bottles'. The latter was useful for their backwards counting.

Towards the end of the first term, around *Toussaint* in November, a Mme Thoreau introduced herself to Margaret and me, as the main English teacher. She invited us to take tea, (quite horrible – a little labelled bag on a string, totally foreign to us then, in warm water, with no milk, only a slice of lemon) and a *patisserie* (quite delicious, and the complete choice of the shop) with her in a posh cake-tea shop on the rue Nationale. So, besides Mesdames Helle, Fournier and Gatineau, whom we tried to avoid anyway, we had another named acquaintance at the school. The rest of the staff were very friendly towards us, smiled, did their best to answer any questions we put to them as they hurried past, but these were superficial relationships. As teachers in France don't have classes all day, they only need to be at school for their lessons each of which lasts an hour. As a result you mightn't see a particular 'prof' for weeks and weeks. I doubt whether I saw all the staff during my year there. After taking us to tea, Mme Thoreau clearly thought her duty towards us had been done and our contact with her thereafter was little more than, "Bonjour Marie. Ça va?"

"*Bonjour, Madame. Oui, ça va merci.*"

No matter that our friendships inside school were sparse, outside, our circle of acquaintances was widening. We'd enrolled at the *Institut de Touraine* and went to lectures when we had an hour free. It was impossible to follow a course as the same teacher taught his programme straight off, then another would take over, so I, at least, had notes on bits of study schemes. We met students here from all over the world. There was Henry Johanssen from Norway whose father ran the Royal Norwegian Yacht Club in Oslo, and who drove in demented manner around Tours, a funny, toy-like car called a Goggomobil. His fiancée, Berit, was with him but they had an 'open' engagement and each, especially her, went out with other fellows. Barbara Blust came from Buffalo, USA, via Georgetown University in Washington and went to Geneva once a month to change her dollars. Blonde Cockney Tony Clarke, who was constantly broke had come to learn *Tourangeau* French from Eltham while Wolfgang and Karl's homes were in Basle and Dortmund.

The chief benefit in enrolment at the *Institut* was not so much for the wellbeing of our minds though, as of our bodies. Once you were a paid-up student, you were issued with cards (requiring more photos) entitling you to eat at the heavily subsidised student restaurant known as the AG (*Affiliation Générale*) in the Boulevard Heurteloup. Here basic, but substantial, meals comprising a cold *hors d'oeuvre* or soup in the evening, fish or meat and a vegetable, *salade*, cheese or yogurt and to finish, dessert or fruit plus bread and water on demand, cost a quarter of something similar in a restaurant.

My initial problem though was that while I could now afford to buy meals, I couldn't eat them. The soup always had vermicelli floating around like white maggots in it: the *camembert* ran across the plate and smelled like dry rot; the *pommes de terre purée* was slushy; the *choucroute garnie* was aloe bitter with fatty lumps of bacon leering through the vinegary cabbage fronds; *steack/frites* sounded great on the menu, but the meat bled blood which soaked into the chips making me realise that is probably the reason the French don't put vinegar on their chips; and on Fridays we were expected to swallow bottle green spinach made into a sort of vegetable blanc-mange – Ugh! I lived on bread, lettuce, fruit and yogurt. My weight fell to seven and a half stone and occasionally I had black-outs. When someone asked me, "What do you do to relax?" I could truthfully answer, "I faint".

People were concerned about me, Mme Fouchaux on one occasion calling her doctor who gave me a lecture, not sympathy, and I was worried about what my mother would say at Christmas. "Oooh! That ol' France! Aren't they feeding you out there? Look at you! There's hardly anything left on your bones! Look Jack, this is ridiculous this is! Oh, fair do's now. She's no bigger than a sparrow. You'll eat proper meals home here my girl! And if you don't put on some flesh, you needn't think you'll be going back, 'cos you won't, so there!"

So I decided to avert my eyes as I gathered up the food on my fork to put in my mouth, think of Wales, and eat everything. I got quite fond of bloody meat. It was all right subdued with lashings of French mustard, but I never could bring myself to swallow the spinach sludge.

After several weeks in France, I desperately missed tea. I longed for a cup, dreamed about it, even estuary-mud coloured as my father drank it, so when I moved to rue de Sébastopol and was paid 20,000 francs salary mid-way through October and had 14,000 left after my rent, I bought a small saucepan and camping stove which burned little white blocks of fuel, to boil water. I couldn't have done this at Mme Carré's – she'd have assumed some evil intent – but even if the tea from the ticketed bags I'd bought was pathetically weak – just off-white with milk added – it was better than nothing and a relief from drinking coffee all the time. I decided I'd import some Welsh tea and a tea-pot after Christmas. I also imported a box of cornflakes and what with these, French strawberry jam, Brittany butter and a fresh *baguette* from Niepceron, the *boulanger* on the Place Jean-Jaurès on my way home from school at 9am, I had very satisfactory breakfasts, continental-adapted so to speak.

Evenings were spent in a variety of ways. There was no marking, apart from dictées corrected during the day, and no work to prepare for classes. There was work to be done in the form of a degree dissertation, 'French Parliamentary Life of the Third Republic, 1875-1914 as depicted in the Novel' which was to be completed and handed in to my tutor Mr Denis Fletcher in the first week of the final year back at Aber. I'd been given a reading list of fourteen writers, Flaubert, Barrès, Maupassant, Melchior de Voguë, Paul Adam, Anatole France etc. But it was a long way off. At least I'd joined the Tours library as a token, and promised myself I'd take out the recommended books one day soon.

Meanwhile Margaret and I met up most evenings after dinner with Bob Miller, Tony, Henry Johanssen, Wolf, Barbara and a French girl Françoise Roubillard from Rennes whose mother was English. We sat around a table on the *terrasse* of the Univers or Hotel de Ville cafes chatting, mutually pledging our *entente* with all the cordials and watching the *Tourangeau* world go by. We wasted hours of time and francs playing *baby-foot* and *flipper* and mostly speaking Franglais with American, cockney and pidgin English thrown in.

About once every two weeks, in winter anyway, we went to the cinema to watch mostly French-made films with Jean Gabin or

Gérard Phillipe, or American films dubbed into French. Since French cinemas didn't open until 9.30 pm, we usually went at the week-end or the night before a bank holiday. Sometimes the film would start at 11 pm so that we'd be returning home around 1 am, "with the Rodneys" as my father would say. *Guerre et Paix* didn't finish until 2 am.

The nearby American-endowed library in the western part of town occasionally held evenings of gramophone concerts, and I became not only well acquainted with the novels of Ernest Hemingway and John Steinbeck during my year in France, but also with the music of George Gershwin, Rodgers and Hammerstein and Lorenzo Hart. The only American I met there though was Barbara and I knew her already.

There was a US army base in Chinon. Off-duty soldiers came to Tours and were always delighted to hear English being spoken in cafés and bars they frequented in the town. Like most Americans they were not slow coming forward and hailed any English speaker, despite meeting them for the first time, as a long-lost friend. We soon came to know some of these; homesick Tony from Chicago who played Frank Sinatra's record of 'Chicago, Chicago, that toddling Town' over and over on the juke-box; Caleb from Pittsburgh always worrying about the scores of the Pittsburgh Steelers or some such, and looking out for their results on the bar's TV and in *The New York Herald Tribune*, a copy of which he was never without; Gerry from Phoenix, the 'cool cat', always frozen, even in summer when he still wore a scarf and several pullovers with the sun-glasses he wore all year round.

Via these roving young men, we, and any English-speaking young women, had invitations to dances at the camp on Thursday evenings whither a bus would be sent to pick us up in Tours and bring us back afterwards. So eight of us travelled for some weeks on Thursdays in this long, charcoal-grey, unmarked, 40 seater bus with portholes for windows along dead-straight, forest-bordered, dusty roads disappearing kilometres ahead into the horizon. There were ups and downs but no bends. Now and then you'd see a speck moving towards you on the road in the distance. It would vanish for a minute or two, then suddenly a cloud of sandy dust would hail its sudden arrival atop a rise. It would speed past and be instantly gone over another gradient in the road.

Hospitality was overwhelming at the camp as was the multitude of soldiers, men outnumbering women by at least 50 to 1. It was difficult to sit out any dance and during the dance there would be half a dozen partners demanding an 'excuse-me'. Drinks of all kinds were on non-stop offer as were sandwiches, crisps, hot-dogs and hamburgers. To celebrate Thanksgiving in November we were invited, before the dance, to a meal of turkey with cranberry sauce and blueberry pie and ice-cream and were glad to have the exercise afterwards. Midway through December the unit moved to Angoulême and my French-American experience was over, despite serious, I think, offers of marriage from Cpl. John Steffenson from Maine and Sgt Danny Mahoney of Stanford University in California.

Before coming to France I'd unwittingly raised the hopes of *M. le Directeur* of the *Collège Technique*, M. Charpentier, that his charges would have an English language *assistante* to chat to, or rather sing and play games with, as it had turned out in reality. When the mistake had been discovered, I was invited to contact him even so. Visiting his family of himself, wife and two teenage sons Yves 12 and Jean-Pierre 15, and sharing the most marvellous meals, became a weekly event. Although for the first hour I'd speak English to the two boys, Jean-Pierre, competent at English, but shy, with little to say, and bubbly, uninhibited Yves who knew little more than, "'Ow arr you today? I am verry well sank you." and " I am glad eet ees fine wezzerr as I like to play footboll" but who never stopped talking and learned fast, this visit was very beneficial for my French. The parents Charpentier, though teachers, knew no English. Their minds were keen, analytic, humorous and enquiring and we discussed, argued, laughed and informed until late evening. Monsieur had served in an inept branch of the French army during the war and many were the tales of bungling and incompetence he had to tell. He was convinced France would have offered more resistance to invasion if there had been no army at all. They were devout atheists and bewildered by the fact that the intelligent British, world-leaders in so many fields of Science, the Arts, Commerce and Industry were so anachronistic as to pay homage to, at the same time as expensively funding, a Royal Family who, according to them, all looked like monkeys. The other thing which baffled them was the Welsh name Llewellyn as in Richard Llewellyn, author of *Qu'elle était Verte, ma Vallee* – a favourite book of theirs. "*Prononciation tout à fait impossible. Il y en a quatre L!*" they'd protest. Every week I'd have to say the name several times. They'd practise diligently, always fail and shake their heads in discouraged amazement. I introduced 'Llanelly' (sic) to them and showed off with 'Llanfairpwllgwyngyllgogerychwndrobwllllantisiliogogogoch', but they snorted, threw up their hands in merriment crying, *"Oh, là là!"* M.Charpentier always gave me a lift back to rue de Sébastopol in his black Citroën Déesse, a most extraordinary, innovative vehicle whose body rose up off its wheels before it would allow him to drive away.

# 23. Reluctant Deportee

Some weekends Florence would come to Tours but more interesting to me were the weekends I'd spend with her in Blois. Her landlady worked in the library of the magnificent *château* and had some nepotistic influence no doubt, for Flor could obtain free entry to it when she so desired. Her house was on the Quai du Foix and her room overlooked the mighty Loire, a powerful, voluminous river at that spot. Usually I caught the train to go there, the Paris (Austerlitz) *rapide* or the slower *express*, climbing the steps up from the ground level platform at Tours station. The *rapide* was like a British train with individual compartments and a corridor, but the *express* had a few long compartments to each carriage and wooden, slatted, uncomfortable seats – in Second class anyway.

It was cheaper, more interesting and hours slower to go by bus – a long single decker, again with slatted seats which resembled school buses in American films only not bright yellow, and having a ladder at the back up which the driver-conductor-guide-amiable fellow climbed to store whatever luggage was being carried. The bus, once everyone had got on, greeted everyone else and settled down, followed the southern Loire road through Montlouis as far as Amboise, stopped for five minutes on the quay under the towering *château*, then crossed the river over the arched bridge to the northern shore road alongside the river flowing in the opposite direction.

People would board and middle-aged ladies especially would chat to you as though you were their next-door neighbour whom they'd known all their lives. You didn't need to say much at such times, a phrase now and then, a *'Oui'*, *'Non'*, nod or shake of the head, they were happy to prattle on about the rising prices of food, gas, transport, the awful government, the effects of the drought on their garden, their children's and sometimes grandchildren's jobs, or lack of them, and taxes which figured largely on everyone's agenda. Then, with a smile and a sigh, "*Oh, alors, c'est la vie, n'est-ce pas? Tant pis! Faut la tolérer! Au 'voir Mademoiselle. Bonne journée!*", the lady would get off busily and be gone for ever. I felt very indigenous at such times travelling in a provincial bus in the heart of the country, being taken for a French person and indeed, finding the French language coming more naturally to me than English in such surroundings.

In Blois, Flor and I would wander through the steep, sleepy, old town with its stairways, small squares, passageways, court-yards, public gardens, narrow paved streets and terraces with wonderful views over the river and the town south of the elegant bridge.

"Cor, you're lucky I dreamed you'd be sent here Flor. I could have had a dream with you being somewhere industrial like Dunkirk or Lille or some God-forsaken little village miles from anywhere."

"Oh well, thanks for your influence. P'raps you could have another dream for me to win the national lottery here, then I'd really think you had connections up above. The school's not got a swimming pool though. Your mysticism or occultism or what-ever 'ism' it was, let you down there."

Blois did have the Poulain chocolate factory though which we visited with Yvonne Lanoe from Guernsey, a friend of Flor's. Yvonne was in Blois as a nanny learning French. Despite her name she could hardly speak a word of the language. We walked through huge halls and rooms watching thick chocolate being stirred in vats, slabs cooling on conveyor belts, lumps of it being chopped up, having nuts, creams and fruit added to it and bars being wrapped by machines. We breathed chocolate oxygen for an hour. The smell inebriated the senses and as a bonus we were given a generous packet of products on the way out.

Florence proudly took me around the castle that the Blesois think is *the* Loire *château*, which stands on a promontory above the north bank dominating the town. Everywhere, on window lin-tels and above doorways was carved the salamander, the symbol of François Premier who extended the fifteenth century-built cas-tle in the sixteenth century.

It was in February that we did the tour and were the only vis-itors, having the guide completely to ourselves. No doubt, not having been called upon to present his drama since the warmer days of the previous autumn, he gave us an enthusiastic, Oscar-winning performance of the assassination arranged by Henri III on Christmas Eve 1588 of the cruel, anti-Protestant, over-power-ful Duc de Guise. Taking all the roles himself he leaped around the room, hid behind the heavy drapes, peeped from behind a screen to finally rush forward with an imaginary sword he thrust into the imaginary, unfortunate duke, whereupon, to our startled glances he himself fell on the floor writhing in an apparent death agony, only to shortly get up, smiling broadly at our spontaneous applause. It was with such pride he showed us, in the courtyard the remarkably beautiful, delicately sculpted, François Premier spiral staircase in its octagonal framework with balconies, that he had to wipe tears from his face. He bade us good-bye after showing us the bed in which the intelligent, cultured, homosexual and weak Henri III slept, probably intending to have a kip there himself after his *tour de force* show.

Florence's Blesois family owned bicycles they were prepared to lend us, so on summer week-ends we ventured wobblingly forth on these sturdy, unpainted metal, gearless cycles with orange-walled tyres and tan leather saddlebags to explore chateau country. Initially we kept (to our near peril) forgetting to *prendre la droite*, especially after a roadside stop to admire a forest or river view, *manoir*, lake, vineyard, garden with peach trees trained on a trellis and would alarmingly, on the mercifully quiet country roads, espy a *deux-chevaux* bouncing rapidly along in a cloud of dust aiming straight at us. The horn would invariably be tooted whatever side of the road we were on but whether in greeting or warning we were never sure. Roundabouts gave us trouble at first, as death-defyingly we unwittingly went the British way round. Eventually though we became experienced on French roads to the extent that on getting back to Aber we couldn't get out of the 'right hand side' habit.

We visited Chambord, the most magnificent of the Loire *châteaux*, seeing it for the first time suddenly, after toiling up a gradient, attacking from the south. We topped the rise and there it was, breathtakingly beautiful a mile away, immense and spread out, creamy stone turrets and towers, balconies and belfries, spires and staircases with roofs shining like pewter gleaming in the sun and reflected in the lake. The uncluttered approach and gentle descent of the road meant we could freewheel while gazing at the unforgettable sight before us which grew larger as we drew nearer.

With bottles of *eau de Vichy* in the saddle-bags, buttered *baguettes*, Ste Maure goat cheese, *saucisson*, huge tomatoes, chocolate bars, usually in a fairly unsolid state, and apples, we cycled to the classical looking, square, hunting château at Cheverny in the middle of the forest and admired especially the outside area with its vast dog kennels and trophy room with thousands of mounted heads of deer. We visited fairy-tale Chaumont and on one marathon ride went as far as Amboise to examine the balcony of the King's Lodging where the Duc de Guise's father, François, husband of Mary Stuart had murdered then hung up there to rot, the corpses of the leaders of the Amboise conspirators. From this vantage point I could see the towers of St Gatien cathedral in Tours. It seemed hardly worth the massive effort of cycling back to Blois to catch the bus home the following day.

Taking a bath in France was a new experience for me. Mme Fouchaux's house did not possess a bathroom such as we know and love in the UK. Adjacent to her bedroom was a washroom with wash-basin, shower and bidet and there was a wash-basin in my bedroom. In Mme Carré's there had been a bidet in my washroom, or foot-bath as I thought. At least, I used it as such to soak tired feet after long walks on hot, dusty roads. "What a good idea these things are!" I thought and wondered why we didn't have them at home. Mme Carré was horrified at the thought of my using more than a cup of cold water for my personal use whether it be for consumption or cleansing and the idea of having to heat water made her positively ill. When I uneasily broached the subject of a bath which I was used to acquainting myself with at least once weekly, "Once a week!" she expostulated like a French version of Lady Bracknell, "That's ridiculous! You'll weaken yourself! However, if you want to take a bath, you must go to the public baths, but I would have thought once a month sufficient." I didn't ask if she'd ever had a bath.

Armed with a towel and toiletries, I sallied forth to the *Bains Publics* in the Avenue de Grammont a little apprehensively, wondering what I'd find. Would there be a football-type bath where everyone leaped in together and cavorted naked in the steaming water? If so I hoped the sexes would be segregated. Would they be communal showers like in the colliery back home or would there be a gracious Roman kind of bath with a man waving fronds and armed with a loofah to scrub your back? Would I find myself in a hip bath, Turkish bath or a sauna affair? I didn't know what to expect.

I paid at the entrance and proceeded through a revolving gate. A row of waiting people sat on chairs with their backs to a tiled wall. Men and women dressed in white jackets, and carrying towels arrived to lead them off. When it was my turn, a white-coated man showed me into a room with a capacious bath and started running the water. I stood watching him, feeling unemployed and foolish. When the bath was threequarters full and steaming, he shut the taps and stood back smiling at me.

"Oh God, what happens now?" I wondered. I smiled at him. Smiles all round.

"*Merci Monsieur,*" I said

"*Ça va Mademoiselle?*" he asked.

*"Oh oui, ça va merci. Très bien merci."*

He didn't budge. His smile was waning now and I was nodding and wondering why on earth he didn't push off. Then, in a flash of enlightment, "Of course, he's waiting for a tip!" Relief flooded through me even though I realised I'd been colossally slow on the uptake. The sight of my purse resuscitated his smile. I gave him 50 francs and he departed bowing and closing the door behind him which I quickly went to lock but couldn't as there was no key, no bolt. The bath was deep, divine, hot and regenerating. Thereafter, I indulged myself weekly.

During the first term and my unhappy time at my initial lodgings, I struck off the days on the calendar to Christmas and my return home. Now it was the reverse. The days, weeks and months were passing too fast.

At Easter, Florence and I had taken the train to the Midi and stayed in youth hostels, some positively palatial with marble accoutrements in bathrooms, down the Rhône Valley and right along the Riviera to the Italian border – Montélimar, Avignon, La Ciotat, Fréjus, Cap d'Ail, Nice, Menton.

At Whitsun we'd gone to Brittany where the hostels were often little more than hovels, frequently with no superintendent. In Lorient we'd drawn water out of the well to also find our supper in the bucket in the form of small fish. We'd cooked chips in the dark and used matches to see if they were done in the absence of any other form of lighting. The next morning we'd left the night's fees under a stone by the front door.

Florence was twenty-one in the June of our year in France. We, together with Margaret Sanderson who'd come for the day, and Yvonne Lanoe, had been to le Clos Lucé where Leonardo da Vinci once lived, then on to the Chanteloup pagoda before returning to a celebration of several kilos of strawberries dipped in sugared *fromage blanc* and washed down with a lot of champagne.

I'd played indoor tennis on a wooden court at the Palais des Sports, representing the foreign students at the *Institut de Touraine* and on two nights I'd been to crowded concerts there, featuring the Platters and Edith Piaf. I'd been taken to see Fritz, '*l'éléphant de Tours*', at the Musée des Beaux Arts, former star of Barnum's Circus who'd gone mad and had to be shot then was preserved in 1902. I'd been to all-night dances ending with croissants and coffee, where I noticed French women didn't shave under their arms but surprisingly preferred to display a thick, dark fuzz which looked somewhat out of place with an elegant dance dress to my British eye. I'd eaten delicious new food – *mille feuilles, religieuses, babas au rhum, pruneaux fourrés, crêpes Tourangelles, paupiettes de veau, rillettes de Tours*. Now my lovely year in lovely France was coming to an end. The owner of the *Alimentation Générale* in our street brought tears to my eyes when I told him I was leaving soon. "But you can't go back to England! You belong here now. So you must stay! You are a real *Tourangelle* girl."

Margaret's landlord and lady, M and Mme Rutard invited us to a meal, "To remember France", before our departure, which began at 12.30 and finished five hours later. There were eight courses with a different wine or liqueur accompanying each one. At midnight, I was sick, more than I'd ever been in my life but I couldn't help thinking I was sick because I was leaving and even when I came back to France it would never be the same again.

Perhaps no-one had had quite the auspicious year in France that John Isaacs, a former Porth County pupil, had spent a few years earlier, playing in the prestigious rugby league final in Paris for Marseilles, but most of us felt at least a quarter French.

But it was time to go home. In April I'd received a letter from my tutor, Mr Fletcher, asking how I was progressing with my dissertation and requesting a synopsis. Progress was in fact zero, although I'd had every intention of borrowing some of the listed novels from the Tours library which I'd joined, but not had time to use. How can a person be sent to France for a year and be expected to stay in, working when there are people to meet, food to sample, sights to see, things to do, a language to speak? I'd invented a synopsis and Mr Fletcher had later replied with a worried letter saying quite kindly that it was more or less, more I suspect, rubbish, and how did I intend advancing from there. He received no reply but I knew the summer would be spent in Cardiff University and the City libraries. Rather more than a few nights would be spent indoors working too.

We didn't all return from France. Anne Tucker from Gowerton, who'd gone to Argelès Gazost in the far south somewhere near Spain, had fallen in love, not only with France, but with a young man who'd given her the opportunity to become Madame Philippe Fialho, and she'd had the good sense to accept.

Oh that I had had a similar chance!

# Acknowledgements

With the publication of *Plateaux, Gâteaux, Châteaux*, the trilogy
of semi-autobiographical musings of growing up in the Forties
and Fifties, and the process through the educational system of the
time, is complete. There are many people to thank: local friends
for their encouragement and kind enquiries as to the progress of
the book, especially Mrs Doreen Jones for her promptings to get
on with it; ex-Porth County pupils, both male and female, who
contacted me after the first books expressing their enjoyment of
them and their nostalgia for bygone years; Gillian Morgan who
rekindled memories of facts and names from university days;
Robin Reeves, editor of the *New Welsh Review* and ex-Aber student who related to me amusing tales, which I have used, of his
collége days; my cousin, Lewis Mann, who told me alot about the
history of Pontypridd; my daughter, Sarah Parnell, for her gift of
a state of the art computer which I didn't get around to learning
to use; John Ash, who cleverly sorted out my incompetently
inputted chapters on my elderly Amstrad; Dr John Baker who,
after patiently reading the word-processed chapters and correct-
ing geological facts, needed a new pair of glasses; all at Seren who
have made publication possible; my son Richard whose unassuming presence has been a continued source of support. To all
my appreciative thanks.

Mary Davies Parnell<br>June 1997